The Global Faculty Initiative's book, *Justi*
logue on the topic of Justice and Rights b
wide range of scholars across disciplines,
captures the essence of the discussions in
if they were part of it. The book is framed
essay for the group, and ends with his gracious and engaging response and
clarifications. This is a unique and rich approach that broadens and enlivens
the reader's engagement with an essential topic of our time. Often scientists
mistakenly see their work as value-neutral. This principled dialogue on justice and rights challenges that notion through embedding the concepts in an
historical and global understanding of definitions and forms of justice that
speak to equity, rights, and obligations informed by a biblical understanding
of justice. Surely such recent experiences as the global COVID-19 pandemic
and the rise of AI should lead all scientists, whether coming from the Christian
community or not, to realize the need for reaching into the deeper wells of
thinking around the intersection of their work and justice. *Justice and Rights*
offers a unique companion for the essential journey that theologians and scientists must take together as we search for truth and wisdom.

Janel Curry
President,
American Scientific Affiliation

This book captivates. It begins a rich conversation that takes off from
Wolterstorff's brilliant opening essay as eminent philosophers, theologians,
and biblical scholars immediately join in. In the form of a dialogue, the conversation quickly branches out to many other disciplines—a historian reflecting
upon how to think about history justly, in light of Christian faith; a political
scientist cautioning against reducing literature and art to the practical category
of justice; an economic historian asking how to bring biblical understandings
of justice to bear in economic frameworks and policy contexts quite different
from the biblical world; an expert on natural disasters insisting on a justice
dimension as societies succeed or fail to cope; a sociolinguistics scholar show-
ing how language and dialect relate to power, in light of Babel and Pentecost;
and on and on to diverse perspectives from the fields of law, environmental

economics, international relations, and medicine, among others. This utterly fascinating, Christian interdisciplinary conversation comes full circle with a postscript by Wolterstorff – whom we find doing one of those rarest of intellectual things, changing his mind about important earlier claims. In sum, this book is a tour de force, exciting and inspiring in every way. May these conversations long continue!

Matthew Levering
James N. Jr. and Mary D. Perry Chair of Theology,
Mundelein Seminary, Illinois, USA
Co-Editor, *International Journal of Systematic Theology*
Co-Editor, *Nova et Vetera*

With Nicholas Wolterstorff's profound insights at its core, this hugely stimulating and wide-ranging book weaves a dialogue between philosophy, theology, and a range of university disciplines. I am struck on the one hand how widely the concept of justice applies, and on the other hand how much more work there is left on the table for Christian scholars to explore. Highly recommended!

Ard Louis
Professor of Theoretical Physics, University of Oxford, UK
Co-Leader, Developing a Christian Mind, Oxford, UK

If you seek inspiration about ways your own research relates to faith, or if you are searching for writings that will energize graduate students or early career scholars to integrate their faith and studies, then I enthusiastically recommend these creatively curated writings brought together in *Justice and Rights,* an all-too-rare academic volume crafted as an extended dialogue. When I first read Nicholas Wolterstorff's superb Theology Brief on Justice and Rights, we were preparing for a study session with graduate students at the University of Oxford, who were part of a spiritual formation group convened by the Oxford Pastorate. I assumed it would engage students working in the social sciences but wondered how those in my discipline, chemistry, would engage with it. In fact, the chemistry students were highly engaged, identifying many connections between the justice issues and their work, including the unequal availability of pharmaceuticals and the environmental impact of chemical industries. Now reaching scholars across the world, I am entirely confident this unique collection of lively and accessible writings will stimulate reflections on justice in the sciences and far beyond, to every corner of the university, for faculty and advanced graduate students alike.

Lorna Smith
Professor of Chemistry and Tutorial Fellow at St. Hilda's College,
University of Oxford, UK;
Co-Convenor, *Christians in Academia*, Oxford Pastorate

This novel volume creatively presents a book in the form of a conversation. It is like listening in to a wide-ranging, intelligent, global exchange among learned scholars, all motivated by the same values – justice and rights – which embrace an extraordinarily wide range of issues in contemporary life and culture. *Justice and Rights* takes the reader on a journey of discovery as eminent philosopher-theologian, Nicholas Wolterstorff, starts a conversation and yet finds his own mind changing and expanding as it proceeds. The different perspectives of the writers, the methodology of the dialogue, the content, and the theme all amply testify to the rich capacity of Christian faith to offer profound and healing perspectives on issues that go right to the heart of our life together across the world today.

The Rt. Revd. Dr. Graham Tomlin
Former Bishop of Kensington
Director, Centre for Cultural Witness, UK

Nicholas Wolterstorff has created the most original and influential Christian theory of justice that the world has seen in the past half century. Here, in a few dozen lucid pages, he distills his account of the natural rights that, in his view, form the foundation of all just societies and the starting point for all loving communities. Wolterstorff has drawn this theory of justice and rights from a profound new reading of Scripture and tradition. And he has applied it – here, and in a score of other titles – to everything from the elementary justice we owe to each neighbor to the massive issues of warfare, apartheid, genocide, racism, sexism, homophobia, poverty, climate change, and more that are crying for just solutions. Such an original and capacious account of justice and rights has invariably raised eyebrows, if not hackles, from many quarters, not least within the Christian tradition. In this judiciously edited volume, four dozen Christian scholars from different fields of study take up and take on Wolterstorff's theory. Some commentators offer small shards of insight from their home disciplines. Others provide several pages of deep engagement with Wolterstorff's biblical exegesis and reading of the tradition. Still others challenge him with alternative accounts of justice, love, and community that deserve consideration. This is the kind of robust and respectful interdisciplinary Christian scholarship that every scholar and student craves. The new Global Faculty Initiative, directed by Terry Halliday and Donald Hay, has created an essential network of Christian scholars from around the world, and has set the scholarly bar very high with this impressive inaugural volume of the Cross-Disciplinary Encounters with Theology series.

John Witte, Jr.
Robert W. Woodruff Professor of Law, McDonald Distinguished Professor,
Faculty Director, Center for the Study of Law and Religion,
Emory University, Georgia, USA

Cross-Disciplinary Encounters with Theology

Series Editors: Terence C. Halliday and K. K. Yeo

The series, Cross-Disciplinary Encounters with Theology, is a scholarly collaboration of the Global Faculty Initiative (GFI), comprising more than 170 professors in research universities worldwide. The book series brings academics across the principal faculties of research universities into conversations with leading theologians. Each book in the series centers on a dialogue between disciplinary scholars and a theologian on a key theme of Christian thought that can be readily accepted as an issue of debate and inquiry in any major university, whatever its religious or nonreligious orientation. The books selectively incorporate five cycles of exchanges between a theologian and disciplinary scholars, from a brief Preview and equally brief Responses, to a more extended yet compact Theology Brief and many Disciplinary Brief reflections, with a Postscript by the theologian. GFI welcomes diverse views consistent with the historic creeds of the Christian faith. Reaching scholars, advanced graduate students, and thoughtful publics on all continents, the series seeks to remedy the challenges faced by academic theologians, whose writings rarely reach the frontiers of disciplinary inquiry in research fields, and by disciplinary scholars who seek intellectual tools to bring theological reflection on their scholarship and academic lives, work, and practices.

Justice and Rights

Justice and Rights

Nicholas Wolterstorff in Dialogue with the University

Edited by

Terence C. Halliday and K. K. Yeo

© 2024 Terence C. Halliday and K. K. Yeo

Published 2024 by Langham Global Library
An imprint of Langham Publishing
www.langhampublishing.org

Langham Publishing and its imprints are a ministry of Langham Partnership

Langham Partnership
PO Box 296, Carlisle, Cumbria, CA3 9WZ, UK
www.langham.org

ISBNs:
978-1-78641-002-3 Print
978-1-78641-080-1 ePub
978-1-78641-081-8 PDF

British Library Cataloguing-in-Publication Data
A catalogue record for this book is available from the British Library

ISBN: 978-1-78641-002-3

Cover & Book Design: projectluz.com

Contents

Contributors..xiii

Acknowledgments.. xvii

Preface..xix

Part I: Preview

Justice *Nicholas Wolterstorff*... 3

Part II: Theology Brief

Justice and Rights *Nicholas Wolterstorff*................................. 9

Part III: Disciplinary Exchanges

1 Justice Debates.. 35

What Is Justice? *Fr. Thomas Joseph White, O.P.* 35

Profound Differences *Oliver O'Donovan* 42

An Alternative Framing of Justice and Rights *Peter Anstey* 43

From Justice Ethics to an Ethic of Care *Eleonore Stump* 43

A Contextual Interpretation of Justice by a Chinese Biblical Theologian *K. K. Yeo* 44

Extending Rights Questions *Jennifer Herdt* 49

On Obligations Rather Than Trust *Casey Strine* 50

Justice and Home *Ryan McAnnally-Linz* 50

Love as the Foundation for Christian Justice *Osam Temple* 51

Are Virtues Necessary to Acting Justly? *Jonathan Brant* 54

Beyond Justice in Relationship *Robert Joustra* 55

Radical Christian Subversion *Chris Watkin* 55

The Justice of God *Brendan Case* 56

2 Society and History.. 61

Doing Justice to the Past: Histories of Rights, Memories of Injustice *John Coffey* 61

Tribal Societies and Collective Rights *Joy Pachuau* 68

Economic Justice and the Politics of Redistribution *Peter Sloman* .. 69

Affinities of Justice with Economic Concepts *Judy Dean* 74

Justice, Rights, and the Quest to Reduce the Risk of Disasters *Ian Robert Davis* 75

Environmental Justice *Erin Goheen Glanville* 79

Just Language *Allan Bell* 80

The Obligations of Justice for Colombia's Displaced Persons *Christopher Hays* 87

3 Law and Society 95
   Restorative Justice *Christopher D. Marshall* 95
   Justice, Judgment, and Virtue in the Law *Nicholas Aroney* 103
      Being Treated Justly in Society and Politics *Karen Man Yee Lee* 111
   Justice, Rights, and Family Relationships *Patrick Parkinson* 112
   Sexual Violence and Sexual Dignity *Anna High* 117
      Justice and Economic and Social Rights *Karen Kong* 120
   Market Failures and Government Agency Rulemaking *Alex Lee* 121
      On Justice in Land Use *Philip Bess* 124

4 International and Global Justice 125
   Climate Change Justice *Donald Hay and Gordon Menzies* 125
   Atrocities, Accountability, and Reconciliation: The Pursuit of Justice in
      International Relations *Cecilia Jacob* 131
   Justice in Transnational Legal Orders *Terence C. Halliday* 137

5 Justice in Biological, Physical, and Medical Sciences 145
   Doing Justice to Nature in Science *Ian H. Hutchinson* 145
      Justice in Biomedicine and Biotechnology *Jeff Hardin* 150
   Justice of Space-Based Communication Architectures *Daniel Hastings* . . 151
   Justice and Public Health *Tyler VanderWeele* 153
      Being Just in Mental Health Care *John Petcet, M.D.* 165
      Mercy, Not Justice, in Medicine *Lydia Dugdale, M.D.* 166
   Vaccine Nationalism During COVID-19 *Benjamin Day* 167

6 Justice and the Academy 173
   Justice in Academic Publishing and the Academic Calling: A Perspective
      from the Global South *Dinesha Samararatne* 173
   Two Thoughts on Justice, Rights, and the Academy *Luke Glanville* . . . 176
      Perversions of Just Relations in the University *Ross McKenzie* 180
   Epistemic Injustice *Carlos Miguel Gómez* 182
      Are Students Treated Unjustly? *Thomas Chacko* 184
   Justice and Trust in Interdisciplinary Research *Claudia Vanney* 185

Part IV: Postscript
   Justice *Nicholas Wolterstorff* 189

   Subject Index 207

   Scripture Index 215

Contributors

Peter Anstey, Philosophy, University of Sydney, Australia

Nicholas Aroney, Constitutional Law, University of Queensland, Australia

Allan Bell, Language and Communication, Emeritus, Auckland University of Technology and Laidlaw College, New Zealand

Philip Bess, Architecture, University of Notre Dame, USA

Jonathan Brant, Theology, University of Oxford, UK

Brendan Case, Theology, Harvard University, USA

Thomas Chacko, Earth and Atmospheric Sciences, University of Alberta, Canada

John Coffey, History, Leicester University, UK

Ian Robert Davis, Architecture and Disaster Risk and Recovery Management, Universities of Amrita, Kyoto, Lund, Oxford Brookes and RMIT Europe

Benjamin Day, International Relations, Australian National University, Australia

Judy Dean, Economics, Brandeis University, USA

Lydia Dugdale, M.D., Medicine, Columbia University, USA

Erin Goheen Glanville, Communications, Simon Fraser University, Canada

Luke Glanville, International Relations, Australian National University, Australia

Carlos Miguel Goméz, School of Human Sciences, University of Rosario, Bogotá, Colombia

Terence C. Halliday, Sociology, Emeritus, American Bar Foundation; Northwestern University, USA; Australian National University, Australia

Jeff Hardin, Biology, University of Wisconsin-Madison, USA

Daniel Hastings, Aeronautics and Astronautics, Massachusetts Institute of Technology (MIT), USA

Donald Hay, Economics, Emeritus, Jesus College, University of Oxford, UK

Christopher Hays, Theology, Scholar Leaders, USA; formerly Fundación Universitaria Seminario Bíblico de Colombia in Medellín, Colombia

Jennifer Herdt, Divinity, Yale University, USA

Anna High, Law, University of Otago, New Zealand

Ian H. Hutchinson, Nuclear Science and Engineering, Emeritus, Massachusetts Institute of Technology (MIT), USA

Cecilia Jacob, International Relations, Coral Bell School of Asia and the Pacific, Australian National University, Australia

Robert Joustra, Politics, Redeemer University, Canada

Karen Kong, Law, University of Hong Kong, Hong Kong

Alex Lee, Law, Northwestern University, USA

Karen Man Yee Lee, Law, La Trobe Law School, La Trobe University, Victoria, Australia

Christopher D. Marshall, Restorative Justice, Emeritus, Te Herenga Waka-Victoria University of Wellington, New Zealand

Ryan McAnnally-Linz, Theology, Yale University, USA

Ross McKenzie, Physics, University of Queensland, Australia

Gordon Menzies, Economics, University of Technology Sydney, Australia

Oliver O'Donovan, Theology, Emeritus, University of Edinburgh; University of St. Andrews, UK

Joy Pachuau, History, Jawaharlal Nehru University, New Delhi, India

Patrick Parkinson, Law, Emeritus, University of Queensland, Australia

John Peteet, M.D., Psychiatry, Harvard Medical School, USA

Dinesha Samararatne, Law, University of Colombo, Sri Lanka

Peter Sloman, Politics, University of Cambridge, UK

Casey Strine, Ancient Near Eastern History and Literature, University of Sheffield, UK

Eleonore Stump, Philosophy, St. Louis University, USA

Osam Temple, Philosophy, Bakke Graduate University, Dallas, USA; formerly Philosophy, American University of Nigeria, Nigeria

Tyler VanderWeele, Public Health, Harvard University, USA

Claudia Vanney, Philosophy and Physics, Universidad Austral, Argentina

Chris Watkin, French Studies, Monash University, Australia

Fr. Thomas Joseph White, O.P., Theology, Pontifical University of St. Thomas (Angelicum), Rome, Italy

Nicholas Wolterstorff, Philosophical Theology, Emeritus, Yale University; Institute for Advanced Studies in Culture, University of Virginia, USA; Australian Catholic University, Australia

K. K. Yeo, Bible, Theology and Culture, Garrett-Evangelical Seminary; Northwestern University, USA

Acknowledgments

In 2007, economist Donald Hay, Fellow of Jesus College and a recently retired Pro-Vice Chancellor of the University of Oxford, spearheaded the Developing a Christian Mind movement for faculty and advanced graduate students within the University of Oxford to elevate the voices and strengthen the community of Christian academics. At roughly the same time, Vinoth Ramachandra, educated as a nuclear physicist at Imperial College London, and for many years the Secretary for Dialogue and Social Engagement of the International Fellowship of Evangelical Students (IFES), initiated a movement for Christian students to Engage the University across more than 150 Christian national student movements worldwide.

As a publication of the Global Faculty Initiative (GFI), this book complements and extends the mission of both movements. It carries the spirit of developing a Christian mind from Oxford into research universities on every continent. It calls upon Christian scholars in those universities to think Christianly about the leading edges of their scholarship and every arena of academic life. It proceeds on the assumption that every corner of the university must be engaged by the Christian faith. To Donald Hay, the Co-Convenor of the Global Faculty Initiative, we express our particular thanks for his vision, inspiration, and wisdom. To Vinoth Ramachandra, and to many other partners in elevating a Christian voice in higher education, we extend deep appreciation.

We are highly indebted to several founding convenors of GFI whose early enthusiasm energized us along the route that led to this volume. Alister McGrath (Oxford), Nigel Biggar (Oxford), Michael Spence (Sydney), Ian Hutchinson (MIT), Ard Louis (Oxford), Nicholas Wolterstorff (Yale), Miroslav Volf (Yale), and Tyler VanderVeele (Harvard) joined numerous others to refine a new form of dialogue between faith and scholarship and to generate the core themes, motifs, and doctrines that GFI injects into thought and conversations among Christian and other scholars in the research university.

Justice and Rights owes a unique debt to Nicholas Wolterstorff. He has exemplified enthusiasm and energy, an experimental spirit, and humble readiness to elaborate and refine each of the superb pieces he has contributed to this volume, all which distill for non-theologians many long years and an extensive corpus of scholarship on justice. He models a theologian's readiness to enter conversations with disciplines and domains of learning far removed from his own, to learn from his peers elsewhere in the institutions of the academy, and even to revise his thought.

This book reflects a sacrificial commitment of time and thought by forty GFI members, most unknown to each other, who have written on the kaleidoscope of topics found in this volume. We are most thankful for their readiness to participate in this experiment, for their humility in revisions, for their grace in modeling respectful conversation among Christians who often differ in their understandings of justice and rights, and for the mix of younger and senior scholars to orient their thought to doctrines introduced by Wolterstorff and debated by his interlocutors. Contributors of Disciplinary Briefs to this volume went the second mile by turning their online study versions into compact forms suitable for the distinctive form of this book.

We thank all those individuals who have led and participated in justice and rights discussions which fed into this volume, whether they be in faculty retreats in Canberra, graduate student groups at Oxford, or online faculty forums in East Asia, among others. A special measure of appreciation goes to the Oxford Pastorate, led by Jonathan Brant until recently, and now by Bethan Willis. The Pastorate's substantive contributions to ways GFI can optimally curate our original writings for research university faculty and graduate students have been invaluable, as have been its contributions to study aids, including a topical guide, study guides and podcasts with *Justice and Rights* authors.

We are grateful, too, for the far-flung sites in which earlier versions of writings in *Justice and Rights* have been a proving ground for dialogues between theologians and scholars in other parts of the university. We celebrate the creativity of study programs and events at the universities of Oxford, Wisconsin, Minnesota, Northwestern, and the Australian National University, and look forward eagerly to the Spirit-infused ways that this book may enable students and faculty alike "to think Christianly" about their work, their academic worlds, and the wider publics and worlds which *Justice and Rights* reaches through the conversations initiated in this book.

Pieter Kwant has been a superlative agent and enthusiast. He has guided us creatively into a genre of publishing that is a new departure from his decades of leadership as Langham's Director of Literature. We likewise are most grateful to Langham Publishing, and Luke Lewis as Director of Publishing, for their readiness to experiment with this innovative genre of academic publication – the series Cross-Disciplinary Encounters with Theology, which *Justice and Rights* launches with promise and expectation for another way to develop a Christian mind, to engage the university, across the research universities of the world.

Preface

Justice and Rights is a different kind of book. It differs in innovative ways from any other scholarly book we have written or edited. It is different, as far as we know, from any book produced by the forty-seven widely published scholars whose writings are featured in this volume. Yet this is an academic book, written by academics for academics, in a form distinctive from conventional academic publications.

Justice and Rights emerges from a dialogue on faith and learning and it is presented here in the simplified form of a conversation. The dialogue is centered on a great issue for the contemporary university on any continent – how shall we understand what is just and what impact might that have on the frontiers of scholarship and domains of academic life in any field of the research university? The dialogue is set in motion by two stimulating writings by the notable philosophical theologian, Nicholas Wolterstorff.

In a crisp, masterful Preview in Part I of this volume, Wolterstorff presented to the then eighty scholar-members of the Global Faculty Initiative (GFI) an evocative set of issues and questions on justice and rights. He asked implicitly which of these issues resonates in any way with any field of scholarship in which you, the disciplinary scholar in architecture, or fine arts, or humanities, or social sciences, or biological and physical sciences, or medicine, or law, among others, are presently thinking, working, and writing? Respond with any fragments of thought, whether a sentence or two or paragraph or two, which can alert me to the reach of justice and rights thought across the faculties of the academy, and additionally, the working of universities themselves and the collegial societies in which all academics are embedded.

From the dozens of responses, Wolterstorff absorbed an astonishing array of topics. They ranged from atrocities in civil wars to domestic economic policies, from space communications to history wars over race and slavery, from restorative justice to treatment of doctoral students, from COVID-19 to Beethoven's sonatas, from psychiatric care to international trade, from climate change to international aid, and many, many more, which are featured as insets in this book.

Upon reflection, Wolterstorff crafted a superb compact essay, his Theology Brief on Justice and Rights, Part II of this volume, to introduce all the scholars in this conversation to a more extended and refined understanding of justice and rights. This distillation of his own extensive writings explicitly sought to equip the academic physicist or nuclear engineer or historian or public health specialist or any other scholar, with theological concepts and tools they might carry into their own work and scholarly lives.

GFI's leaders invited members to join this conversation more deeply, to engage with Wolterstorff's and their GFI peers' writings, by penning Disciplinary Briefs or Notes of their own. These more extended expressions of thought, presented in compact form in Part III of this volume, variously extended, questioned, disagreed, applied, refined, and explored Wolterstorff's theological sketch across many of the most prominent areas of inquiry in the contemporary research university, not to mention the headline issues of our times. Theologians O'Donovan and White offered alternative theologies of justice. Disciplinary scholars connected Wolterstorff's themes to climate change and language dialects, to displaced persons and natural disasters, to urban planning and palliative care, to government regulations and sexual violence, to welfare systems and refugees, among others. What proved especially exciting was the readiness of disciplinary scholars to engage and to observe the breadth of theological reach as it has been perceived from almost every corner of the university.

The dialogue did not end there. Donald Hay and Terence Halliday, GFI's Co-Convenors, invited Wolterstorff to reflect on all fifty or so responses to his Preview and Theology Brief. Did the theologian hear anything new from his interlocutors across the university that might refine his theology, learn of any other places in the academy or society where his thought might be extended, find himself compelled to rethink any of his own work? In a brilliant Postscript, Part IV of this volume, Wolterstorff models academic humility and generosity of spirit. He expresses surprise, for instance, that a theology of justice extends to language, as New Zealand sociolinguist Allan Bell argued; or that rights issues were somewhat turned on their head in the internal dislocations of Colombia's simmering civil war, as New Testament scholar Christopher Hays observed. Wolterstorff explicitly revises his views about Ulpian's thought in relation to the Christian tradition. He responds to gentle requests with an eight-point set of postulates about biblical teaching on justice and rights. And he concludes with the powerful assertion that rights-thinking long precedes the Enlightenment, insofar as Christian theologians have elaborated it since the early church and medieval Catholicism through the Reformation and into the early modern period of European history.

Readers will see that we have maintained the overall arc of a conversation in the organization of the book. In Part III, we have bundled the disciplinary side of the dialogue into five broad categories: chapter 1, Justice Debates; chapter 2,

Society and History; chapter 3, Law and Society; chapter 4, International and Global Justice; chapter 5, Justice in Biological, Physical and Medical Sciences; and chapter 6, Justice and the Academy.

If the dialogic structure of *Justice and Rights* marks a perceptible difference from conventional academic publishing, another departure is our decision to bring into intellectual engagement the authoritative with the exploratory. Many scholars bring years and decades of deep thought on justice and rights. Yet we have encouraged others to offer short pieces of instantaneous reaction or the glimmerings of previously unrecognized connections between the theologian's offering and our fields of academic expertise and specialization. However, as the dialogue unfolded, we could see that a few sentences opened a window, or a short Disciplinary Note set off a spark, not only for the author but for the rest of us. It took only a few words for Daniel Hastings at Massachusetts Institute of Technology to point us to the fact that the rush to a global space communications infrastructure raises profound issues of justice, especially for poor countries. In a radical contrast of scale, in a paragraph or two, Harvard psychiatrist John Peteet draws justice and rights issues inside the therapeutic consultation, and Columbia University's physician Lydia Dugdale proposes that mercy rather than justice marks so much of medical practice. Justice reaches inside the home, says Ryan McAnnally-Linz, while India's Nehru University historian Joy Pachuau points to the collective rights of India's tribal societies. Very rarely do such compact ruminations make it into print. Here we feature them as insets in the text, interspersed among the longer pieces.

This is a book of risks. In contrast to conventional academic publishing, which proceeds through rigorous rounds of proposals and drafts and refereeing and revision, the GFI process encourages disciplinary scholars in particular to risk thinking in a new way about our work. More than that, it invites scholars to go public with their thoughts in a most uncharacteristically early stage of reflection. Every GFI scholar and our research university colleagues achieve their standing by adhering to the rigors and training, research and writing that are modal for our fields. *Justice and Rights*, and the Dialogue on Faith and Learning on which it builds, dares disciplinary scholars to think in ways a substantial number of us are ill-equipped to do. We are asked to think theologically about our work. *Justice and Rights* thereby takes the bold step of revealing what is a weak hand for so many of us. Numbers of scholars in this volume have taken the risk of appearing naïve or wrong or under-developed in our thought. As Editors, we applaud what is a kind of academic courage—to go into print with new and possibly unfamiliar ideas in order to bring our Christian faithfulness more fully into conversation with our disciplinary expertise.

This book is different, too, because it curates in book form an antechamber of scholarship usually invisible to the outsider. Of course, many of the contributions here reflect long years of distinguished scholarly writings as they are brought into conversation with justice and rights. For more than a few of us, however, we reveal to outside audiences states of reflection before migrating to the status of working papers or conference presentations, before they mature into publications as refereed articles or make their way to print in books. We agree to publish the sorts of initial notes we make at the early and earliest stages of project development; we open up to distant readers the sorts of things we would normally discuss only with trusted colleagues or put on the table in workshops for rudimentary ruminations or maybe launch initially at an academic society conference. We do so not only for our own sakes, as we take small or new steps to think theologically about our work. We do so because we seek to encourage every reader of this book to begin to jot down and share initial thoughts about ways a theology of justice and rights might shake up, unsettle or revise our current research and writing, academic, and professional practices.

Many readers of *Justice and Rights* will therefore recognize that this book, in the rather static form of a print volume, captures on paper what so many of us longed for when we entered the doors of the academy. We wanted to sit in conversation with the "greats," the veterans, of our field. We hoped to witness emerging and junior scholars breaking old molds. We imagined we might be present during spirited exchanges when new ideas were placed on the table and old ideas were being stretched, qualified and even discarded. We wanted to be in the birthplace of new schools of thought, of new traditions, of exciting revisionisms, of new data, new findings, new theories that turned us in new directions. *Justice and Rights* simulates that excitement.

And, in contrast to very many books on faith and scholarship, *Justice and Rights* spans not only the disciplinary organizations of the university and the collegial institutions of the academic community, but also across the world. A law professor in Otago, New Zealand, encounters an architect in Oxford; an urban planner in the USA rubs shoulders with a chemist in Hong Kong; international relations specialists at the Australian National University are brought into conversation with great theologians at St. Andrews and Yale; a philosopher in Argentina encounters a law professor in Sri Lanka; an historian in Leicester speaks in effect to a philosopher from Nigeria.

But herein lies another distinctive of this book. It invites a different kind of reading. In *Justice and Rights* readers will encounter eminent scholars who are distilling a lifetime of thought and publication. They will read pieces by some disciplinary scholars who are already versed in theology. But not a few of us are reflecting for the first time, and at the earliest of stages, on Wolterstorff's views of justice and rights. As a result, what may be a profound new realization for one scholar, thinking far outside her usual domain, may be elementary to another. What may be a generative spark for a scholar who has never ventured this far from his home ground, can be seen as an enormously complex well-studied matter for a sophisticate or a veteran.

As a result, we urge readers of *Justice and Rights* to encounter the volume with the humility we see in Wolterstorff's Postscript. We encourage empathetic reading, an openness to surprise, a willingness to applaud a scholar who is prepared to reveal publicly how new or how late in their career is this fresh way of expanding their faith and intellectual horizons. We admire a scholar, customarily writing in equations, as he or she seeks to reach the rest of us in words. We appreciate the artist, for switching into a different medium so we fellow-travelers in other departments of the university gain a new comprehension of justice and rights in walkways and seminar rooms far from the usual paths we tread or settings we inhabit, even in our home institutions. As Wolterstorff argues so eloquently in his Theology Brief, let us give the appropriate recognition, what is due, to every scholar who has dared to think outside their usual box – and to do so in public.

We may therefore think of *Justice and Rights* as a site for our own cultivation of Christian virtues. It may inspire us with models of writing that are most uncharacteristic of our usual academic rhetorical style. It may bring a nod of appreciation for the scholar who takes a leap beyond their comfort zone. It can energize us with ideas that can be cultivated in our own work. It can humble us with admiration for those whose academic portfolios or modes of expression exemplify ideals to which we aspire. And most of all, it can equip each of us with broadened perspectives on the ubiquity of these integral biblical themes central to the long Judeo-Christian tradition, themes that might infuse our own scholarship or scholarly practices in ways that could inspire us to new chapters in a faithful calling to the research university and beyond.

Terence Halliday and K. K. Yeo

Part I

Preview

Justice

Nicholas Wolterstorff

Philosophical Theology, Emeritus, Yale University;
Institute for Advanced Studies in Culture,
University of Virginia, USA; Australian Catholic University, Australia[1]

Essential to any discussion of justice is the distinction between two fundamentally different forms of justice – call them *first-order justice* and *second-order justice*. First-order justice consists of justice in our ordinary interactions with each other: teachers and students treating each other justly, merchants and customers treating each other justly, and so on. Second-order justice becomes relevant when there has been a violation of first-order justice, that is, when someone has treated someone unjustly, wronged him or her. It consists of reprimands, punishments, and the like.

Many people, when they hear the word "justice," think exclusively of second-order justice. The term "justice" connotes for them prisons, fines, condemnations. First-order justice is basic, however, in that, if there were no such thing as first-order justice and injustice, there would be no such thing as second-order justice. For that reason, I will focus my discussion on first-order justice.

Justice is fundamental in Christian Scripture. Over and over in the Old Testament we read, "I the LORD love justice" (e.g. Isa 61:8), and over and over the ancient Israelites were instructed to "seek justice" (e.g. Isa 1:17). When the writer of the Gospel of Matthew explains who this mysterious person Jesus is, he identifies him as the one who is fulfilling "what had been spoken through the prophet Isaiah." He "will proclaim justice to the Gentiles" and will "bring justice to victory" (12:17–20).

An important point to note about what the Old Testament writers say about justice and injustice in ancient Israel is that, though on occasion they have individual cases in view, usually it is social (systemic) justice that they urge and social (systemic) injustice that they condemn – that is, justice and injustice in the laws and social practices of Israel.

What is justice? Coming down to us from antiquity are two fundamentally different ways of thinking of justice. One comes to us from the Greek

---

1. gfiweb.net/contributor/9

philosopher Aristotle, who explained justice as equity or fairness in the distribution of benefits and burdens. The other comes to us from the Roman jurist Ulpian (ca. 170–223 CE), who defined justice as *rendering to each what is his or her right, or due* (Latin: *ius*). I prefer Ulpian's definition, for the reason that not all cases of injustice consist of the inequitable distribution of benefits or burdens. Suppose that I violate your privacy; then, even if I do nothing with what I learn, I have wronged you, treated you unjustly. But I have not in any way distributed benefits or burdens inequitably. The Ulpian formula tells us that treating someone justly consists of rendering to that person what is his or her right or due – treating that person as he or she has a right to be treated. Justice is grounded in rights. But what are rights?

As one would expect, there is a good deal of disagreement on the answer to this question. My view, shared by many, and explicit in the UN documents on rights, is that rights are grounded in the worth (excellence, dignity) of the rights-bearer. Two fundamental facts about human beings are that we all have worth in certain respects and to certain degrees, and that there are ways of treating human beings that show due respect for their worth and ways of treating them that do not show due respect. I have a right to be treated a certain way when, if I were not treated that way, I would not be treated with due respect for my worth. Rights are what respect for worth requires.

Scholarship and teaching are inherently communal activities. In our engagement with students and colleagues we are called, one and all, to act justly – to treat our students and colleagues as they have a right to be treated, to treat them with due respect for their worth. It is evident to all who work in the academy, however, that the call to treat the other person justly is pervasively violated. In the vaunting by professors of their positions of authority, and in the competitive struggle of scholars to get ahead, they ride roughshod over the rights of others. But the biblical call to act justly is relevant not only to how professors and scholars treat each other and their students. In many disciplines and areas of inquiry, considerations of justice belong within the subject matter under consideration. This seems obvious for such disciplines and areas of inquiry as economics, political theory, management, health care, and gender studies, since these all deal directly with interactions among human beings. I say, "This seems obvious." It does not seem obvious to everyone. In the work of a good many scholars in these areas, utilitarian considerations of power, efficiency, and so on, are so prominent that justice is never brought into the picture.

A bit of reflection shows that considerations of justice are also relevant in disciplines and areas of inquiry where the relevance is not immediately obvious, since they do not deal directly with interactions among human beings. Architecture, for example. The focus of architecture is on buildings. But it is human beings interacting with each other who determine what is built and where. And what is built shapes, for good or ill, the lives of the human beings who inhabit those buildings and of those who must cope with them. Considerations of justice pervade architecture. Consider those disciplines and areas of inquiry that deal with the arts. Here too, while it may not be immediately obvious that considerations of justice are relevant, a bit of reflection shows that they are. Works of the arts are not just "out there" somewhere; they are made and engaged by human beings. And the ways in which they are made and engaged perforce raise issues of justice and injustice. Is it just, for example, that only the relatively well-to-do can afford to attend performances of the local symphony orchestra and choral society? And what colonialist studies of literature have shown us is that the worlds projected by literary works – how characters are portrayed and how society is pictured – raise profound issues of justice: gender, racial, class, economic, religious justice.

The same point could be developed for, say, environmental studies. But rather than developing that point, let me formulate the principle toward which we have been moving: considerations of justice are relevant to any discipline or area of inquiry that deals, in whole or in part, either directly or indirectly, with the interactions of human beings. And that covers most of what takes place in our colleges and universities. It does not cover theoretical physics as such – but it does cover how physics is developed and applied. It does not cover mathematics as such – but it does cover how mathematics is developed and employed.

When one looks at what scholars study and what professors teach, almost everywhere one sees that they are dealing, in part at least, directly or indirectly, with interactions among human beings. And whenever human beings interact with each other, they are divinely called to treat each other justly.

Part II

Theology Brief

Justice and Rights

Nicholas Wolterstorff

Philosophical Theology, Emeritus, Yale University; Institute for Advanced Studies in Culture, University of Virginia, USA; Australian Catholic University, Australia[1]

How may Christian academics engage justice and rights in their scholarship and the academy? The theme of God's love of justice recurs repeatedly in the Old Testament and it is integral to the teaching of Jesus and the apostles. Consistent with this teaching, I distinguish between first-order justice, where agents, individuals, and institutions act justly in their ordinary affairs; and second-order justice, which concerns the laws, sanctions, and systems that secure first-order justice. I focus on first-order justice as structurally basic. First-order justice is best understood as each person or institution rendering to others what is their right or what is due to them. A right is a morally legitimate claim to something, an entitlement. There are conferred rights, such as those attached to a position or a promise or by law or social practice; and non-conferred rights grounded in the excellence (goodness, worth, dignity, praiseworthiness) of the rights-bearer, such as natural rights and human rights. I show why the recognition of rights-talk is important and how it has an intrinsic connection with duties and obligations. First-order justice should play a pervasive role in the university. On the one hand, since the university is an intensively interactive institution, it is imperative to be alert to justice and injustice, including racism and sexism, in the fine texture of teaching, research, academic administration, and collegial interactions. Justice pertains also to relations of scholars and the university with funding agencies, governments, social institutions, and publics. On the other hand, considerations of justice belong in the subject matter of most disciplines, in scholarly agendas, methods, and theory. I conclude with questions every scholar might ask about the salience of justice and rights for his or her own research and scholarship and for the character of the academic institutions in which we serve.

---

1. gfiweb.net/contributor/9

My project in this essay is to bring to light the role of justice for the academy and the importance of being alert to that role. In order to do that, it will be necessary first to discuss the nature and importance of justice as such.[2]

Justice is fundamental in Christian Scripture. Over and over, dozens of times, the writers of the Old Testament declare God's love of justice. "I the LORD love justice," writes the prophet Isaiah (61:8). And over and over the writers set forth God's injunction to Israel to join God in loving justice. In a well-known passage the prophet Micah writes,

> [The LORD] has told you, O mortal, what is good;
>   and what does the LORD require of you
> but to do justice, and to love kindness,
>   and to walk humbly with your God? (6:8)

An important point to note about what the Old Testament writers say about justice and injustice in ancient Israel is that almost always it is social (systemic) justice that they urge and social injustice that they condemn – that is, justice and injustice in the laws and social practices of Israel. When condemning injustice, they seldom name names of individual wrongdoers. Another important point to note about justice in the Old Testament is that, over and over, the writers connect justice with *shalom*. Shalom consists of flourishing in all dimensions of one's existence: in one's relation to God, to one's fellow human beings, to the natural world, to oneself. Insofar as one is a victim of injustice, one is obviously not flourishing in that respect. Justice is thus intrinsic to shalom. However, one might be justly treated by all and yet not be flourishing; one might be seriously ill, or the victim of widespread famine. Justice is, as it were, the ground floor of shalom.

The claim has rather often been made by Christian theologians and ethicists that, though justice is indeed prominent in the Old Testament, in the New Testament justice has been superseded by love. Jesus, it is noted, issued a love command; he did not issue a justice command. The classic statement of this position is the 1930s publication *Agape and Eros* by the Swedish Lutheran bishop Anders Nygren. What this position implies, of course, is a dispensationalist understanding of God's work in history.

I hold that this is a serious misreading of the New Testament. Let's look at just two of the many relevant New Testament passages. In the Gospel of

---

2. A brief preview of this essay published above attracted around fifty responses from scholars in the Faculty Initiative Convening Panel and Collaborating Network. I thank them for the extraordinarily rich body of suggestions that they offered for topics to be discussed in the essay itself.

Luke we read that shortly after Jesus began speaking in public, he attended the synagogue in Nazareth on a Sabbath and was invited to read Scripture and comment on what he had read. He was given the scroll of the prophet Isaiah, unrolled it, and, on Luke's narration, read the following:

> The Spirit of the Lord is upon me,
>> because he has anointed me
>> to bring good news to the poor.
> He has sent me to proclaim release to the captives
>> and recovery of sight to the blind,
>> to let the oppressed go free,
> to proclaim the year of the Lord's favor.

Luke reports that Jesus then "rolled up the scroll, gave it back to the attendant, and sat down. The eyes of all in the synagogue were fixed on him," writes Luke, expecting him to offer some comment on what he had read. Jesus then said, "Today this scripture has been fulfilled in your hearing" (Luke 4:18–20).

What Luke reports Jesus as reading is an adaptation of the opening verses of Isaiah 61, which read as follows:

> The spirit of the Lord GOD is upon me,
>> because the LORD has anointed me;
> he has sent me to bring good news to the oppressed,
>> to bind up the brokenhearted,
> to proclaim liberty to the captives,
>> and release to the prisoners;
> to proclaim the year of the LORD's favor,
>> and the day of vengeance of our God. (Isa 61:1–2)

The passage is a close parallel of a passage in an earlier chapter in which the prophet spoke explicitly of God's demand for justice:

> Is not this the fast that I choose:
>> to loose the bonds of injustice,
>> to undo the thongs of the yoke,
> to let the oppressed go free,
>> and to break every yoke? (Isa 58:6)

The import of Jesus's declaration "Today this scripture has been fulfilled in your hearing" is unmistakable: Jesus identified himself as the one anointed by God to proclaim to the poor, the captives, and the oppressed the good news of the inauguration in his person of "the year of the Lord's favor" (the Year of Jubilee), when justice will reign.

In Matthew's gospel, Jesus has already been teaching and healing for some time when the writer intrudes himself into the story he has been telling to offer his interpretation of Jesus's identity – the same interpretation as that which Jesus himself offered in the synagogue. Jesus is "to fulfill what had been spoken through the prophet Isaiah," namely,

> I will put my Spirit upon him,
>> and he will proclaim justice [*krisis*] to the Gentiles.
>> . . .
> He will not break a bruised reed
>> or quench a smoldering wick
> until he brings justice [*krisis*] to victory. (Matt 12:17–20)

Why the De-justicizing Interpretation of the New Testament?

Why is it that, in spite of the passages I have quoted, and a good many others that could be cited as well, it is rather often claimed that justice has been superseded in the New Testament by love? Let me offer a few suggestions.

In many writers, perhaps most, what accounts for their supersessionist interpretation is primarily their understanding of the meaning of "love" (*agapē*) in the New Testament. *Agapē* is understood as gratuitous benevolence: seeking the good of the other person out of sheer benevolence, rather than because justice (or anything else) requires it. This was Nygren's interpretation of New Testament *agapē*, as it was that of the American theologian Reinhold Niebuhr throughout his career (for more, see Wolterstorff 2011a).

Intrinsic to this way of thinking of *agapē* is the claim, or assumption, that justice and agapic love are incompatible: if one acts out of agapic love, one does not act as one does because justice requires it; and conversely: if one acts as one does because justice requires it, one does not act out of agapic love.

Is this interpretation of *agapē* in the New Testament correct? Might it not be the case that some actions are instances of both agapic love and acting justly? I hold that that is indeed the case. The matter deserves a lengthy discussion; here let me introduce just one consideration.

All three Synoptic Gospels report the episode in which Jesus cited the two love commands (Matt 22:34–40; Mark 12:28–34; Luke 10:25–37). In Matthew's account of the episode, the Pharisees learned that the Sadducees had been unsuccessful in their attempt to trap Jesus, so they decided to see what they could do. "One of them, a lawyer, asked him a question to test him: 'Teacher, which commandment in the law is the greatest?'" Jesus replied:

"You shall love the Lord your God with all your heart, and with all your soul, and with all your mind." This is the greatest and first commandment. And a second is like it: "You shall love your neighbor as yourself." On these two commandments hang all the law and the prophets.

Matthew reports no response on the part of the lawyer or his Pharisee colleagues. Jesus got it right!

The first love command is to be found in Deuteronomy 6:5; the second, in Leviticus 19:18. Nothing in the context in which the commands occur in the gospels helps us in determining the meaning of *agapē*. Perhaps the context in which they occur in the Torah does help. The second love command is the one relevant to our purposes here.

In Leviticus, the command to love one's neighbor as oneself concludes a long list of specific injunctions to Israel as to how it is to live. Jesus and his interlocutors did not regard the love command as just one among others on that long list. It is "the greatest." And not just the greatest. Its function in the Leviticus passage is to sum up the preceding injunctions: "In short, love your neighbor as yourself."

For our purposes, what's important to note is that among the long list of injunctions summed up by the command to love one's neighbor as oneself are injunctions to act justly: "You shall not render an unjust judgment; you shall not be partial to the poor or defer to the great: with justice you shall judge your neighbor" (19:15).

The conclusion is inescapable: acting justly is not incompatible with acting out of agapic love; it's an example of such love. Love and justice must be understood in such a way that love incorporates justice. Later I will suggest how to understand justice so as to fit this requirement. As for how love should be understood: I suggest that love should be understood not as gratuitous benevolence that pays no attention to what justice requires, but as *care* – not care *for* but care *about*. When I care about you, I seek to promote your good, including the good of your being treated by myself and others as justice requires. Agapic love, understood as care, incorporates acting justly. Its comprehensive goal is shalom.

A Matter of Translation

The adjective *dikaios* and the noun *dikaiosynē* occur hundreds of times in the Greek text of the New Testament. When those same words occur in the classical Greek writers – Plato, Aristotle, and so on – they are almost always translated into English as "just" and "justice," respectively. When they occur in commonly used English translations of the Bible, they are almost always translated as "righteous" and "righteousness."

I take it as obvious that, in present-day idiomatic English, "righteousness" is not a synonym of "justice," nor is "righteous" a synonym of "just." "Righteousness" denotes a certain trait of personal character. In everyday speech we don't often, nowadays, describe a person as *righteous*; when we do, what we suggest is that the person in question is scrupulously concerned with his or her personal rectitude. Justice, by contrast, is an interpersonal normative state of affairs, specifically, the state of affairs that obtains when people treat each other justly. And a just person is one who habitually treats his or her fellows justly.

When we look at the contexts within which the terms *dikaios* and *dikaiosynē* occur in the Greek New Testament, we have to conclude that the reference is seldom to the interior character trait of righteousness. Almost always there is a reference or allusion to action – sometimes, to *just action*, sometimes, less precisely, to *right action*. Let's look at just two occurrences of the terms, out of hundreds, and judge, in the light of their context, how they are best translated; one doesn't have to know Greek to do this (Wolterstorff 2008, ch. 5; Wolterstorff 2013, chs. 14–16). I will use the NRSV translation.

In the Beatitudes as reported in Matthew we read, "Blessed are those who hunger and thirst for righteousness, for they will be filled" (5:6). The Greek word translated as "righteousness" is, again, *dikaiosynē*. This translation strikes me as strange. Does one hunger and thirst for a certain character trait? *Striving* for righteousness, for personal rectitude – that makes sense. But *hungering and thirsting for it*? One wants to say: "Don't just hunger and thirst for rectitude; act uprightly." By contrast: whether justice is present in society is mostly out of one's control; it depends on what others are doing. That is why one hungers and thirsts for justice. Jesus is blessing those who hunger and thirst for justice in society.

In Romans 1:16–17, Paul states the main theme of the letter that follows: The gospel "is the power of God for salvation to everyone who has faith, to the Jew first and also to the Greek. For in it the [*dikaiosynē*] of God is revealed through faith for faith; as it is written, 'The one who is [*dikaios*] will live by faith.'" In most commonly used translations, *dikaiosynē* is translated as "righteousness" and *dikaios* as "righteous." But when we read the letter that follows, what we learn is that God offers justification impartially to Jews and Greeks alike. "God shows no partiality" (2:11). To distribute a benefit impartially is to act justly. The main theme of Romans is not about God's righteousness – whatever that might be – but about God's justice.[3]

Two Types of Justice

In one of the psalms we read:

> Happy are those who observe justice,
> who [act rightly] at all times. (106:3)

In the law code delivered by Moses to Israel, and recorded in the Old Testament book of Deuteronomy, we find this passage:

> You shall appoint judges and officials throughout your tribes, in all your towns that the LORD your God is giving you, and they shall render just decisions for the people. You must not distort justice; you must not show partiality; and you must not accept bribes, for a bribe blinds the eyes of the wise and subverts the cause of those who are in the right. Justice, and only justice, you shall pursue. (16:18–20)

Moses is clearly referring to a fundamentally different type of justice from that to which the psalmist is referring. The psalmist is referring to justice in how we treat others in our ordinary affairs – justice in how people "conduct their affairs." "Happy are those who observe justice . . . at all times." Moses, by contrast, is referring to justice in judicial proceedings – the type of justice that becomes relevant when someone has not "conduct[ed] their affairs with justice."[4]

That there are these two fundamentally different types of justice was noted already by Aristotle. The traditional terms for them are "distributive justice" and "retributive justice." I think neither term is satisfactory. Let me explain here why I think the term "distributive justice" is not satisfactory; a bit later I will explain why the term "retributive justice" is not.

---

3. The New Testament scholar N. T. Wright 2011, in his recently published translation of the New Testament, renders the passage as follows: "The good news [is] God's power, bringing salvation for everyone who believes – to the Jew first, and also, equally, to the Greek. This is because God's covenant justice is unveiled in it from faithfulness to faithfulness. As it says in the Bible, 'the just shall live by faith.'"

4. O'Donovan 1996 contends that "justice" (*mišpāṭ*) in the Old Testament refers almost exclusively to justice in judicial proceedings, and that even when, on rare occasions, it does not refer to justice in judicial proceedings, "it has still not lost touch with the context of litigation." I engage O'Donovan's claim in Wolterstorff 2013, 68–75.

Aristotle held that justice of both types consists of the equitable (fair) distribution of benefits and/or burdens; injustice, of an inequitable distribution. As one would expect, what constitutes equity of distribution has been the subject of extended discussions among philosophers. Aristotle's idea, in the words of the contemporary American political philosopher Joel Feinberg, was that "justice requires that relevantly similar cases be treated similarly, and relevantly dissimilar cases be treated dissimilarly in direct proportion to the relevant differences between them" (Wolterstorff 2011a, 209). I have elsewhere argued that there is no one thing, neither equity nor anything else, that accounts for what makes distributions in general just. Distributions are just (and unjust) for a variety of different reasons.

Be that as it may, the reason I hold that the term "distributive justice" should be rejected for that type of justice which consists of agents acting justly in their ordinary affairs is that, though such justice is often to be located in how benefits and/or burdens are distributed, that is not always the case. Rape is a profound violation of justice, a profound wrong. But what fundamentally makes it wrong is not that benefits and burdens have been mal-distributed – though they have been. What makes it wrong is that the victim has been violated, treated with indignity. Another example: Suppose the government secretly invades my privacy without warrant. It has violated justice, wronged me. But there has been no distribution of benefits or burdens, and hence no *mal*-distribution.

I propose calling the type of justice that consists of agents acting justly in their ordinary affairs *first-order* justice: universities treating their support staff justly, teachers and students treating each other justly, banks treating justly people of color who are seeking loans, and so on. Justice in the distribution of benefits and/or burdens is one among other forms of first-order justice.

First-order justice encompasses both systemic justice and "one-off" cases of just action. And the term "agents," in the formula for first-order justice that I offered above, must be understood as encompassing not only individuals but also social entities such as institutions, organizations, groups, and the like. There is justice and injustice in the relation between banks and corporations, between a coal-burning plant and an asthmatic child in the area, between a Syrian refugee and an affluent European country, between health providers and patients, between states at the center of geopolitics and tiny Pacific island states – and on and on. It's because social entities can act unjustly and be treated unjustly that they can sue and be sued.[5]

When there has been a violation of first-order justice, there are just and unjust ways of responding to that violation; I shall call just ways of responding *second-order justice*. Punishment is a common form of second-order justice; but there are many other forms as well, such as fines, restitution, censure, banishment, reprimands, pardons, and forgiveness. A type of second-order justice that has become popular in the last fifty years or so is so-called *restorative justice*, this typically including the wrongdoer acknowledging that he or she did wrong and apologizing, the victim or his or her representative offering forgiveness in response to the apology, and restitution by the wrongdoer when that is possible.

It is my impression that many people, when they hear the word "justice," think primarily, if not exclusively, of second-order justice; they think of police, court proceedings, punishment, prisons, and the like. Second-order justice is obviously of fundamental importance – not only for its own sake but also because, given our human proclivity for wrongdoing, first-order justice cannot flourish without the support of a just and effective system of second-order justice. A just and effective legal system will institute both a system of laws and sanctions aimed at securing first-order justice among individuals and social entities, including justice in how the state treats its citizens, and a system of laws and procedures aimed at securing a just exercise by the state of second-order justice.

Though first-order and second-order justice are intertwined, first-order justice is structurally basic in that, if there were no such things as first-order justice and injustice, there would be no such things as second-order justice and injustice. Given this structural connection between the two types of justice, only if one understands first-order justice can one understand second-order justice. For that reason, I will focus my attention, in what follows, on first-order justice. Much of what I say will apply, however, to second-order justice as well.

Lest my single-minded focus on justice in this essay leave readers with the wrong impression, let me emphasize that loving God above all and one's neighbor as oneself are fundamental; justice is a component of neighbor love, not an alternative. Furthermore, not only is justice never the only virtue

---

5. The fact that both individuals and social entities can act and be treated justly and unjustly generates four possibilities: justice and injustice in how social entities treat other social entities, in how social entities treat individuals, in how individuals treat social entities, and in how individuals treat individuals.

exercised (or not exercised) in our interactions; acting justly *requires* the exercise of other virtues. To name just a few: it requires attentiveness to the worth and dignity of others, it requires empathy with the condition of others, it requires humility.

What Is Justice?

The biblical writers do not explain what justice is; they assume we understand what they are talking about when they speak of justice. They do not offer a "theory" of justice. For an explanation of what justice is, a theory, we have to turn to philosophers.[6] Christians will, of course, require of a philosophical theory of justice that it be, among other things, compatible with what the biblical writers say about justice – and more than compatible: that it illuminate what they say.

Coming down to us from antiquity are two fundamentally different accounts of what justice is. One comes from Aristotle who, as we saw, explained justice as equity (fairness) in the distribution of benefits and/or burdens.[7] The other comes from the Roman jurist Ulpian (ca. 170–223 CE). Referring to the virtue of being just, Ulpian says that justice (*iustitia*) is a steady and enduring will to render to each his or her *ius* (*suum ius cuique tribuere*).

How should we translate Ulpian's term *ius* into present-day English? A common translation is "right": justice is rendering to each what is his or her right. An alternative translation would be "due": justice is rendering to each what is his or her due. Ulpian's thought is that the virtue of justice (being just) is a steady and enduring will to render to each what is his or her right, or due. Justice understood as a state of affairs in society consists, correspondingly, of each individual or social entity rendering to each what they have a right to, what is due them.

I have already indicated why Aristotle's account will not do. Not all instances of first-order justice are cases of an equitable distribution of benefits and/or burdens, nor are all instances of injustice cases of an inequitable distribution of benefits and/or burdens. Ulpian seems to me to have gotten it right. All instances of first-order justice are cases of an agent rendering to another what is the other's right or due; all instances of first-order injustice are cases of an agent not rendering to another what is the other's right or due.

---

6. Someone might suggest that theologians also offer theories of justice. I think not; what they offer is, rather, a systematic account of how justice fits into God's "economy."

7. This is how John Rawls understands justice, in his much-discussed Rawls 1999.

But what are rights, and what accounts for agents having the rights they do have? The answer to this question is a subject of deep controversy among philosophers. To the best of my knowledge, all parties agree that a right is a morally legitimate claim to something; rights are entitlements. And as to what accounts for agents having the rights they do have, all parties agree that individuals possess certain rights because of official positions that they occupy, that individuals and social entities possess other rights because of some speech act directed toward them, such as a promise, and that individuals and social entities possess yet other rights because they have been conferred, by law or social practice, on all individuals or social entities of a certain standing. My right to a monthly Social Security check from the United States government is an example of this last sort. Rights of this last sort have traditionally been called *positive* rights; rights of the other two sorts have no common name. Let me call rights of all three sorts *conferred* rights.

However, by no means are all rights conferred. We have some of our rights just by virtue of being the sort of creature that we are – a person needing food, clothes, respect, and so forth – and standing in the sort of relations in which we do stand. So what accounts for the fact that one has a *nonconferred* right to some ways of being treated that would be a good in one's life whereas one does not have a right to other such ways of being treated? This, in my judgment, is the most difficult and controversial question that a theory of rights has to face.

Begin with the fact that what one has a right to is always a good in one's life, a life-good, never a life-evil. A life-good to which one has a right is, or implies, a way of being treated. That is not always evident on the face of things. My purchase of a ticket gives me the right to a seat on the plane; and that, obviously, is not a way of being treated! However, what's implied by my right to a seat on the plane is that I have a right to the airline officials *permitting* me to take a seat on the plane; and that is a way of being treated. The right to free exercise of one's religion is, similarly, the right to be *permitted* to exercise one's religion freely; it is a *freedom* right, of which there are many others as well: the right to freedom of speech, for example, the right to assemble, to vote, to start a business.

Though that to which one has a right always is, or implies, some life-good of being treated a certain way, the converse is not the case: there are many ways of being treated that would be a good in one's life to which one does not have a right.

A view on the matter that is currently prominent in the literature is that such rights are all either conditions for the enjoyment of, or specifications of, our fundamental nonconferred right to autonomy – that is, our fundamental nonconferred right to form for ourselves a plan of life and to enact that plan.[8] Popular though this theory is, it has to be rejected. One problem confronting the theory is explaining what that purported nonconferred right to autonomy amounts to. Clearly nobody has the right to do whatever he or she sees fit; so what, then, is that purported right to autonomy? I judge that no autonomy theorist has succeeded in answering this question. But we don't have to read around in the discussions surrounding the nature of autonomy to see that the theory won't do. I trust that everybody reading this essay will agree that to torture imprisoned criminals as a way of punishing them is to wrong them; they have a nonconferred right not to be punished by torture. To employ torture as a method of punishment is to treat them unjustly. But what makes it wrong is not that their autonomy is thereby impaired; their autonomy is already impaired; they are locked up. What's wrong about torturing them, I suggest, is that their dignity as human beings is violated.

And in general, it's my view, shared by many and explicit in the UN rights documents, that nonconferred rights are grounded in the excellence (goodness, worth, dignity, praiseworthiness) of the rights-bearer. I have a right to the life-good of being treated a certain way just in case, were I not treated that way, I would be treated in a way that does not befit my worth, my dignity, my praiseworthiness. The philosopher Jean Hampton put it well: A person wrongs another, treats that person as he or she has a right not to be treated, "if and only if (while acting as a responsible agent) she treat him in a way that is objectively . . . demeaning, that is disrespectful of [that person's] worth" (quoted in Wolterstorff 2008, 296).

Two fundamental facts about human beings are that we all have excellence in certain respects and to certain degrees, and that there are ways of treating us that show due respect for some excellence that we possess, and other ways of treating us that do not show due respect. Nonconferred rights are what respect for excellence requires. For example: if an election official rejects my ballot for the irrelevant reason that my signature did not include my middle name whereas my driver's license does, I am not being treated with due respect for my being a duly registered adult citizen of the state of Michigan.

The praiseworthiness that grounds the right to the gold medal of the person who has won the race is an acquired praiseworthiness. But not all rights-grounding excellences are acquired. Some we have on account of some property we naturally possess, such as bearing the image of God, being capable of speech (which grounds one's right to freedom of speech), and being religious (which

---

8. A good example of this line of thought is Griffin 2008.

grounds one's right to free exercise of one's religion). The rights grounded by such excellences have traditionally been called *natural* rights. An important subset of natural rights are *human* rights – rights that one has just by virtue of being a human person or human being.[9] An example of an excellence that grounds a natural right that is not a human right is *having exceptional mathematical ability.* This sort of praiseworthiness is not acquired; the right of such a person to due respect for his or her mathematical ability is, accordingly, a natural right. But it's not a right he or she has just by virtue of being a human. It's a right he or she has by virtue of being a particular sort of human; so it's not a human right. Two excellences of human persons that ground genuinely human rights are the capacity to interpret oneself and the reality in which one finds oneself, including interpreting it religiously, and the capacity to perform an action for the reason that one judges it to be good or obligatory (the Kantian tradition singled out this excellence) (Wolterstorff 2012).

Why the Recognition of Rights Is Important

It would be a mistake to move on without taking note of the fact that there is hostility in many quarters nowadays to talking about rights, including in Christian quarters. This hostility has many roots, the most common being, so it appears to me, the conviction that rights-talk is made to order for expressing one of the most pervasive and malignant diseases of modern society – namely, the mentality of possessive individualism. It's made to order, so it is said, for an "entitlement society" such as ours in which individuals place themselves at the center of the moral universe, focusing on their own entitlements to the neglect of their obligations toward others and to the neglect of the cultivation of those virtues that are indispensable for the flourishing of our lives together. It both encourages and is encouraged by the possessive individualism of the capitalist economy and the liberal polity. The theologian Joan Lockwood O'Donovan puts the point crisply: "the modern liberal concept of rights belongs to the socially atomistic and disintegrative philosophy of possessive individualism" (Wolterstorff 2008, 51).[10] To the best of my knowledge, all those who espouse this critique of rights-thought and rights-talk claim, in support

---

9. By the term "human person" I mean a human being capable of functioning as a person. Tiny infants, those in a coma, those sunk deep into dementia, are human beings but not human persons.

10. The theological ethicist Oliver O'Donovan shares this view of rights. I discuss their view of rights in part 1 of my Wolterstorff 2008, titled "The Archeology of Rights."

of their interpretation of rights, that the idea of natural rights was devised by the secular individualist philosophers of the Enlightenment. The medieval intellectual historian Brian Tierney showed decisively in his 1997 publication *The Idea of Natural Rights* that this historical claim is mistaken. He shows that the canon lawyers of the twelfth century were explicitly employing the idea. It was from the seedbed of medieval Christendom that the concept of natural rights emerged, not from the eighteenth-century Enlightenment.[11]

No doubt rights-talk is often employed in exactly the way the critic charges. But being employed in this way is not intrinsic to rights-talk; it's an abuse. Every component of our moral vocabulary is subject to abuse. The correct response to the abuse of some moral concept is not to toss out that concept – we would have no moral vocabulary left – but to do what one can to correct the abuse.

When you and I interact with each other, our normative situation is symmetrical: I have a morally legitimate claim, a right, to being treated in certain ways by you, and you have a morally legitimate claim, a right, to being treated in certain ways by me. One of the respondents to the preview for this essay made this point nicely by saying that we are called to be not only *claimants* for justice but *agents* of justice. The possessive individualist employs the language of rights to focus on the former to the neglect of the latter. It's the mentality of possessive individualism that is the culprit in such cases, not the language of rights. And let's recall a point made earlier: not only do individuals have rights; social entities such as institutions, organizations, and communities also have rights. My bank can wrong me, but I can also wrong my bank.

Here is perhaps a good place to note that there is an intrinsic connection between rights and duties (obligations): if you have a right to my treating you a certain way, then I have an obligation to treat you that way; and conversely. Given this correlation, it turns out that justice, on the Ulpian conception, consists equally in agents honoring the rights of others and in agents honoring their duties to others.

But if rights and duties are correlative in that way, and if rights-talk is often abused in the way indicated, why not eliminate rights-talk from our moral vocabulary and make do with talk about duties, obligations, and responsibilities?

Certain things of great importance would be lost if we eliminated rights-talk from our moral vocabulary. The moral order has two dimensions, distinct but intimately connected: the *agent dimension*, the dimension of what we do, where the language of duty, obligation, responsibility, guilt, and so on, is for bringing to speech this dimension of the moral order; and the *patient*

---

11. I discuss what I call this "contest of narratives" in Wolterstorff 2008, ch. 2.

dimension, the dimension of how we are done unto, where the language of rights, of what is due one, of being wronged, is for bringing to speech this dimension of the moral order. In some situations, it's important to bring to speech the agent dimension by speaking of responsibilities; in other situations, it's important to bring to speech the patient dimension by speaking of rights.

Consider the abused wife. With the language of duty, guilt, and so on, she can bring to light the agent dimension of the situation, the moral significance of what her husband is doing. He is failing in his responsibilities to her, his duties; he is guilty. But she cannot bring to light the patient dimension of the situation, the moral significance of how she is being done unto. For that, she needs the language of rights: she is being wronged, her rights are being violated, she is not being rendered what is due to her.

It's no accident that all the great social justice movements of the twentieth century, struggling against one or another form of systemic injustice, employed the language of rights: women's rights, labor rights, civil rights, and on and on. It was their use of such language that enabled the members of those movements to bring to speech the moral condition of those who were being systemically wronged.

There is something else of great importance that would be lost if we eliminated rights-talk from our moral vocabulary. A feature of rights that I have thus far not taken note of is what is sometimes called their *trumping* force, or sometimes, their *peremptory* force. The idea is this: if you have a right to my treating you a certain way, then, no matter how many good things I might bring about by not treating you that way, I am morally required to treat you that way.

The best way to see that rights do indeed have this trumping force is to recall the connection, noted above, between rights and duties. If you have a right to my treating you a certain way, then I have an obligation to treat you that way. But if I have an obligation to treat you that way, then I am morally required to treat you that way, *period*, no matter how many good things I might bring about by not treating you that way. Nothing trumps obligation!

The twentieth century was rife with authoritarian regimes pursuing policies that they claimed to be for the greater good over the long haul: Hitler, Stalin, Pol Pot, the Afrikaners. If we do not have available to us the language of rights to call attention to the fact that, no matter how much good such policies might bring about, they are nonetheless morally unacceptable because they are trampling on the rights of people, we have no way of putting the brakes on such (self-perceived) benevolence. The point is relevant at the micro level as well. All too often, benevolence is extended in such a way as to violate the dignity of the recipient; it humiliates. We need the recognition and language of rights for putting a brake on paternalistic benevolence.

The question has also been raised: Can living creatures other than human beings have rights – animals and plants? When discussing the nature of nonconferred first-order rights I said, with my eye on human beings, that a right one has is always to a way of being treated that would be a good in one's life – a life-good.[12] Animals and plants have lives, and there are goods in their lives – states and happenings in their lives that contribute to their flourishing in their own distinct way, including ways of being treated by human beings that would be goods in their lives.

At least some of these goods are good in that they contribute to the good of a human being: *instrumental* goods. Perhaps one thing good about your dog is that it provides you with companionship; that's an instrumental good. But are animals *intrinsically* praiseworthy in certain respects, not just instrumentally? My own conviction is that they are. In the opening chapter of the book of Genesis we read that on the sixth day of creation, before the creation of human beings, God stood back, contemplated what had been created, and "saw that it was good" (Gen 1:25).[13] Aldo Leopold's *A Sand County Almanac* (Leopold 1970) is a treasure trove of extraordinarily perceptive celebrations of the praiseworthiness of the wild plants and animals in his surroundings. The question that needs deep reflection, so it seems to me, is not whether animals and plants are intrinsically praiseworthy in certain ways and to certain degrees, but what form due respect for their excellence should take.

Justice in the Academy

It is time that we turned our attention to the role of justice in and by and for the academy, and to the importance of being alert to that role. My discussion will be little more than suggestive. My aim is to point to the pervasive role of justice in the academy and to the pervasive presence of injustice.

---

12. A question that naturally arises here is whether social entities have lives. Literally speaking, they do not. But they can flourish, and there can be enhancements and diminutions in their flourishing, and that makes it possible for them to have rights.

13. A full discussion of what Scripture tells us about the intrinsic praiseworthiness of animals and plants would take note of the repeated declaration that God's glory is revealed in creation.

As an Institution

First-order justice pertains to how agents engage each other, how they interact. Teaching is an inherently interactive activity: teachers and students interacting with each other. Scholarship is inherently interactive: scholars interacting with other scholars in their discipline. Academic administration is inherently interactive: administrators interacting with faculty, students, and staff. Laboratory research is interactive. In all these interactions, we are called to act justly – and to seek the well-being of our fellows and institutions in ways that go beyond what justice requires.

The present-day American academy, for instance, is pervaded by instrumentalist appraisals, that is, appraisals in terms of one or another form of success and failure. What proportion of those who graduate from the college with a pre-med degree are getting into medical school? What proportion of those who graduate from the university with a PhD in English are getting tenure-track positions within a year? How many citations have there been over the past year of publications by members of the philosophy department? And so on. The academy is an arena of success and failure. But it's also an arena of justice and injustice. And it is at least as important to appraise academic life in terms of justice and injustice, in terms of doing right and being wronged, as it is in terms of success and failure.

In making such appraisals, it's imperative that we be alert not only to the racism, sexism, and sexual abuse that pervade the academy, but also to justice and injustice in the fine texture of our interactions. Anyone who has participated in the academy for any length of time has heard about, or witnessed, teachers giving unfair tests, teachers humiliating students to whom they have taken a dislike, senior scholars blackmailing young scholars whom they perceive as potential competitors, faculty badmouthing administrators, administrators being rude and heartless to staff. All such actions, and others like them, are instances of injustice, instances of someone being wronged. Those who have heard the biblical call for justice will themselves refrain from all such actions and will seek to halt the injustices they witness.

Justice pertains not only to interactions within the academy but to interactions of academic institutions, and their faculty and staff, with individuals and social entities outside the academy – scholars interacting with fund-granting entities and publishers, professors functioning as consultants or as public intellectuals, universities interacting with other universities and with state legislatures, policymakers and international organizations, universities interacting with sports associations – the list goes on and on.

Consider research funding and agenda-setting. One of the respondents to the prospectus for this essay wrote,

> Research priorities are skewed. . . . Most studies on global health inequality consider unequal health care and socio-economic conditions but neglect inequality in the production of health knowledge. . . . Conditions common to developed countries garnered more clinical research than those common to less developed countries. Many of the health needs in less developed countries do not attract attention among developed country researchers, who produce the vast majority of global health knowledge. (McKenzie 2020)

On Scholarly Frontiers

The relevance to the academy of considerations of justice is not limited, however, to how academic institutions and their members treat each other and how they engage with individuals and social entities outside the academy. In many disciplines and areas of inquiry, considerations of justice belong within the subject matter of the discipline and a scholar's area of inquiry. This is obvious for those that deal directly with interactions among human beings and social entities, such as economics, political theory, business and management, sociology and social work, health care, and gender studies. I say, "This is obvious." Apparently it is not obvious to everyone. In the work of a good many scholars in these disciplines, utilitarian considerations of power, efficiency, cost, preference, and so on, are so pervasive that justice is never brought into the picture.

Those who have heard the biblical call for justice will see it as their responsibility to do what they can to resist such reductionism. Those whose specialty is public health will go beyond considerations of cost and efficiency to ask what justice in health care calls for – attending especially to justice for "the little ones." Those whose field is economics will not be content, when appraising the economic health of a society, with determining its Gross National Product (GNP) but will ask whether that GNP is justly distributed among members of the society. Those who work in the field of education will explore what it is to teach justly, and will ask whether access to quality education is justly distributed within a school district, a city, a county, a state; they too will attend especially to the fate of "the little ones." Those who work in political theory and international relations will ask what a just refugee and immigration policy would look like.

History is both similar to and different from the disciplines mentioned above: similar in that it deals directly with interactions among individuals and social entities, different in that it does not make policy suggestions. Historians who have heard the biblical call for justice will not write hagiographical Great Men histories in which the flaws of the "great man" are airbrushed away and the fate of "the little people" ignored. They will show human history for what it is: a mixture of the noble and the ignoble, of the just and the unjust. And they will narrate not only the accomplishments of the elite and powerful but also the lives of the ordinary people.

A bit of reflection will make clear that considerations of justice are also relevant in disciplines and areas of inquiry that do not deal directly with interactions among human beings and social entities. Architecture, for example. The focus of architecture is on buildings and the space within buildings. But it is human beings interacting with other human beings who design buildings and spaces, deciding, in doing so, for what use and by whom they will be designed and where they will be located. Considerations of justice pervade the practice of architectural design.

Once buildings have been built, they shape the lives of those who inhabit those buildings and the lives of those who must cope with them. Considerations of justice are relevant at these points as well. Redlining, zoning, gentrification, and government housing projects are just four of many examples that could be given of building practices that raise profound issues of justice and injustice.[14]

Engineering and environmental studies raise issues of justice and injustice similar to those raised by architecture. But I must move on. Consider those disciplines and areas of inquiry that deal with arts other than architecture: music, drama, literature, visual art. That considerations of justice are relevant here is even less evident than it was in the case of architecture. But again, a bit of reflection shows that they are.

Gender and colonialist studies of literature have shown, in recent years, that the worlds projected by literary works – how characters are portrayed, how society is pictured, and so on – raise profound issues of justice: gender justice, racial justice, class justice, economic justice, religious justice. Traditional aesthetics, with its exclusive focus on the aesthetic properties of works of art, ignores such issues.

---

14. The Inner City Christian Federation in Grand Rapids, Michigan, is an excellent example of a private nonprofit organization that consistently employs considerations of justice in its renovation and construction of inner-city housing.

Add to this that works of art are not just "out there" somewhere. They are made, performed, displayed, and engaged by human beings; and the ways in which they are made, performed, displayed, and engaged perforce raise issues of justice and injustice. Is it just, for example, that only the relatively well-to-do can attend performances of the local symphony, the local opera, and the local choral society? Does injustice lurk behind the fact that so few of the composers who people the canon of Western classical music are women and so few, people of color?

Let me formulate the principle toward which we have been moving: considerations of justice are relevant to the subject matter of any discipline or area of inquiry that deals, in whole or in part, either directly or indirectly, with the interactions of human beings and social entities. And that covers most of the disciplines and areas of study in our colleges and universities. It does not cover theoretical natural science as such; but it does cover how physics, chemistry, biology, computer science, and so on, are developed, supported, taught, and applied. Neither does it cover mathematics as such; but it does cover how mathematics is developed, supported, taught, and applied.

When one looks closely at what scholars study and professors teach, one discerns that, outside mathematics and the natural sciences, they all deal, in part at least, directly or indirectly, with interactions among human beings and social entities. Considerations of justice are relevant to all such interactions.

I wrote the initial draft of this section of my essay on the very same day, 30 July 2020, that the final written words of John Lewis, great American civil rights activist and congressman, appeared in *The New York Times* (p. A23). His brief essay included the following words:

> I heard the voice of Martin Luther King Jr. on an old radio. . . .
> He said it is not enough to say it will get better by and by. He
> said each of us has a moral obligation to stand up, speak up and
> speak out. When you see something that is not right, you must
> say something. You must do something.

King was referring to civil society. His words are as applicable to the academy as they are to civil society.

The Scholarly Pursuit of Justice

In this essay I have posed many questions that I could not address on this occasion. I have had to skip lightly over the verdant terrain of justice and its role in the academy. Much more could be said. Let me conclude with questions that every scholar might ask that bring the theology and ethics of justice and rights into the fullness of the academy and scholarship.

Research and Scholarship

Is there any aspect of my current research, writing, or academic performance where the question "Is it just?" has salience (e.g. in my scholarly agenda or method or theory I bring to bear on it)?

To what extent does my discipline in general, and my research topic in particular, incorporate interactions between people and/or groups?

- What are the rights of the parties to those interactions (being studied? doing the studying?)? What might be the main sources of injustice in those interactions?
- What rules and institutions are in place to implement justice, in the sense of redressing wrongs, or even better, preventing those wrongs occurring? Are they adequate to deliver justice?
- How far are the interactions mediated through (academic?) institutions, and what powers do those institutions have over persons? What ensures that they act justly?
- Are there just or unjust ways that my scholarly products may be applied or utilized?

Academic Institutions

To whom does the scholar in my field owe a duty or obligation – within the academy and beyond the academy?

Do my academic practices, or do academic practices in my discipline, give all persons their due, affirming and cultivating their excellence (e.g. in acknowledgments, attributions and citations, authorship, mentorship, collegial support, teaching and training)?

In my experience, how just are the core institutions of the academy: recruitment of students and faculty, academic governance, scholarly publishing, academic societies, academic award-giving, academic promotion?

In the interactional spaces of my scholarly field, where is there manifest injustice, that is, a failure to express love through giving others their due or enhancing the quality of their "life-worlds"?

Agencies funding research must establish priorities on topics, research institutions, qualifications of researchers, and so on. Are you personally cognizant of what you judge to be injustices in the setting of such priorities?

References and Further Reading

Brunner, Emil. 1945. *Justice and the Social Order.* New York: Harper & Brothers. A classic example of a theological account of justice.

Finnis, John. 1980. *Natural Law and Human Rights.* Oxford: Oxford University Press. An attempt to ground human rights in natural law.

Goodman, Lenn E. 2008. *Love Thy Neighbor as Thyself.* Oxford: Oxford University Press. A discussion from a Jewish perspective of justice in the Old Testament and the command to love one's neighbor as oneself.

Griffin, James. 2008. *On Human Rights.* Oxford: Oxford University Press. An attempt to explain human rights as conditions and/or specifications of the fundamental right to autonomy.

Keller, Timothy. 2013. *Generous Justice.* New York: Penguin. An excellent discussion of all the relevant New Testament passages on justice.

Leopold, Aldo. 1970. *A Sand County Almanac.* New York: Ballantine.

McKenzie, Ross. 2020. "Preview Response. Justice/ Physical & Biological Sciences." https://www.facultyinitiative.net/content_item/262 [pp. 180–181 in this volume]

Niebuhr, Reinhold. 1935. *An Interpretation of Christian Ethics.* New York: Harper & Brothers. Niebuhr's development of the position that justice is for situations of conflict and love for situations of harmony.

Nygren, Anders. 1953. *Agape and Eros.* Translated by Philip S. Watson. London: SPCK. See for Nygren's contrast between pagan *eros* and Christian *agapē*, and for his influential contention that justice is superseded in the New Testament by *agapē*.

O'Donovan, Joan Lockwood. 1997. "The Concept of Rights in Christian Moral Discourse." In *Protestants, Catholics, and Natural Law*, edited by Michael Cromartie, 143–56. Grand Rapids: Eerdmans.

———. 1998. "Natural Law and Perfect Community: Contributions of Christian Platonism to Political Theory." *Modern Theology* 14, no. 1 (January): 19–42. In these essays, O'Donovan argues that the idea of rights that are not conferred is intrinsically expressive of possessive individualism.

O'Donovan, Oliver. 1996. *Desire of the Nations.* Cambridge: Cambridge University Press. Discusses justice in the Old Testament, contending that it is almost always judicial proceedings that the writers have in view.

———. 2005. *The Ways of Judgement.* Grand Rapids: Eerdmans. A theological discussion of justice very different from Emil Brunner.

Rawls, John. 1999. *A Theory of Justice.* Rev. ed. Cambridge: Harvard University Press. Rawls's hugely influential attempt to explain justice as equity in the distribution of benefits and/or burdens.

Tierney, Brian. 1997. *The Idea of Natural Rights: Studies on Natural Rights, Natural Law and Church Law 1150–1625.* Atlanta: Scholars. A detailed defense of the claim that the idea of natural rights can be traced back to the writings of the canon lawyers of the twelfth century.

Tuck, Richard. 1979. *Natural Rights Theories: Their Origin and Development.* Cambridge: Cambridge University Press. Tells the story of appeals to natural rights in the late Middle Ages and the early Renaissance.

Witte, John. 2007. *The Reformation of Rights.* Cambridge: Cambridge University Press. Shows in rich detail that the idea of natural rights was employed extensively by the second-generation Reformers and their successors.

Wolterstorff, Nicholas. 2008. *Justice: Rights and Wrongs.* Princeton: Princeton University Press. A detailed treatment of many questions raised in the Theology Brief, including: *chapter 2* on the contest of narratives between those who claim that the idea of natural rights has its origins in eighteenth-century Enlightenment thought and those who claim that it has its origins in the canon lawyers of the twelfth century; *chapter 5* on translation; and *part 2,* "Theory: Having a Right to a Good," on alternative accounts of nonconferred rights.

———. 2011a. *Justice in Love.* Grand Rapids: Eerdmans. A detailed discussion of the relation between justice and love.

———. 2011b. Essays in *Hearing the Call,* edited by Mark R. Gornik and Gregory Thompson. Grand Rapids: Eerdmans: "The Moral Significance of Poverty," on the rights of the poor (pp. 287–96); "Has the Cloak Become an Iron Cage: Love, Justice, and Economic Activity," on justice in the operation of business in the modern world (pp. 372–94); "Justice, Not Charity: Social Work through the Eyes of Faith," on the role of justice in social work (pp. 395–410).

———. 2012. *Understanding Liberal Democracy.* Oxford: Oxford University Press. On various excellences of human beings that ground human rights.

———. 2013. *Journey toward Justice.* Grand Rapids: Baker Academic. On issues of New Testament translation (chs. 14–16) and the New Testament case against retribution.

———. 2018. "Why There Is a Natural Right to Religious Freedom." In *Homo Religiosus? Exploring the Roots of Religion and Religious Freedom in Human Experience,* edited by Timothy Samuel Shah and Jack Friedman, 195–229. Cambridge: Cambridge University Press. On the right to freedom of religion.

Wright, N. T. 2011. *The Kingdom New Testament: A Contemporary Translation.* New York: HarperCollins.

Part III

Disciplinary Exchanges

1

Justice Debates

What Is Justice?

Fr. Thomas Joseph White, O.P.

Theology, Pontifical University of St. Thomas (Angelicum), Rome, Italy[1]

Prof. Wolterstorff helpfully points out that justice is based on healthy and well-ordered relationships between persons. For Thomas Aquinas, the medieval theologian influenced by Aristotle and Augustine, such order emerges from natural human inclinations to seek happiness in virtuous and constructive ways, through relationships of affability and love of friendship, within the framework of collective lives based around goods shared in common. (See *Summa Theologiae* II-II, Q58, 61.) A human family, for example, is a kind of common good in which each person can flourish through affable and caring relationships, friendships of the spouses and parental friendships with children in their care. Based on such relations, an order of justice emerges. Parents, for example, normally owe certain standards of care and education to their children. Spouses normally owe one another a certain degree of engagement and genuine fidelity. The relationships between persons in this context amount to more than relationships of justice but they include and are supported by fundamental relations of justice. Aristotle notes that friendship and love are more than justice can provide but they cannot be sustained without basic justice.

---

1. gfiweb.net/contributor/163

Three Forms of Justice

This first case is familial but one could extend the examples to include collective organizations of work, education, or statecraft. In any of these cases, one may speak analogically of various forms of justice, not one form alone. There is justice that results from (1) the part to the whole (which I will call participatory justice), (2) the part to the part (which he calls commutative justice), and (3) the whole to the part (distributive justice). However can we illustrate each of these cases inductively from examples?

1. Participatory Justice: The Part to the Whole

The person (considered as part) who participates in a larger common good (the whole life of the city, the family, the workplace, the university) incurs obligations and responsibilities toward the whole, precisely as a beneficiary participant. In this case each person has a role to play in contributing to the larger group. It is reasonable, for example, that a city or state ask its citizens to pay taxes, or that a family ask its children to participate in a common family outing. An academic is expected to creatively contribute to the university in teaching and writing or in administrative work. Diverse nation states need to work together collectively within the framework of a larger international common good, so that all states contribute constructively to peace, international justice, and economic prosperity.

2. Commutative Justice: The Part to the Part

Each member of the collective community has obligations and rights vis-à-vis one another as individuals. The most common example of this is in exchanges, as when one is expected to pay a just price for something one purchases or one is owed a just wage for work one does. However, this notion is flexible and somewhat analogical, applying to various forms of equality. The spouses have equal rights and responsibilities in justice to one another within a marriage bond. Two academics who write a paper or edit a book together have a kind of equal share in the reputation and effect of the book. Two nation states need to show mutual respect and just concord in relations with one another, be they economic or political.

3. Distributive Justice: The Whole to the Part

The whole has obligations to each individual, depending upon the needs and capacities of the individual in question. This is the kind of justice that typically comes to the forefront in questions of political policy. Any common good has some representative leadership that represents the whole and makes decisions in view of the common good of the whole. In doing so they have to think about the qualities, capacities, and limitations or needs of individuals and subgroups. Parents in a family need to think of the just distribution of needs for an infant versus a teenager who may need tutoring versus a child with athletic or artistic talents they legitimately wish to develop. A university administration can distribute scholarships prudently in view of a diverse representation of students, and can distribute grants, honors, or responsibilities among academics in view of representative academic excellence. The state has social obligations to various groups of people who are more vulnerable or who require distinct kinds of advocacy: those with disabilities, the poor, the socially marginalized. Any given country needs to respect the subsidiary and self-determination of small collective groups and institutions within its polity. Wealthier or more powerful nation states should think rightly of how to incorporate more materially disadvantaged or less developed nations within the larger collective common good of deliberation and exchange.

Justice and Personhood

This idea of justice presupposes some form of human exceptionalism: there is a reason human beings are agents and recipients of justice, due to their dignity as intellectual and free animals, able to live constructively or destructively with one another. This means that any realistic notion of justice cannot be merely procedural or formal, politically convenient or conventional, but must be grounded in a viable claim about what human persons are, and what they are genuinely meant to live for (and not live for). The Christian intellectual tradition typically has argued that the human being has a unique dignity because he or she is made in the image of God, and has spiritual powers of intelligence and free will. The Thomistic tradition has argued that this truth claim is at least in part verifiable and defensible by means of philosophical argumentation. (See in this respect Madden 2013 and Stump 2005, noted below.) One can analyze and explain key facets of human reason and free decision-making so as to show why human beings are agents of moral responsibility and, more profoundly, why they are spiritual animals. They are constituted not only by bodies possessing (highly evolved) animal powers but also by a spiritual principle or "soul" that is the formal cause of personal identity. Does one have to go all the way into such metaphysical speculation to retain a rich conception of human justice? Some would say no. I agree with philosophers like Augustine, Aquinas, Hume, and Nietzsche that it matters very much that we determine first what human beings are if we wish in turn to evaluate their ethical nature.

Justice and Mercy

From this line of thinking about justice one also might suggest that the search for justice is integrally related to the search to love or care for others personally in responsibility, and the need of the community not only to punish or rehabilitate but also to forgive and have mercy. Mercy entails a love that passes beyond the mere requirement of justice, so as to care for a person when he or she is suffering *in extremis* or failing ethically. Mercy helps us recall what interpersonal relations are about fundamentally, the communion of persons in love of friendship. Mercy can seek to reconstitute communion even after people have failed to attain the due measure of justice, even while acknowledging justice. In this sense there is no mercy without justice since mercy is more apparent when love passes beyond merely "what is due" to another. At the same time, justice without mercy readily becomes a caricature of itself, a kind of ethical false coinage. Just relations between persons exist in view of love of friendship, cooperation that is personal, and in view of a civilization of human charity. When one weaponizes justice in uncharitable ways so as to exclude or destroy persons and harden society abrasively, one creates an unmerciful and in effect unloving society. War does this, even just war, to some extent (though one may still commend one's enemies to the eschatological mercy of God). But it is an error to construe civic and political life as always being on a war footing. The truth is that all human beings are unjust at times, even radically so, so in a society that loses a sense of mercy, justice will eventually become intolerable and so even a culture of justice will be difficult to sustain. The wielders of justice, if they are not perfect, which they will not be, will appear arbitrary or inconsistent in their justice, so their notions of justice will become suspect. Those who want a culture of justice should strive also to create a culture of mercy, rehabilitation, and reasonable penance. Indeed, penance is important for the harmony of justice and mercy, so that confession, forgiveness, and reconciliation can be a dimension of human social life.

Historically the cultural belief in the centrality and practice of mercy as a qualifying feature of justice is of Christian ancient and medieval origin, and there are noteworthy exponents of it who developed their ideas against the backdrop of a Christian eschatological and theocentric vision of the human person and of society. We can think here of Augustine, Aquinas, Catherine of Siena, and in more recent times, Pope Leo XIII, Elizabeth Anscombe, and Pope Francis. Christian intellectuals should think not only of human justice but also of the transcendent divine justice and mercy of God publicly revealed in Christ. The latter idea is not merely a private or individual truth, unless one holds to an erroneous conception of it. In the New Testament we are intriguingly told that God himself has justified humanity. That is to say, in the person of Christ, God has revealed a deeper mystery and order of justice unfolding in human history, in which God seeks to repair our ties of weak or self-interested love (individual or collective), to reestablish and reframe our human common life, by the power of his grace.

Christians need not be reticent to speak about this mystery of divine love and justice, unveiled in Christ, in the university today. Historically speaking, the very idea of Christian atonement (literally: at-one-ment) gave rise to the aspiration of a genuinely universal culture of learning and love of God and others, at the heart of the medieval university. In our contemporary academic context characterized by ideological heterogeneity and by an often contested search for new grounds of ethical normativity, this distinctively Christian notion of universal love and personalistic justice can provide a helpful resource in the ongoing shared human search for the truth.

Speaking of Justice in the Wider Academy

Is it really possible to speak about such matters with people who do not share a common assent to the central truth claims of Christianity? I think it certainly is, at least in part. We might note some of the key claims made above that one could openly propose or discuss with colleagues not prone to share any particular convictions regarding God or Christianity.

1. Justice may be considered broadly as the rendering to each what is due to him or her, but this is in fact analogically denoted, as we have noted above, in diverse ways. One cannot apply notions of distributive justice to situations that entail the norms of commutative justice, or participatory justice. Justice within the family can be analyzed using any of these three forms of justice, depending on the relations in question, but what justice is in the family is different from what it is in the university or workplace, the city, the state,

the nation, or the international order. *Distinct common goods entail distinct relations and forms of responsibility.*

2. This means that the determination of what justice is, is not merely a question of intuition or emotivism (though our intuitions or emotions may or may not tell us something about it, imperfectly). *Thinking about justice is an intellectual discipline* marked by care for truthfulness, analytic depth, clarity of analysis, and fairness, as well as the search for concord, love, and appreciation of persons. One can invite non-Christians to this vision of things.

3. It is mysterious that we as human animals are subjects able to be just who are characterized by responsibility. What does this say about us as beings, open in freedom to do what truth requires, but also able to evade or ignore the truth in our actions? To converse about justice is to ask in reality what a human being is, a fact that Plato already saw so well in the Gorgias. *The travails of modern university culture in regard to this question are new opportunities to return to the sources of classical reflection on this key question. What is a person?*

4. What about justice within the larger complex dynamic of human existence, marked by moral failure (sin), evil, the need for repentance, forgiveness, and rehabilitation? Anyone who sustains meaningful human relationships knows he or she needs some form of forgiveness to play a life-giving role in his or her relations to others. What does this unavoidable drama of human good and evil say to us and to our contemporaries? Does our experience of ethical fragility (and for some at times even torment) open us up to religious questions, or should it? Here again we face a perennial question. To ask about justice is also to ask ultimately who in this universe is on trial by whom? Is the court of history constituted merely by passing human beings, who judge us in the hours before they in turn die, and leave the standards to others who may change them? Or are we ultimately on trial before a transcendent standard, the mystery of God in his truth and justice? In this latter case, would the trial, execution, and death of Christ have something to tell us about our relationship to God and one another? Is it a piece of romantic lore or is it Logos made flesh, divine reason unveiled in human history? We might also courageously invite our secular colleagues in the university today to ask this question of Christ himself, doubtful or agnostic though they may be. After all, he can and often will answer

them directly, since he is now risen from the dead. We crucified him, but on the other shore of our injustice, *he provides an unyielding horizon of hope, bearing in on us, inviting us to a new and strange regime of justice, mercy, and charity.*

Further Reading

Budziszewski, J. 2016. *Commentary on Thomas Aquinas's Treatise on Law*. Cambridge: Cambridge University Press. An excellent contemporary introduction to Aquinas's moral theory that leads the reader through one of his main analytic treatments of ethics.

Dewan, Lawrence. 2006. *Wisdom, Law, and Ethics: Essays in Thomistic Ethics*. New York: Fordham University Press. An intellectually dense but accessible treatment of many contemporary problems in ethics making use of Aquinas's moral principles.

Hittinger, Russell. 2003. *The First Grace: Rediscovering the Natural Law in the Post-Modern World*. Wilmington: ISI. This work engages with the challenge of contemporary perspectivalism or relativism and asks how one might recover a basic sense of universal ethics.

Madden, James. 2013. *Mind, Matter and Nature: A Thomistic Proposal for the Philosophy of Mind*. Washington, DC: Catholic University of America Press. A splendid and clear defense of the immaterial powers of the human person, in engagement with contemporary analytic philosophy, while keeping in mind modern scientific understanding of the material body.

Pinckaers, Servais. 1995. *The Sources of Christian Ethics*. 3rd ed. Washington, DC: Catholic University of America Press. A most famous and influential modern work on ethics, arguing that the medieval virtue-based approach was eclipsed by utilitarianism and deontology, giving rise to much of the confusion that we experience today in public life. This work presents a eudaimonistic (happiness-based) account of the pursuit of goodness, and situates virtue and law in that context.

Stump, Eleonore. 2005. *Aquinas*. London: Routledge. A major contemporary work of analytic philosophy taking profound inspiration from Aquinas. Notions of personhood and human understanding and freedom are explored here that are relevant to our contemporary conversations on the ontological foundations of ethics and notions of justice.

Profound Differences

Oliver O'Donovan

Theology, Emeritus, University of Edinburgh; University of St. Andrews, UK[2]

It will be no news to my friend Nicholas Wolterstorff, I am afraid, that I have profound difficulties with his approach to the topic of justice. The essence of justice lies in what he calls "second-order justice," that is, in the act of judgment which distinguishes innocence from guilt and creates a new public context of right. Many of the biblical texts that refer to "justice" are in fact referring to the "act of justice" – which is Aquinas's name for judgment. Judgment is performed primarily by God, and by humans as authorized under God. Justice is the name for the condition established by judgment.

The overarching normative moral category governing interactions among persons considered apart from the exercise of judgment is not justice, but love. That our day-to-day interactions may be qualified as just is determined by the fact that they are, in fact, always governed by divine judgment that precedes them. The "ordinary" interaction is never prior to the act of judgment. It is for this reason that human interactions qualified primarily by other virtues may and must also display justice as well as the other virtues. So while I agree with Wolterstorff in his claims for the comprehensiveness of justice as a criterion for all kinds of interaction, I think he fails to explain how it is that a relation clearly normed by the virtue of wisdom, such as that between teacher and pupil, must also display justice.

Also, justice is always a public state of affairs, a set of relations among or between different agents, and cannot be accounted for as a sum of subjective rights held by individual or particular agents. The conception of subjective rights is a medieval development, and it has its areas of usefulness. But rights derive from justice, not justice from rights.

2. gfiweb.net/contributor/130

An Alternative Framing of Justice and Rights
Peter Anstey
Philosophy, University of Sydney, Australia[3]

I do not believe that speaking about justice in terms of rights is always helpful: first, because the notion of rights is foreign to Scripture; and second, because, in my view, rights are derived from more fundamental moral concepts, and analyzing moral issues in terms of rights can result in one losing touch with the more fundamental concepts. For example, take the passive right of a child to be cared for by his or her parent. This right is founded on the duty of care that pertains to the parent: take away the duty of care and the right disappears. Here the fundamental moral concept is duty of care. Once we have that, there is a sense in which the child gets the right "for free." In some contexts, rights-speak seems to be helpful, but I would certainly advise against using it as a term of reference for understanding the nature of justice.

From Justice Ethics to an Ethic of Care
Eleonore Stump
Philosophy, St. Louis University, USA[4]

In recent decades, at least in certain philosophical circles, justice has lost some of its luster as a virtue for establishing and sustaining good relationships in a society. In the view of some feminist philosophers, for example, ethics based on justice needs to be supplemented, or even supplanted, by an "ethics of care." One of the problems faced by those who think an ethics of care should supplant, rather than supplement, an ethics of justice is that it is not immediately apparent how to ward off certain sorts of exploitation on an ethics of care alone, without reference to justice. I think Aquinas's account of justice has the resources for dealing with the problem.

---

3. gfiweb.net/contributor/30
4. gfiweb.net/contributor/133

A Contextual Interpretation of Justice by a Chinese Biblical Theologian

K. K. Yeo

Bible, Theology and Culture, Garrett-Evangelical Seminary; Northwestern University, USA[5]

Prof. Nicholas Wolterstorff has written an insightful Theology Brief on "Justice and Rights" (hereafter NWTB). Any response to such a rich, dense, and evocative piece is mainly an expression of my gratitude for the gift of friendship afforded by the Global Faculty Initiative (GFI) platform.

A Dialogue with NWTB from a Biblical Interlocutor
Two Different Methods of Two Theological Fields

There are two different methods by which theologians may bring Scriptures and the theologies that derive from them to disciplinary scholars. One is NWTB's approach of a "systematic" or constructive theologian who introduces a philosophical category, then looks to its scriptural supports, logic, and argument, and offers a critical analysis and constructive synthesis. The merits of this approach are that it is comprehensive in scope of the topic examined, persuasive in its method of inquiry, and winsome in finding biblical support for its thesis.

An alternative approach, that of a biblical theologian, is to start with the biblical text, examine its particulars of time and place and situation, and then move up to more variegated biblical texts and their contexts, as a biblical theology is summarized and constructed to be applied to new contexts (or disciplines).

My approach emphasizes "context" or "culture" in at least three areas:

1. The salience of the cultural context of the Bible and its authors in biblical exegesis;

2. Culture itself or the social location of the initial and subsequent readers as a lens to receive the biblical messages;

3. That the cultural contexts of the Bible are *part of the content* in the Bible as well as in our contemporary biblical interpretations.

---

5. gfiweb.net/contributor/88

The benefits of this approach are attentiveness to contexts and nuances; and the conscious effort to extrapolate from one context/discipline so as to make the biblical message more fitting to new situations in the course of history.

Let me illustrate this alternative approach, beginning with the meaning of the word "upright"/"righteous" (in the sense of making right or acting for neighborly good) in Habakkuk 2:4 (see table).

Hebrew Bible [MT, ca. 538 BCE][6]	Greek Old Testament (OT) [LXX, ca. 250 BCE]	New Testament (NT, 1st century CE, NRSV)
Habakkuk 2:3–4: For the vision is yet for an appointed time, but at the end it shall speak, and not lie: though it tarry, wait for it; because it will surely come, it will not tarry. Behold, his soul which is lifted up is not upright in him: but the **righteous** shall live by *his* faith.	Habakkuk 2:3–4: For the vision is yet for a time, and it shall shoot forth at the end, and not in vain: though he should tarry, wait for him; for he will surely come, and will not tarry. If he should draw back, my soul has no pleasure in him: but the **righteous** shall live by *my* faithfulness.	Galatians 3:11: Now it is evident that no one is justified [set right] before God by the law; for **"The one who is righteous will live by faith."** Romans 1:17: For in it the righteousness of God is revealed through faith for faith: as it is written, **"The one who is righteous will live by faith."** Hebrews 10:37–38: For yet "in a very little while, the one who is coming will come and will not delay; but **my righteous one will live by faith."**

These are complex texts. The word "righteous" (*ṣaddîq/dikaios*) in the Old Testament context is first and foremost not a *psychological-moral* (inner trait) category, but a *theological* one, which refers to a people who are justified or *set right* before God in the Abrahamic covenant (Gen 12; Rom 4; Gal 3). This people are called "righteous" or "just" not because of their own moral fortitude or sinlessness but because of God's faithfulness ("*my* faithfulness" in the Greek OT, ca. 250 BCE). The book of Habakkuk in its original context (Hebrew Bible, ca. 538 BCE) is addressing the question stated in 1:1–4: "Why are God's elect, called the righteous or just, allowed to suffer in their captivity under the arrogant and unjust Babylon?" Habakkuk 2:3–4 replies that God is not pleased with the person who is not upright (i.e. unjust Babylon), but the

---

6. Unless otherwise indicated, all translations of biblical texts are the author's.

members of the covenant characterized by their Torah obedience "shall live by *his* faith" in God.

Without a contextual reading, one easily slips into a historical theology perspective, notably the Reformation debate regarding whether it is the believer's faith or the believer's works that bring the salvation of God. The context of Martin Luther in sixteenth-century Europe is about whether the purchase of a letter of indulgence (works) will guarantee salvation or whether salvation comes simply by "faith alone." The Reformers are doing biblical interpretation that is *cross-culturally* biblical.

Further, the phrase "those who are hungry and thirst for [uprightness or justice: *dikaiosynē*]" in Matthew 5:6 (predominantly Jewish community) has a different meaning from "you who are hungry" in Luke 6:21 (predominantly mixed community), though they are parallel texts – the "Beatitudes" – describing the same teaching of Jesus, albeit in two different literary styles and with differing nuances. Matthew's gospel overall has certain features that focus on the set-right life of being God's people, such as pursuing uprightness (the word appears seven times in Matthew, not at all in Mark, once in Luke, twice in John) *as a quality of life in the Spirit of God* (Matthew chs. 5–7). In contrast, Luke's gospel overall has certain features that focus on the social-political transformation of the gospel through the mission of God's people, such as "peace on earth and goodwill to all people" (2:14), and to "proclaim good news to the poor, release the captives, recover the sight of the blind" (4:18).

This contextual reading of Matthew and Luke allows us to let both texts stand without the need to change Matthew's meaning ("one hungers and thirsts for uprightness") into Luke's (one "who is poor" and "hungers" for justice). I see the contextual readings of Matthew and Luke as speaking to the beauty and power of diversity in the biblical revelation and its embrace of the creative tensions of differences within the biblical canon, thus enabling biblical conceptions of justice to speak to myriad contexts.

Toward a Biblical Theology of Justice and Uprightness

The larger and variegated contexts of the biblical canon grant us a more robust understanding of justice than a few texts can. Due to limited space, let me offer briefly my view on meanings of justice/judgment (*mišpāṭ/krima*) and righteousness/rightness (*ṣĕdāqâ/dikaiosynē*) in the Old Testament (see Pedersen 1926 and 1959; Krašovec 1999; Reimer 2014).

Justice (*mišpāṭ/krima*) is one of the *attributes* of God (Deut 32:4; Isa 28:6; 51:4–5; Jer 9:24; Ezek 34:16) the Judge (Pss 67:4; 96:13; 98:9), whose character is fairness (without prejudice) and (up)rightness in his dealings with people. "He is the Rock, his works are perfect, and all his ways are just. A faithful God who does no wrong, upright and just is he" (Deut 32:4 NIV). So the biblical language of justice is primarily *theological* (about who God is and what God does), *covenantal* (about the relationship God has with people), and *legal* (about laws or ordinance).

Righteousness (*ṣĕdāqâ*/*dikaiosynē*) in the Old Testament is neither *simply* a legal concept nor the quality of religious observance, but rather about a relationship with God that requires a fulfillment of conditions of integrity, trustworthiness, and uprightness which contribute to the peace and prosperity and flourishing of all (Job 29:16; 31:21; Prov 8:18; 14:23; 31:9). This idea of righteousness and its vocation extends from the Old Testament's "people of God" to the New Testament's "kingdom of God" and the church.

Justice Applied to the Academy

The Bible affirms that the relationship God has with all people and the whole creation is established and maintained in equity or fairness (Isa 1:27: "Zion will be redeemed with justice") and what is right (2 Chr 12:6; Neh 9:33). Justice is God's concern for the shalom of all, and the Bible has a *universal* scope of justice. God's people, who are called "the righteous" or "the just," are expected to keep the covenant as a way to maintain their identity of being God's people (Ps 37:28; Prov 28:5) for the sake of goodness to the world. "My justice will become a light to the nations. My righteousness draws near speedily, my salvation is on the way, and my arm will bring justice to the nations" (Isa 51:4–5 NIV). God uses his people, scholars among them, as an instrument to bring about justice in the world. Whoever else participates in the mission of a just God then aligns with the vision of God's reign on earth (Mark 9:40).

Three Frames for Conversing with Other Disciplines on Justice

There are three cultural frames about shalom (well-being) in biblical theology that will enable us to see justice (what is right and what is due) in more fulsome language and elaborate a vision that can then be applied to the research interests of many disciplines.

1. The first frame is that of a *truthful and legal universe*, and much of NWTB focuses articulately on this frame. Justice is about obeying the rules of life, abiding by the laws of God, and following the orders of

the cosmos – be they moral, political, economic, and so on. Injustice is missing the mark (*hamartia*), or doing wrong (*ḥāṭā'*). The Mosaic laws have a lot to say about this, as do the Psalms, providing more or less direct biblical guidance on key issues in disciplines:

- How can the "love your neighbor" commandment of Leviticus 19 be practiced by architects to design buildings that promote community life, to construct spatial justice etched with hospitality, especially to the vulnerable?
- In finance and banking, how can "love your neighbor" overcome poverty and challenge zero-sum games, for example in offering lower-interest loans (e.g. in microfinancing) or the zero interest of cooperatives (e.g. Basque cooperatives, Israeli *kibbutzim*) in sharing of capital for, say, small business startups?

2. The second frame is that of a *moral universe* that highlights the heavenly order of inherent goodness – though some cultures view the order of this moral universe as oscillations or roles of yin and yang, cycles of good and evil, and justice is *li* (cosmic order). Justice in this frame is viewed as the health benefits due to a person, animals, plants, outer space; and injustice is viewed as illness, toxic wastes, space trash. Therefore we can ask:

- How can the fields of deep ecology and climate change and carbon cycle studies envision justice-oriented programs to restore the health of our habitat, ecology, outer space? Will they in turn generate justice for humanity?
- In the fields of language studies, do we have a duty to overcome bigotry, bullying, and toxic language?

3. The third frame is that of a *holy and beautiful universe*, one that is covered with its creator's presence and glory. "Honor everyone. Love the brotherhood. Fear God" (1 Pet 2:17 ESV) is considered justice in this frame, because what is due to everyone is "honor" (shaming others is injustice); what is due to friends is "love" (hatred is injustice); and what is due to God is "fear/reverence, glorifying." In contrast, injustice, as sin, has "fall[en] short of the glory of God" (Rom 3:23). We can raise pertinent questions:

- How can astronomy and physics attract scientists to honor the excellences of minorities or people of color, and by so doing *advance* the fields?

- In music, mathematics, and photography, is the "golden ratio/ mean" universal or culturally defined in terms of what is aesthetically pleasing or morally just?

References and Further Reading

Krašovec, Jože. 1999. *Reward, Punishment, and Forgiveness: The Thinking and Beliefs of Ancient Israel in the Light of Greek and Modern Views.* Leiden: Brill. Esp. ch. 28 on the legal and theological understanding of justice in the ancient world.

Pedersen, Johannes. 1926 and 1959. *Israel: Its Life and Culture I–II.* Copenhagen: Povl Branner, 1926; and *Israel: Its Life and Culture III–IV.* [Denmark]: Dyva & Jeppesen, 1959. Thorough cross-linguistic and contextual understanding of justice (*mišpāṭ/krima*) and righteousness (*ṣĕdāqâ/dikaiosynē*) in the OT and its complex world.

Reimer, David J. 2014. "*sdq.*" In *New International Dictionary of Old Testament Theology and Exegesis,* edited by Willem A. VanGemeren, vol. 3, 744–69. Grand Rapids: Zondervan. Nuances of "right/righteousness" in word and theological studies of the OT.

Wolterstorff, Nicholas. 2015. *Justice in Love.* Grand Rapids: Eerdmans. A companion volume to his *Justice: Rights and Wrongs,* the author examines the thick but harmonious relationship between justice and love.

Yeo, K. K. 2018. *What Has Jerusalem to Do with Beijing? Biblical Interpretation from a Chinese Perspective.* 2nd ed. Eugene: Pickwick. Ten cross-cultural biblical interpretation essays which read the Chinese cultures biblically and read the Bible contextually and indigenously; a number of essays on justice, righteousness, and love.

Extending Rights Questions
Jennifer Herdt
Divinity, Yale University, USA[7]

Defenders of inalienable natural rights (e.g. Locke, Frederick Douglass) often insist that while these natural rights cannot be taken away, they can be forfeited, together with the dignity of humanity. What is secured by theological affirmations of the *imago Dei* and of universal human dignity if theological justifications for the forfeiture of that dignity can and are often given?

---

7. gfiweb.net/contributor/98

On Obligations Rather Than Trust
Casey Strine
Ancient Near Eastern History and Literature, University of Sheffield, UK[8]

I want to query whether "rights" is the appropriate term for what Wolterstorff advocates. Would it not be more appropriate to maintain that the value (or worth, as it is said in the preview) of every human being means all people have obligations in how they treat others? This reverses the perspective of the language in the essay – focusing on the Other rather than the Self – and seems to better reflect what is said in the final five paragraphs (of the Preview) in my reading of them. This change would also engage other relevant texts (e.g. Gen 9:6; Matt 22:39 *et passim*).

Justice and Home
Ryan McAnnally-Linz
Theology, Yale University, USA[9]

Wolterstorff's rights-based account of justice has significant bearing on the ethics of homemaking and home maintenance, particularly in a world where there are millions who have no house to call home, no land that will treat them as belonging, or highly insecure habitations. It pushes in the direction of asking what, if any, quality of home is *due* to a human being and to whom the correlative duty of providing such a home belongs.

---

8. gfiweb.net/contributor/81
9. gfiweb.net/contributor/64

Love as the Foundation for Christian Justice

Osam Temple

Philosophy, Bakke Graduate University, USA;
formerly Philosophy, American University of Nigeria, Nigeria[10]

Introduction: Why Must I Be Interested in Justice?

Professor Wolterstorff's Theology Brief on "Justice and Rights" demonstrates deep Christian thinking on a very important subject. Not only does it reinforce the centrality of justice in both the Old and New Testaments, it also shows the nexus between justice and rights, and makes the pertinent point that Christians need not be negative about discussions on rights since the roots of natural rights discussions can be traced to the "seedbed of medieval Christendom." All of these lead to the crucial point that questions of justice and rights underlie the subject matter of our academic disciplines.

This Theology Brief should challenge Christian scholars to search deeper within the boundaries of their academic disciplines. It should motivate us to reposition ourselves and find our voices amid the concatenation of anti-Christian voices that dominate life in academia today.

An important plank in the brief is the emphasis on first-order justice. The focus on Ulpian's perspective on justice brings home the salient points that connect the concept of justice to obligation as well as to the inherent worth of individuals. These are strong themes that should guide Christian academics to excel and be relevant wherever they find themselves.

There are, however, questions that need to be addressed in our discussion of justice. What is the source and nature of justice from a Christian perspective? Are there no distinctly Christian approaches to justice and rights? How does my interest in justice differ from that of an atheist, a Buddhist or a Muslim? What is in my Christian faith that should motivate me to be interested in justice in my institution? Why should I be interested in the questions of justice that arise in my teaching and research? Is our interest in justice aimed at building a good and moral society? After that, what? Is the gospel message only about building a fair and moral society? Will any fair and moral society in the world be considered Christian? What is the overall purpose of this discussion anyway? Is there no salvific or missional purpose to the Christian interest in justice?

---

10. gfiweb.net/contributor/84

Love – the Missing Link

In my opinion, the real challenge for Christian scholars today is not merely to be engaged in issues of justice in their universities, but to understand the compelling reasons for this engagement. We need to develop a robust theory of justice that is biblical and relevant to our world today. The Theology Brief does not take this path because it rejects a very important perspective in the discussion, which is that in the New Testament, justice has been superseded by love and that Jesus did not issue a justice command but a love command. Of course, as Professor Wolterstorff puts it, "acting justly is not incompatible with acting out of agapic love; it is an example of such love. Love and justice must be understood in such a way that love incorporates justice." This is a valid point, but it further highlights that love supersedes justice. There is no love without justice but there can be justice without love. You can give everyone their due even when you do not love them. You can do justice not out of conviction but out of the fear of the law and punishment. It is for that reason that Christian scholars must always have the love commandment on their radar. If this is the case, if love must incorporate justice, then our discussion of justice should lead us to explore the concept of love. This is what I think may be missing in our Christian approaches to justice.

Jesus Situates Justice on Love

Professor Wolterstorff states that biblical writers do not explain what justice is and they do not offer a "theory" of justice. Therefore, he suggests that "for an explanation of what justice is, a theory, we have to turn to philosophers." I agree that there is a rich corpus of resources on justice in philosophic history from which we can draw, but should this be our guide? Is it true that the Bible does not give us a guide to a theory of justice?

Let us return to Matthew 22:37–40 for better insight:

> Jesus said unto him, Thou shalt love the Lord thy God with all thy heart, and with all thy soul, and with all thy mind.
> This is the first and great commandment.
> And the second is like unto it, Thou shalt love thy neighbour as thyself.
> On these two commandments hang all the law and the prophets.
> (KJV)

What did Jesus mean when he said, "On these two commandments hang all the law and the prophets"? I think that what he was really saying is that "on these two commandments hang the entire scope of justice." He was actually laying the foundations of a justice theory and demonstrated it through his life. The true origin of justice is in the nature of God. What Jesus did was to situate justice in the womb of love. He didn't philosophize about it; he lived it. It was left for Paul to lay down a full-blown theory of love in 1 Corinthians 13:

> Love is patient, love is kind. It does not envy, it does not boast, it is not proud. It does not dishonor others, it is not self-seeking, it is not easily angered, it keeps no record of wrongs. Love does not delight in evil but rejoices with the truth. It always protects, always trusts, always hopes, always perseveres. (1 Cor 13:4–7 NIV)

The Superiority of Love-Based Justice

The motivation of the Christian scholar to stand for justice should therefore rest on just one principle, love – the love of God, love of humankind, love of academia, love of students and colleagues, love of our institution, and so on. It is this commitment to love that can motivate Christian academics to take action when confronted with injustice in society. Any concept of justice that is not rooted in love will end up finding its roots in law or the constitution, and the legal system is subject to periodic changes and amendments. When Jesus requires us to be just, is he simply asking us to obey the constitution? There is a huge gap between love-based justice and law-based justice.

In my experience as a Christian scholar, I have observed some of my colleagues display a commendable sense of justice. But in some cases, the Christian sense of justice ends up in a strict adherence to rules even when they are no longer reasonable. Therefore, the Christian witness, through the adherence to rule-based justice, sometimes becomes negative. The impression is given that Christians are rigid and not open to dialogue. I believe that if we practice true *agapē*, we can teach the world the true meaning of justice. The problem however is that we have not given sufficient thought to the concept of love. And we ought to do so! In the modern day, *eros* is confused with *agapē* and the chief formulators of the concept of love are now in Hollywood.

The Missional Angle

Once again, I ask: What is the purpose of my interest in justice? If my interest in justice has no missional or salvific purpose, how far can I go? The whole point about Christianity is to redirect humanity back to the love of God. What is it about love that makes it redemptive? This is a question that Christian scholars should reflect on. From the life of Christ and the teachings of the apostle, we can infer that love is sacrificial and selfless; it preserves the truth, the good and the beautiful; it draws people closer and promotes human solidarity. Therefore, it creates space for sincere engagement with the world, and increases the possibility of expanding the kingdom of God.

As individuals in our various institutions our primary focus ought to be the kingdom of God. Everything God did for humankind was motivated by love. Our interest in justice should also be motivated by love. Our interest in reconciling fallen humanity to God should motivate us not only to be just in our dealings with others (first order) but to seek to transform our institutions with Christian values. Justice in this case, therefore, is not an end but a means to an end. The end will be to demonstrate through our activities the love of God and give all men and women an opportunity to reconcile with God.

In my opinion, justice without this salvific purpose is pointless. Furthermore, if we do not rest justice on love, we may surrender our commitment to a thoroughly Christian concept to secular philosophers or artists. Philosophers can give us only a limited perception of justice, and not a full picture. This is because justice is based on the nature of God, which is love. And this theory was there before Plato's theory of justice.

Are Virtues Necessary to Acting Justly?
Jonathan Brant
Theology, University of Oxford, UK[11]

If justice is about "interactions between human beings" then the "actors" or the "agents" are clearly important, opening up an interesting question: What virtues might be necessary to underwrite the ability to interact justly – honesty, humility, gratitude?

---

11. gfiweb.net/contributor/39

Beyond Justice in Relationship
Robert Joustra
Politics, Redeemer University, Canada[12]

As a political scientist, while I appreciate this renaissance in justice as a driving category across disciplines, I also worry that this renaissance can preclude what other disciplines are really *for*. I agree with Nick that justice is a feature of every relationship, but it may not be the defining or central aspect. If we read literature, or participate in art, or theater, and all of these simply become a vehicle for conversations about justice, or – even worse – become largely utilitarian mediums for partisan or political commentary, we have suffered a real loss on the intrinsic nature of these activities. None of this is to say that justice, as a right relationship, should not be a constant partner, but by raising questions of art and history and music into a central, driving question about justice, I fear we lose what some might call the "leading aspect" of these areas, reducing them to a medium for activism, rather than appreciating their full worth.

Radical Christian Subversion
Chris Watkin
French Studies, Monash University, Australia[13]

I'm interested in how social contracts are being extended today to include nonhuman parties: animals, particular features of the environment. Wolterstorff states that "considerations of justice are relevant to any discipline or area of inquiry that deals, in whole or in part, either directly or indirectly, with the interactions of human beings," which I take to mean between two or more human beings. What about human interactions with nonhuman actors? Can I treat my dog unjustly, if no other human is concerned? Can I treat a river unjustly, if my interaction with it has no effect on other human beings? I think a Christian approach has unique things to say about this.

---

12. gfiweb.net/contributor/57
13. gfiweb.net/contributor/19

The Justice of God

Brendan Case

Theology, Harvard University, USA[14]

Nicholas Wolterstorff's Theology Brief on "Justice and Rights" offers a characteristically lucid distillation of some key themes from his wide-ranging work on justice as (in Ulpian's classic definition) "rendering to each his [or her] right (or due)."[15] In particular, Wolterstorff argues convincingly, both in his brief and at greater length in his books, that God's concern for justice as equitable or impartial treatment is evident throughout the Old and New Testaments. In this brief, I want to consider a related question, which arises from Wolterstorff's reflections on justice in the Scriptures, but which he does not address directly: Does God abide by the principles of justice to which he holds his creatures? Does he "render to each according to his right"? As we'll see, the Old and New Testaments each offer prima facie challenges to this idea, first in Exodus's insistence that God "visits the iniquity of the fathers upon the sons" (Exod 20:5), and then in Paul's insistence that "no human being is justified through works of the Law" (Rom 3:20). The former might suggest that God treats us unjustly; the latter, that he treats us, not with justice (which could only condemn us), but instead with mercy and grace.

"Correct Justice" in the Old Testament

Let's begin with a brief overview of Wolterstorff's conception of justice, which, on his view, is centrally concerned with equitable treatment: the virtue of justice disposes its possessors to recognize one's duty to respect others' legitimate claims to noninterference (permission rights) or to the active provision of some good (claim rights). Wolterstorff emphasizes the prominence within the Old Testament of injunctions to do "justice" (*mišpāṭ*), a term which "is often paired with 'ṣĕdāqâ,' standardly translated as righteousness" (Wolterstorff 2011, 69); the conjunction of the two might be translated, following David Novak's

---

14. The following is adapted, with permission, from Case 2021. Brendan Case's areas are theology and biblical studies, and he now serves as the associate director for research at the Human Flourishing Program, Harvard University (gfiweb.net/contributor/154). Unless otherwise indicated, all translations of biblical texts are the author's.

15. Cf. Wolterstorff 2009 and 2011.

suggestion, as "correct justice."[16] Throughout the Old Testament, *ṣĕdāqâ* and *mišpāṭ* are repeatedly related to attitudes, practices, and institutions shaped above all by fairness and impartiality.

In the Torah, as still today, both attributes are depicted as embodied first and foremost in law courts: "You shall not render an unjust judgment [*mišpāṭ*]; you shall not be partial to the poor or defer to the great: with justice [*ṣĕdāqâ*] you shall judge your neighbor" (Lev 19:15; cf. also Exod 23:2 and Deut 1:16–17). This requirement of impartiality was married to a concern for proportionality in sentencing: not only should each person be treated equally to others who are like him or her in the relevant respects, but each person should be treated in a manner commensurate with his or her own actions: "You shall give life for life, eye for eye, tooth for tooth, hand for hand, foot for foot" (Exod 21:23–24). And in Deuteronomy, this requirement of proportionality is used to rule out any notion of inherited or transferrable guilt: "The fathers shall not be put to death for the children, neither shall the children be put to death for the fathers: every man shall be put to death for his own sin" (Deut 24:16 KJV).

Does God Render to Each According to His or Her Right?

Does God abide by this standard of "correct justice" to which he holds us? Does he render to each according to his or her due? The early Judahite exiles to Babylon had real doubts about this, at least as they were depicted by the prophets Jeremiah and his younger contemporary, the priest Ezekiel. Ezekiel 18 in particular consists of an oracle addressed to Israel by God himself, and opens with God's own complaint about a proverb – "The fathers ate sour grapes and the children's teeth are set on edge" – then current among the exiles (18:2–3; cf. Jer 31:28–30). The proverb's meaning is clear: "Our fathers sinned, but only we are punished."

The exiles, it must be said, had some grounds for this complaint: at Sinai, after all, God had promised to "visit the iniquity of the fathers upon the sons, even to the third and fourth generations" (Exod 20:5). Indeed, the author of the Kings cycle brings this apparent incongruity to the surface of his narrative. "Before [Josiah] there was no king like him," he observes, "who turned to the LORD with all his heart, with all his soul, and with all his might, according to all the law of Moses." Nonetheless, "the LORD did not turn from the fierceness of his great wrath, by which his anger was kindled against Judah, because of all the provocations with which Manasseh had provoked him" (2 Kgs 23:25–26).

---

16. *Natural Law in Judaism*, quoted in Wolterstorff 2011, 69.

In Ezekiel 18, however, the Lord emphatically repudiates this visitation of one person's sins upon another: "As I live, says the Lord GOD, this proverb [about the sour grapes] shall no more be used by you in Israel" (18:3). He insists instead, "Behold, all souls are mine; the soul of the father as well as the soul of the son is mine: the soul who sins shall die" (18:4 ESV). God also respects the judicial principle set out in Deuteronomy 24:16: if the son of a just man works evil, then that son will die (18:10–13). But if that son has a son who turns away from his father's evils and does what is right, then he shall live (18:14–17). In short, "the son shall not bear the iniquity of the father, neither shall the father bear the iniquity of the son: the righteousness of the righteous shall be upon him, and the wickedness of the wicked shall be upon him" (18:20 KJV). This nontransference of evil and righteousness applies even within the life of an individual: past righteousness will not ensure a favorable judgment for the one who turns to wickedness, and by the same token, past wickedness is no bar to a favorable judgment in the one who repents and does what is right (18:21, 24).

If justice is rendering to each according to his or her due, then the Lord is just; like the judges he raises up for Israel, he is impartial, treating each according to the same standard, namely, what is owed to each (*ta opheilōmena*) as a result of his or her works. But this justice is equally merciful, an expression of God's love. "A man's work is his character," as George MacDonald observes, "and God in his mercy is not indifferent, but treats him according to his work" (MacDonald 1907, 132).

A Pauline Dilemma Regarding Judgment According to Works

Ezekiel and the psalmist insist that God does in fact abide by correct justice in his dealings with us; he renders to each according to his or her works. Nonetheless, might not this Old Testament insistence on the justice of God be less a promise than a threat of the law, whose fearsome commands cannot be borne, and which must be superseded by the gracious and forgiving gospel? Doesn't the New Testament teach that God treats us not with justice, but rather with mercy and grace? After all, if God rendered to each according to his or her works, who could be saved?

Paul did, of course, write that "no human being will be justified in his sight by works of the law" (Rom 3:20), which Martin Luther famously read as teaching that "a Christian has all he needs in faith and needs no works to justify him" (Luther 1968, 39), and about which he wrote, "If that article stands, the

Church stands; if it falls, the Church falls."[17] But then, Paul wrote this injunction just one chapter after quoting Psalm 62's declaration that God "will render to each one according to his works" (Rom 2:6 ESV), and then insisting, "It is not the hearers of the law who are just before God, but the doers of the law who will be justified" (2:13), a statement which might seem to be more at home in the Epistle of James (cf. 1:22; 2:24) than in Romans. In short, the juxtaposition of Romans 2:13 with Romans 3:20 seems to present us with a dilemma: In the divine law court, is my case dismissed on the basis of my faith, apart from "works of the law," or am I instead acquitted as a "doer of the law"?

In his *Justice in Love*, Wolterstorff acknowledges the apparent tension between these passages, and seeks to interpret Paul's talk of the reward given to "those who do good" (Rom 2:10) so as to make it consistent with Romans 3:20:

> Who are these people who patiently do good and who are, on that account, given eternal life, glory, honor, and peace [cf. Rom 2:10]? They cannot be those who, in the words of 3:20, do all the "deeds [*ergōn*] prescribed by the law," since there are none such, Christ excepted. . . . I think the conclusion is irresistible that the people Paul has in mind when he speaks of those who patiently do good are those that he will shortly speak of as people who have faith in God; they are the ones who see fit to acknowledge God. (Wolterstorff 2011, 274)

But this rereading of Romans 2:10–13 runs into the difficulty that Paul immediately goes on, perhaps in Romans 2:14–15, but certainly in Romans 2:26–29, to describe a class of Gentiles who "keep the ordinances of the Law" (2:26) and who possess the Spirit (2:29), that is, who are Gentile Christians like those in his own congregation.

Justification Is Not Through "What the Law Does"

It seems to me, however, that there is a more excellent way of resolving the apparent contradiction between Romans 2:13 and 3:20. Recall that, in Romans 2, Paul describes the Gentiles who "keep the just requirements of the Law" (2:26) as possessing "the circumcision of the heart, in the Spirit, not the letter" (2:29). Here the contrast is not between "faith" and "works of the law," but rather between circumcision "in the Spirit" and "in the letter." Paul alludes

---

17. "Isto articulo stante stat Ecclesia, ruente ruit" (*Luthers Werke*, Weimar Ausgabe 40/3.352.3, quoted in McGrath 2005, 189).

here to a distinction he states more clearly in 2 Corinthians 3:6: in itself, as a mere external letter, the law kills (*gramma apoktennei*, 3:6), but as written on one's heart by the Spirit (3:3), it gives life (*pneuma zōopoieî*, 3:6).

The problem of the law's inflaming sin is arguably in view in the context of Romans 3:20, which maintains that "by works of the Law no flesh will be justified." Paul here discusses a particular activity of the law, which is to address its subjects so as to shut every mouth (3:19) and to usher in the knowledge of sin (3:20). Indeed, it seems reasonable to view the chain of Old Testament passages on human sinfulness Paul assembles in Romans 3:10–18 as supplying the content of "what the law says" (3:19). But in that context, a sudden comment on "[human] works according to the law" would imply a change of subject twice in the span of two verses. By contrast, interpreting *erga nomou* as "the law's works" yields a single, seamless line of thought in Romans 3:19–20: the law silences humanity in their sin and makes them liable before God (3:19), and so we aren't justified through what the law does (3:20a), since the law brings only the knowledge of sin (3:20b).

So there is no ultimate contradiction: none are justified by what the law does (3:20), despite the fact that it is the doers of the law who will be justified, when God renders to each according to his or her works (2:6, 13).

References

Case, Brendan. 2021. *The Accountable Animal: Justice, Justification, and Judgment.* London: T&T Clark.

Luther, Martin. 1968. "The Freedom of a Christian." In *The Protestant Reformation*, edited by Hans Hillerbrand, 31–58. New York: Harper, 2009.

MacDonald, George. 1907. "Justice." In *Unspoken Sermons*, Series 3, 109–62. London: Longmans, Green, & Co.

McGrath, Alister. 2005. *Iustitia Dei: A History of the Christian Doctrine of Justification.* New York: Cambridge University Press.

Wolterstorff, Nicholas. 2009. *Justice: Rights and Wrongs.* Princeton: Princeton University Press.

———. 2011. *Justice in Love.* Grand Rapids: Eerdmans.

2

Society and History

Doing Justice to the Past: Histories of Rights, Memories of Injustice

John Coffey

History, Leicester University, UK[1]

Humans are storytelling animals, and our debates about justice involve debates about history. As Nicholas Wolterstorff observes in his Theology Brief "Justice and Rights," there are rival accounts of the genealogy of human rights. This is high-stakes history, and hence we find philosophers, theologians, and political theorists joining historians to argue over the past. Alongside this academic debate over the intellectual history of rights, we are witnessing public "history wars" over past injustice, especially racial injustice. Once again, this is a contest that divides Christians as well as the larger public. While many look back with nostalgia from our godless age to a Christian past, others point out that the Christian past was marred by slavery, segregation, and racial discrimination.

My own historical research touches on these issues, so I want to offer a Christian reflection on how we remember the past.[2] I will focus on the stories we tell about the history of justice and injustice, beginning with the

---

1. gfiweb.net/contributor/25

2. See my book Coffey 2014, which explores the importance of the exodus story within Anglophone political culture, from Protestant Reformers and Puritan revolutionaries to abolitionists and civil rights leaders.

genealogy of rights discourse, and then turning to how we remember (or forget) historic injustice.

Reconstructing the Genealogy of Rights

The intellectual history of natural human rights offers a case study in why the past still matters. Both critics and champions of rights discourse fight for control of historical terrain. Each constructs a historical narrative to explain what's right or wrong with rights. Against modernist genealogies, and in line with a growing number of scholars, Wolterstorff maintains that the idea of natural (or nonconferred) rights has a long and distinguished pedigree in the Western tradition, going back beyond early modernity into medieval and even patristic thought (Edelstein 2019; Siedentop 2014). He denies that this concept is a byproduct of possessive individualism, or of liberalism and capitalism. And he contends that the recognition of rights is important: "It is no accident that all the great social justice movements of the twentieth century, struggling against one or another form of systemic injustice, employed the language of rights." I would concur with this point and take it further. The language of natural rights has mattered to Christian social justice activists for a very long time, as three case studies from Anglo-American history suggest.

The Leveller Movement and the Rights of Citizens

The Levellers wrote during the English Civil Wars of the 1640s, decades before the "early Enlightenment" of Spinoza, Locke, and Bayle (who in any case were themselves steeped in the Hebrew and Christian Scriptures). Yet the intellectual historian David Wootton has argued that the Levellers were the first movement to argue for

> a written constitution in order to protect the rights of citizens against the state. The first with a modern conception of which rights should be inalienable: the right to silence . . . and to legal representation; the right to freedom of conscience and freedom of debate; the right to equality before the law and freedom of trade; the right to vote and, when faced with tyranny, to revolution. The Levellers are thus not merely the first modern democrats, but the first to seek to construct a liberal state. (Wootton 1992, 71)

If this makes the Levellers sound thoroughly modern, their sources were often antiquated and eclectic: Greco-Roman texts, the Bible, the tradition of natural law theory, and ideas of Anglo-Saxon liberty. When it came to individual natural rights, their reasoning was theological. John Lilburne argued that because God had created humankind "after His own image" – enduing them with "a rational soul" – "every particular and individual man and woman that ever breathed in the world since" was "by nature all equal and alike in power, dignity, authority and majesty." (Taken from Coffey 2017, 20) Natural rights were grounded in human dignity which derived from the *imago Dei*. By invoking rights, the Levellers sought to defend the weak against the mighty. The Levellers saw defense of the marginalized as a biblical imperative. In their writings, the Bible was read as history from below, viewed from the vantage point of the vulnerable (Coffey 2017).

The Tolerationist Movement and the Right to Religious Liberty

The Levellers drew much of their support from religious minorities such as the Baptists, and there was one right above all that they sought to protect: the right to freedom of conscience and worship. Nowadays, we think of this as a global norm, embodied in the UN Declaration of Human Rights (1948). Yet this is a right under threat in many parts of the world, and it was rarely respected in post-Reformation Europe. If we trace how the idea of "rights of conscience" emerged, we find that it developed from within the Christian tradition. While Robert Wilken has argued that we can see it in church fathers such as Tertullian, who believed it was "a privilege inherent in human nature that every person should be able to worship according to his own convictions" (Wilken 2019), it was most forthrightly pioneered by persecuted religious minorities on the fringes of seventeenth-century Christendom before making its way from the margins to the center, thanks in part to thinkers such as Locke and Bayle. In the eighteenth century, the century of the Enlightenment, the principle of inalienable rights of conscience went mainstream (Coffey 2021).

The proponents of religious liberty reached for natural rights language to assert the dignity of personal conscience and the limits of state power. They made their case on theistic grounds. The rights of the individual were based on duties to God. Because the individual was duty-bound to worship God according to his or her own conscience, he or she could not transfer (or alienate) power over conscience to the magistrate. The kind of worship that was acceptable to God was free and uncoerced. Thus, the individual's natural duty to God generated a natural right to liberty of conscience (Forst 2013, ch. 4). The radical Protestant provenance of this theory of religious liberty has generated suspicion among various critics, from conservative Roman Catholics to postcolonial theorists. For the most part, however, it has "far more often been a weapon of the weak than a technology for the powerful" (Philpott and Shah 2016, 388).

Abolitionism as a Human Rights Movement

Our final example is antislavery activism. Historians have always recognized that abolitionism had religious roots, especially among Quakers such as Anthony Benezet, devout Anglicans such as Granville Sharp and Thomas Clarkson, and black evangelicals such as Olaudah Equiano and Ottobah Cugoano. We find these early abolitionists speaking of a natural right to freedom before the Declaration of the Rights of Man. For Equiano, slave traders (whether African or European) were "destroyers of human rights," "invaders of human rights" (Equiano 1789). The slave trade was a violation of the natural right to liberty and thus a defiance of the law of God and nature. Abolitionism, in the words of the Anglican poet Hannah More, was a campaign to see "human rights restored" (More 1788). It is not surprising that abolitionism is often regarded as the first international human movement (Martinez 2012).

In the 1790s, rights language was tarnished by association with the Jacobins and Thomas Paine, and partly for that reason it was a marginal feature in the writings of Wilberforce and other establishment abolitionists. What *was* central to them was a doctrine of human dignity: slavery was unjust because it degraded persons. Wilberforce had a strong sense of the "claims" and "privileges" owed to the human person as "a rational and immortal being" with "moral dignity": not just food, clothing, lodging, and medical care, but also "personal independence" and the power to pursue one's chosen occupation or habits of life (Wilberforce 1823, 45–46). In the writings of African American abolitionists such as Frederick Douglass, this assertion of the "claims" of currently enslaved persons to liberty was couched, emphatically, in the language of what Wolterstorff calls "nonconferred" rights: "natural rights," "inalienable rights," "the rights of man," "human rights." Douglass thought of these as "God-given rights." He also asserted women's rights on the basis of their natural equality with men: he was one of the male delegates to attend the Women's Rights Convention at Seneca Falls in 1848, the seminal event of American feminism.[3]

---

3. This is a theme of the Pulitzer Prize-winning biography by Blight 2018.

Religious Roots of Human Rights

Why does this slice of intellectual history matter? It matters because both Christians and secularists are prone to forget the religious roots of human rights. Both underestimate the extent to which Christianity continued to shape Western intellectual culture during the Enlightenment and into the nineteenth and twentieth centuries. Non-Western critics are often more alert to the Christian ancestry of human rights, though they tend to tie it too closely to Western imperialism (Mahmood and Danchin 2014; Massad 2015). In reality, Christian activists had long spoken the language of human rights to protect the weak from the strong. Reformers were fired by a Christian moral imagination.[4] Understanding this history might make secular citizens more aware of their debts to Christianity; it might also nudge Christians away from the temptation to be too dismissive toward liberal democracy.

Remembering Historic Injustice

If debates about the genealogy of rights engage public intellectuals, disputes about historic injustice are now front-page news.[5] How we remember past evils has become one of the most hotly contested battlegrounds in our current culture wars.

Black Lives Matter and the History of Racial Injustice

In the wake of the Black Lives Matter movement, the UK and the US have been confronting uncomfortable questions about historical memory. Statues of slave traders, imperialists, and Confederates have been flash points. The *New York Times* provoked a backlash when it published the "1619 Report," asserting that 1619 (when the first enslaved Africans were landed in British North America) was "the country's true birth date, the moment that its defining contradictions first came into the world." In response, President Trump's 1776 Commission issued a counterblast: "The 1776 Report." "Team 1619" urged Americans to lament the past; "Team 1776" told them to celebrate it. On this too, we find Christians – even Christian academics – in rival camps. Trump's

---

4. The case has been made with forceful eloquence in Tom Holland's bestselling book *Dominion: How the Christian Revolution Remade the World* (London: Little, Brown, 2019). The UK subtitle omits the Christian element: "The Making of the Western Mind." See also Witte and Alexander 2010; Shah and Hertzke 2016.

5. See the cover story "The History Wars" in *Time* magazine (5–12 July 2021), with an article by Olivia Waxman on "The Politics of Teaching America's Past."

1776 Commission initially included two senior Christian historians – Wilfred McClay and Allen Guelzo – while other Christian scholars have been highly critical of the new drive for "patriotic" history.[6]

Biblical Narrative and Self-Critique

In a recent paper on "Difficult Histories," I have argued that Christian memory ought to be shaped by biblical narrative (Coffey 2020). Israel's Scripture is undoubtedly patriotic, yet as the former Chief Rabbi, the late Jonathan Sacks, observed: "The Hebrew Bible is the supreme example of that rarest of phenomena, a national literature of self-criticism. Other ancient civilisations recorded their victories. The Israelites recorded their failures" (Sacks 2015, 52). Biblical narrative contrasts with the celebratory stories we prefer to tell about our national, imperial, or ecclesial pasts. Biblical history is frequently dark, confronting the worst episodes in Israel's past; biblical history is written from the margins, by a people exiled or colonized; biblical history contains searing self-critique; biblical history is concerned with justice and oppression. Western histories have often ignored the victims, and even celebrated the perpetrators. The current reckoning with that past is overdue. Biblical memory challenges our tendency to count ourselves among the righteous, whether as chauvinists or censors. Throwing the first stone is a dangerous business. Everyone needs redemption.

A Third Way for Authentic Christian Memory

An authentically Christian memory, shaped by biblical narrative, suggests a third way beyond our "history wars." In remembering the past, we should avoid reducing it to its worst features; equally, we should not turn a blind eye to the worst of the past. Christian scholars have a role to play in the cultivation of a less selective memory. Since we acknowledge our own need for forgiveness, we do not set ourselves up as self-righteous censors passing judgment on lesser mortals or past generations. Yet we do have a duty to counteract historical amnesia and the historical nostalgia that celebrates past triumphs but overlooks historic injustice.

The novelist Marilynne Robinson, whose own thought and writing is infused with a Christian sensibility, exemplifies the bittersweet quality of Christian memory and of biblical narrative. She argues that we owe past generations

---

6. See the exchange between Abram Van Engen and Os Guinness in du Mez 2020.

"great pity" and "very great respect" but also moral critique. There is much in the past that is worthy of retrieval and conservation (including a tradition of Christian human rights activism), but there is much to deplore (including centuries of Christian complicity with racial slavery and segregation). Yet we ought to approach our ancestors in chastened mood, with a sharp sense of our own shortcomings. In that way, we might (as we say) "do justice" to the past. And we might be better equipped, in the words of the prophet Micah, "to act justly and to love mercy and to walk humbly with [our] God" (6:8 NIV).

References and Further Reading

Blight, David. 2018. *Frederick Douglass: Prophet of Freedom*. New York: Simon & Schuster.

Coffey, John. 2014. *Exodus and Liberation: Deliverance Politics from John Calvin to Martin Luther King, Jr.* New York: Oxford University Press.

———. 2017. "State Democracy and Church Democracy: The Levellers and the Bible in the English Revolution." *Transmission* (Autumn 2017): 18–20. https://www.biblesociety.org.uk/content/explore_the_bible/bible_in_transmission/files/2017_autumn/State_democracy_and_church_democracy.pdf.

———. 2020. "Difficult Histories: Christian Memory and Historic Injustice." *Cambridge Papers* 29, no. 4. https://methodistic.org.uk/wp-content/uploads/2021/03/P_CP_Dec20_web-compressed.pdf.

———. 2021. "How Religious Freedom Became a Natural Right." In *From Toleration to Religious Freedom: Cross-Disciplinary Perspectives*, edited by Marietta van der Tole et al., 23–56. Oxford: Peter Lang. This essay traces how the language of rights was applied to religious liberty in early modern English political thought and then considers the claims made by postcolonial critics of religious liberty.

Edelstein, Dan. 2019. *On the Spirit of Rights*. Chicago: University of Chicago Press.

Equiano, Olaudah. 1789. *The Interesting Narrative of Olaudah Equiano*. London.

Forst, Rainer. 2013. *Tolerance in Conflict: Past and Present*. Translated by Ciaran Cronin. Cambridge: Cambridge University Press.

Holland, Tom. 2019. *Dominion: How the Christian Revolution Remade the World*. London: Little, Brown.

Mahmood, Saba, and Peter Danchin. 2014. "Politics of Religious Freedom: Contested Genealogies." *The South Atlantic Quarterly* 113: 1–8.

Martinez, Jenny S. 2012. *The Slave Trade and the Origins of International Human Rights Law*. New York: Oxford University Press.

Massad, Joseph. 2015. *Islam in Liberalism*. Chicago: University of Chicago Press.

Mez, Kristin du. 2020. "Dangerous Christian Nationalism? A Conversation between Abram Van Engen and Os Guinness." Patheos, 20 August. https://www.

patheos.com/blogs/anxiousbench/2020/08/dangerous-christian-nationalism-a-conversation-between-abram-van-engen-and-os-guinness/.

More, Hannah. 1788. *Slavery: A Poem*. London.

Philpott, Daniel, and Timothy Samuel Shah. 2016. "In Defense of Religious Freedom: New Critics of a Beleaguered Human Rights." *Journal of Law and Religion* 31: 380–95.

Sacks, Jonathan. 2015. *Not in God's Name: Confronting Religious Violence*. London: Hodder & Stoughton.

Shah, Timothy, and Allen Hertzke, eds. 2016. *Christianity and Freedom*. 2 vols. Cambridge: Cambridge University Press.

Siedentop, Larry. 2014. *Inventing the Individual: The Origins of Western Liberalism*. London: Allen Lane.

Waxman, Olivia. 2021. "The Politics of Teaching America's Past." *Time*, 5–12 July.

Wilberforce, William. 1823. *An Appeal to the Religion, Justice and Humanity of the Inhabitants of the British Empire in Behalf of the Negro Slaves in the West Indies*. Cornell University Library.

Wilken, Robert Louis. 2019. *Liberty in the Things of God: The Christian Origins of Religious Freedom*. New Haven: Yale University Press.

Witte, John, and Frank Alexander, eds. 2010. *Christianity and Freedom*. 2 vols. Cambridge: Cambridge University Press.

Wootton, David. 1992. "The Levellers." In *Democracy: The Unfinished Journey*, edited by John Dunn, 71–89. Oxford: Oxford University Press.

Tribal Societies and Collective Rights
Joy Pachuau
History, Jawaharlal Nehru University, New Delhi, India[7]

There are many societies in the world, especially those that have been designated "tribal," where social solidarity and individual rights are at the expense of each other. The societies that I have in mind are also Christian. A lack of social solidarity can mean at one level a loss of identity for the individual and yet it can come at the cost of individual rights. How does one approach the issue of justice and rights under such social circumstances?

---

7. gfiweb.net/contributor/131

Economic Justice and the Politics of Redistribution

Peter Sloman

Politics, University of Cambridge, UK[8]

Nicholas Wolterstorff's Theology Brief offers a stimulating analysis of how the Old and New Testaments should shape a Christian approach to justice and rights. Prof. Wolterstorff argues that a strong emphasis on social (or systemic) justice not only pervades the Mosaic law and the prophetic tradition in the Old Testament, but continues into Jesus's ministry and the teachings of the early church, in a way that is often obscured by the common translation of *dikaiosynē* as "righteousness." I find his argument persuasive, and also welcome the defense of "rights-talk" which Prof. Wolterstorff develops in the second half of his paper. It is always salutary to remember that Western liberalism has been deeply shaped by Christian thought, even if that connection has waned somewhat over the last century.

In this response, I write from my perspective as a historian of modern Britain, with a particular interest in the politics of economic and social policy. I want to suggest that the distinction Prof. Wolterstorff draws between first-order and second-order forms of justice offers us a valuable tool for understanding some of the trade-offs which social policymakers face in rich "Western" countries today.

First-Order Justice in Economic and Social Policy

Prof. Wolterstorff uses the term "first-order justice" to describe "the type of justice that consists of agents acting justly in their ordinary affairs," including (but not restricted to) "justice in the distribution of benefits and/or burdens" (p. 16). As I understand it, this conception of just *action* is deeply rooted in a vision of a just social *order* – a world in which human beings are treated fairly and in which their rights are respected by other individuals and social entities. First-order justice, in this sense, "is structurally basic," whereas second-order justice is designed to redress violations of it. Public policy, Prof. Wolterstorff suggests, can be directed *both* toward the achievement of "first-order justice among individuals and social entities" *and* to the development of "laws and procedures" which ensure that punishment and restitution are carried out

---

8. gfiweb.net/contributor/80

consistently and fairly. Prof. Wolterstorff's conception of second-order justice is primarily a judicial one, exemplified by "police, court proceedings, punishment, prisons, and the like" (p. 17). However, he is clear that second-order justice can be *restorative* as well as *punitive*, and I think the concept might productively be extended to include the forms of compensation, restitution, and redistribution which the state carries out in the economic sphere.

The vision of economic justice which the Old Testament gives us is set out primarily in first-order terms. The Mosaic law provides for economic security through the distribution of the land, underpinned by the principle of the Jubilee, which acts as a safeguard against both excessive concentration of agricultural property and permanent alienation from economic resources (Lev 25). The prophet Micah, too, relates economic security to property ownership, looking to a time when "everyone will sit under their own vine and under their own fig tree, and no one will make them afraid" (Mic 4:4 NIV). At the same time, the provision for gleaning, which gives "the poor and . . . the sojourner" an implicit right to food (Lev 19:9–10 ESV), shows a frank recognition that not everyone will enjoy such material security. Throughout the Bible, the people of God are also enjoined to be just and generous in their economic relations, particularly toward those in need. In other words, economic justice is to be achieved *both* through the structure of the social order *and* through a distinctive social ethic, grounded in respect for other humans and recognition of one's own dependence on God.

The agrarian subsistence economy of ancient Israel is, of course, a world away from the economic structure of contemporary Western states. Well into the modern era, however, I think it is fair to say that economic rights have been conceptualized in concrete terms which would not have been wholly unfamiliar to the biblical writers. Land reform has been a perennial subject of political debate, and remains so in many parts of the world; even in the UK, it is barely a century since David Lloyd George's plans for land taxation provoked a constitutional stand-off with the House of Lords, and Liberal Party meetings resounded with the Land Song ("God gave the land to the people"). Likewise, cheap food was a major theme of British politics right up to the 1970s, held up as one of the main benefits of free trade – as Frank Trentmann (2008) has shown – and allegedly imperiled by the UK's entry into the European Economic Community. The notion of "a fair day's wage for a fair day's work" was central to trade union activity, often equated (in a male-breadwinner era) with a "family wage" – an income sufficient to support a man, his wife, and three children. Notions of a "just wage" and a "just price" structured what E. P. Thompson (1971) called a "moral economy," rooted in everyday custom and practice but often also reflected in government policy. Catholic social theorists and economists such as Michael Fogarty (1961) were particularly active in translating these concepts of economic justice into an industrial context.

Until the middle of the twentieth century, then, economic rights were largely understood in academic as well as popular discourse in terms of a specific set of human needs: food, fuel, housing, clothing, education, and health care. Governments sought to make the real economy "fair" in a way that their citizens understood through policies such as price subsidies, rent controls, centralized systems of wage bargaining, and direct forms of social provision such as council housing.

From First-Order to Second-Order Economic Justice

Since World War II, however, this "first-order approach" to achieving economic justice has been steadily eroded by the influence of neoclassical economics and the growth of increasingly abstract conceptions of poverty and inequality. Postwar liberal thinkers have generally held that collective provision of goods and services is economically inefficient and morally paternalistic (except in specific fields such as health and education) and that cash transfers are therefore preferable. With the onset of deindustrialization since the 1960s and 70s, governments' ability to meet expectations of "fair work" – particularly for male manual workers – have also waned. As a result, social policy has increasingly been structured by a logic of *compensation* in which cash transfers bridge the gap between what the market economy delivers and what citizens or policymakers think is "fair." John Kay (1996) has characterized this approach as "redistributive market liberalism," and I have suggested in my book *Transfer State* (2019b) that it explains much of the popularity of proposals for a Negative Income Tax or Universal Basic Income.

The practical implications are perhaps best illustrated by the way Tony Blair's government framed its child poverty strategy in the early 2000s. Child poverty was conceptualized in relative income terms (a child was "poor" if he or she lived in a household whose equivalized income was less than 60 percent of the median equivalized income), and Gordon Brown's strategy for eliminating it by 2020 revolved around an expansive system of tax credits for low-income families with children. Such policies helped to take the edge off the sharp rise in inequality which the UK had experienced during the 1980s and 1990s onward as a result of deindustrialization and free-market economic policies. While the Gini coefficient (which measures the degree of inequality in a country) for *market* incomes rose from 0.38 in 1975 to 0.52 in 2010, the

Gini coefficient for *disposable* incomes rose only from 0.27 to 0.34. Despite historically high employment levels and a spate of austerity measures since 2010, cash transfers have continued to play a major role in supplementing earned income not only for the unemployed and those with disabilities, but also for many low-paid workers with children (Sloman 2019a). The logic of the US Earned Income Tax Credit and Child Tax Credit is very similar. As Elizabeth Popp Berman (2022) has put it in the US case, social policy has been reshaped by the increasingly pervasive influence of an "economic style of reasoning."

From a policy perspective, the shift from a first-order to a second-order approach to economic justice arguably makes a good deal of sense. After all, the practical record of state intervention in labor and product markets has been distinctly uneven, so if politicians can achieve their social objectives without risking politically damaging forms of government failure, that is bound to be appealing to policymakers. The decoupling of economic security from paid work might also be desirable on normative grounds, since the Fordist labor-market model of the twentieth century was premised on a male-breadwinner family structure and tended to reinforce gendered patterns of dependency within the household. Likewise, we might welcome the fact that cash transfers expand citizens' autonomy and choice, while insisting that a Christian conception of moral agency will always entail much more than control over private consumption.

Contemporary Debates and Concluding Questions

A strong current of recent scholarship has argued, however, that the politics of redistribution is politically weak and is liable to face a growing legitimacy crisis (Anderson 1999). The problem is threefold:

- First, once economic rights are untethered from the concrete goods required for subsistence (or flourishing) and from people's daily experience of making a living, they are likely to seem increasingly abstract and arbitrary: a matter of political fiat rather than the expression of a deeper moral economy.
- Second, the pattern of production, prices, and rewards produced by the market is likely to appear increasingly normal and natural – at least to its beneficiaries – since citizens cannot easily see the ways in which market outcomes are shaped by government policies.
- Third, the process of redistribution requires constant government activity: if at any point the transfer machine is turned off, the market

is likely to produce quite extreme concentrations of wealth and economic power.

The practical result is that center-left politicians have found it increasingly hard to justify patterns of redistribution, especially in periods of actual or perceived fiscal crisis. This can be seen not only in the contested politics of "welfare" but also in debates over foreign aid spending. The UN target of spending 0.7 percent of gross national income on overseas development assistance appears arbitrary because it is arbitrary. On the other hand, it is not easy to see how a first-order vision of global economic justice might be operationalized as a basis for public policy.

This paper has moved some way beyond the focus of Prof. Wolterstorff's Theology Brief in an attempt to think about how the categories he uses might be applied to contemporary economic and social policy issues. I conclude, then, by inviting readers to consider two questions:

- First, is it useful to apply the distinction between first- and second-order justice to the economic sphere in this way, or am I stretching the concept too far? (Perhaps I am.)
- Second, is there any *theological* reason for Christians to prefer policies which seek to achieve economic justice by acting directly on the real economy rather than by the "second-order" means of redistributive transfers, or is this choice simply a matter of economic judgment and political strategy?

References and Further Reading

Anderson, Elizabeth S. 1999. "What Is the Point of Equality?" *Ethics* 109: 287–337.

Berman, Elizabeth Popp. 2022. *Thinking Like an Economist*. Princeton: Princeton University Press.

Fogarty, M. P. 1961. *The Just Wage*. London: Geoffrey Chapman.

Kay, John. 1996. "Staking a Moral Claim." *New Statesman*, 11 October: 18–20.

Rogan, Tim. 2017. *The Moral Economists: R. H. Tawney, Karl Polanyi, E. P. Thompson, and the Critique of Capitalism*. Princeton: Princeton University Press. Examines how moral and ethical concerns permeated twentieth-century critiques of capitalism.

Saunders, Robert. 2018. *Yes to Europe! The 1975 Referendum and Seventies Britain*. Cambridge: Cambridge University Press.

Sloman, Peter. 2019a. "Redistribution in an Age of Neoliberalism: Market Economics, 'Poverty Knowledge,' and the Growth of Working-Age Benefits in Britain,

c. 1979–2010." *Political Studies* 67, no. 3: 732–51. https://doi.org/10.1177/0032321718800495.

———. 2019b. *Transfer State: The Idea of a Guaranteed Income and the Politics of Redistribution in Modern Britain*. Oxford: Oxford University Press. Explores how attitudes to redistribution have changed in the UK over the last century and how these ideas have shaped policy responses to poverty and inequality.

Thompson, E. P. 1971. "The Moral Economy of the English Crowd in the Eighteenth Century." *Past & Present* 50: 76–136.

Tomlinson, Jim. 2016. "Distributional Politics: The Search for Equality in Britain since the First World War." In *The Contradictions of Capital in the Twenty-First Century: The Piketty Opportunity*, edited by Pat Hudson and Keith Tribe, 167–91. Agenda: Newcastle upon Tyne. Offers a lively analysis of approaches to equality in UK public policy.

Torry, Malcolm. 2016. *Citizen's Basic Income: A Christian Social Policy*. London: Darton, Longman & Todd. Develops a Christian case for a Universal Basic Income.

Trentmann, Frank. 2008. *Free Trade Nation: Commerce, Consumption and Civil Society in Modern Britain*. Oxford: Oxford University Press.

Waldfogel, Jane. 2010. *Britain's War on Poverty*. New York: Russell Sage Foundation.

Affinities of Justice with Economic Concepts
Judy Dean
Economics, Brandeis University, USA[9]

Nicholas Wolterstorff's excellent discussion of justice grounded in rights – with rights being "what respect for worth requires" – closely links up with the equitable "distribution of [economic] benefits." Economic efficiency can actually be a strong ally for justice, especially for the poor. In a world of scarce resources and great need, good stewardship requires us to be efficient so that nothing is wasted. Freer international trade promotes this efficiency globally, reflecting our respect for the worth of people in other countries, and their flourishing as well as our own.

---

9. gfiweb.net/contributor/45

Justice, Rights, and the Quest to Reduce the Risk of Disasters

Ian Robert Davis

Architecture and Disaster Risk and Recovery Management, Universities
of Amrita, Kyoto, Lund, Oxford Brookes and RMIT Europe[10]

Justice and Mercy

I have often pondered on the issues that Nicholas Wolterstorff has lucidly raised during almost fifty years of working to reduce disaster risks. The key passage in Micah chapter 6 has always presented a powerful challenge for anyone working in the disaster field – how to balance the need for "doing justice" and providing "loving kindness" (or mercy) – not one or the other, but *both*. The need is to seek for both justice and mercy, often within the same project or work program, while maintaining a humble relationship with a loving God.

The aims and practice of disaster protection and recovery need to expand beyond the delivery of relief provision – well beyond the bare statistics of numbers of safe houses rebuilt, jobs created, and infrastructure protected. Wolterstorff reminds us that justice is the "ground floor of shalom" and shalom consists of "flourishing."

In this paper I would like to comment on disasters as the product, or consequence, of the relationship between hazards and vulnerability and to highlight some of the justice issues described by Wolterstorff that relate to this collision and the quest for safety.

Corruption Kills

Unresolved issues of justice and rights pervade the subject at all levels and in all sectors. Typical ethical questions that have attracted the attention of international conference delegates, academics, and political leaders include the following: Why are certain groups of people exposed to disaster risks? What are the links between offering mercy and working for justice? How are disaster risks generated, maintained, and expanded? Who secures protection from disaster risks and why? Do communities have intrinsic rights to safety, and who confers such rights?

---

10. gfiweb.net/contributor/119

The collective focus of concern has centered on ways to counter an oppressive vulnerability and exposure and in many cases an acute lack of justice for vast millions of people suffering from unjust – often criminal – policies and practices. Professor David Alexander has recognized the pervasive corruption that lies at the root of a high percentage of disaster deaths, injuries, and property damage:

> Corruption is an insidious problem that affects all societies, rich or poor. It defies easy characterization and direct measurement, yet it can have very clear, concrete effects. These are mainly of four kinds:
>
> (a) failure to observe rules, laws, regulations, and standards that relate to safety and protection of the public;
>
> (b) exploitation and lack of protection of vulnerable members of the public;
>
> (c) propagation of vulnerability to hazards through failure to take appropriate risk reduction measures, or weakening of existing measures; and
>
> (d) undermining representation of the people, human rights, and community cohesion.
>
> From this it can be seen that there are sins of both omission and commission. Failure to protect the public is one of the former, while exploitation of people and undermining of standards are examples of the latter. (Alexander 2016, 16)

Such failures relate to Wolterstorff's challenge to us to ponder how Christ's proclamation of bringing "good news to the oppressed . . . [and] liberty to the captives" relates to our varied disciplines. In my case this applies to architecture, engineering, urban design, planning, land-ownership, and official land and housing policies. The justice issues noted in this paper are all in the "second-order justice" category that has been proposed.

Pre-disaster Issues Concerning Justice
Siting of Settlements

Communities that live or work in highly unsafe sites are vulnerable to multiple hazards. Examples of such sites are steep slopes subject to rockfalls and landslides that can occur in high rainfall or with earthquake impact, and shorelines subject to river or coastal flooding or tsunamis. Such sites may be occupied by communities living illegally on prohibited sites, or in some situations the authorities may have actually provided the land for housing development on sites they know to be highly dangerous.

Unsafe Construction

Dangerous construction practice is a common feature exposed in disaster damage assessments. Examples abound and include reinforced concrete with the corrupt omission of vital steel reinforcement, or the substitution of sea sand (costing nothing) containing corrosive salt in the concrete mix in lieu of prescribed pure sand (which has to be purchased). Dangerous construction can also result from ignorance concerning good, safe construction practice.

Corrupt Practice to Avoid Regulations

Government building safety construction bylaws or land-use planning controls are often sidestepped by the taking of bribes by enforcement officials. The situation is often "regularized" by governments paying such officials low wages based on the assumption they will top them up by the receipt of bribes.

Withholding Risk Data

Governments often possess detailed assessments of potential risks facing their citizens, but for reasons of political control fail to share this data with affected communities. This data may relate to risks associated with unsafe buildings, such as the structural safety of schools, or the occupation of unsafe sites as noted above. In other situations, unscrupulous landowners have sold land knowing the risks while withholding the risk assessment data from house purchasers or house renters. (The blood pressure of the prophet Amos would have risen to boiling point over such evil practices!)

Risk Transfer

A common problem in the management of river flooding is that an upstream community may build safety measures for themselves that can increase downstream flooding – thus transferring and intensifying the risks facing others. In complex river catchments that cross national boundaries this practice can result in hostilities or "river wars."

Inaction by Governments

Governmental action is often found wanting, and this "sin of omission" is certainly an issue of justice. Professor Ian Burton has noted that

> decision makers often find themselves faced with pressures *not* to act or to delay decisions perhaps indefinitely. There is often a power structure and a set of political interests to which decision makers respond or comply with and fail to act in the best interests of the community as a whole in terms of risk and damage reduction. This power structure and political interests can be local, national and international (global) and there can also be expressions of private sector interests. (Quoted in Davis 2015, 83)

Can Justice and Rights Challenge Deeply Entrenched Causes of Disasters?

I conclude with the reminder that the root causes of deeply entrenched causes of disasters include fundamental justice issues of poverty and inequality. These underlying causal factors relate to corrupt practice and the denial of access of marginal, disadvantaged communities, or sections of communities such as women, to representation, resources, power, and knowledge. Each of these risk drivers presents a formidable challenge for any concerned individual, local church, concerned agency, or government. But we need to remind ourselves that we serve a living God who cares for any vulnerable, exploited community and takes positive delight in our faith and obedience to "move mountains." "If you have faith as small as a mustard seed, you can say to this mountain, 'Move from here to there,' and it will move. Nothing will be impossible for you" (Matt 17:20 NIV).

References and Further Reading

Alexander, D. 2016. "Corruption and the Governance of Disaster Risk." *Oxford Research Encyclopedia of Natural Hazard Science*. New York: Oxford University Press. Published online October 2017. https//DOI: 10.1093/acrefore/9780199389407 .013.253.

Davis, I., ed. 2015. *Disaster Risk Management in Asia and the Pacific*. Asian Development Bank Institute (ADBI). Abingdon: Routledge.

Davis, I., and D. Alexander. 2016. *Recovery from Disaster*. Abingdon: Routledge. On problems and possible solutions in the complex recovery process following disaster events, including a long-term case study of positive urban recovery in India by a Christian Agency.

Davis, I., and M. Wall, eds. 1992. *Christian Perspectives on Disaster Management: A Training Manual.* Teddington: Interchurch Relief and Development Alliance (IRDA) and Tearfund. Used in NGO training courses from the 1980s and 90s in disaster management. https://desastres.unanleon.edu.ni/pdf/2002/agosto/PDF/ENG/DOC3788/DOC3788.HTM.

Wisner, B., P. Blaikie, T. Cannon, and I. Davis. 2003. *At Risk: Natural Hazards, People's Vulnerability and Disasters.* 2nd ed. London and New York: Routledge. On root causes and the nature of vulnerability of people to extreme hazards. https://www.preventionweb.net/files/670_72351.pdf.

Environmental Justice
Erin Goheen Glanville
Communications, Simon Fraser University, Canada[11]

What is the place of environmental justice insofar as resource extraction is closely connected to human displacement? But beyond that link, there is an element of in/justice even in our relationship to the nonhuman creation. Is there a third-order justice that recognizes "undue burdens" on the land?

---

11. gfiweb.net/contributor/48

Just Language

Allan Bell

Language and Communication, Emeritus, Auckland University of
Technology and Laidlaw College, New Zealand[12]

Nicholas Wolterstorff's stimulating Theology Brief on "Justice and Rights" majors on justice as rendering persons their right in light of their worth or dignity or excellence. He comments rightly that the Old Testament focuses on social or systemic injustice rather than on individual cases, and that it therefore critiques the laws and social practices of ancient Israel. I want to pick that up from my disciplinary perspective as a sociolinguist, and comment on the ways in which the concepts of "voice" and language are intertwined with justice and are, in my view, a core component of doing justice.

The God who made the profusion of creation is also the God of the treasures that we find in human language and voice. Genesis 1 bears witness to the unstinting abundance that God created, and John 1 places the Word at the heart of that creation. In language, a plenitude of voices meets us everywhere. Language is an identity-bearer, implicated in the shape of society. Our voice in particular is always embodied, personal, situated. Language is wholly interactive (in accord with Wolterstorff's stress on the centrality of interaction), a bridge between self and others, central to communication. But as well as a truth-teller, language can also be a deceiver. Social inequities produce linguistic inequities, and language reproduces injustice in many areas of society: structures, demographics, power, gender, ethnicity.

Not all the voices of society are easily or equally heard. The founding sociolinguist Dell Hymes was concerned for how linguistic justice is evidenced in the voices of society – who speaks, who is listened to, who is valued, who is disregarded. "One way to think of the society in which one would like to live is to think of the kinds of voices it would have," he wrote (1996, 64). Such a sociolinguistics of voice invites and requires engagement in society, including intellectual engagement. It is a continuation of the Old Testament tradition where the prophetic voice was central to guiding and correcting Israel in the ways of justice.

---

12. gfiweb.net/contributor/33

What Is a Language?

Linguistic justice begins with a most basic question: What is a language? It turns out that this is not a simple or objective matter.

Languages Are Sociopolitical

There are languages that have different names but are linguistically very similar – Hindi/Urdu, Serbian/Croatian. They are kept apart by political rather than linguistic boundaries. There are other clusters of linguistic codes which bear a single name (such as Arabic or Chinese) but are so diverse that some are not mutually intelligible. They are held together by political rather than linguistic factors. "A language is a dialect with an army and navy" is an axiom credited to the early twentieth-century Yiddish linguist Max Weinreich. Sociopolitical rather than linguistic factors give a language its status.

Language in Colonization

The notion of identifiable languages (and often, their identification with a nation) is in fact an eighteenth-century Enlightenment construct, but one that was imposed on the rest of the world through European colonizers. These – including Christian missionaries – enthusiastically distinguished, defined, and named "languages" wherever they went. Groups were assumed to be monolingual, but clean boundaries between them could be mapped only by ignoring the prevailing multilingualism. The imperial payoff for such idealizations was that territories and their peoples were identified, segmented, and ready for governance. Wolterstorff refers to the ways in which elitist and colonialist practices promote injustice. In language, the fruits of inequitable colonial, postcolonial, and quasi-colonial ideologies are still manifest in today's world. The requirement to speak English or Mandarin or Indonesian at the expense of local languages indexes how some voices are stifled by unconscious attitudes or intentional policies.

Language Ideologies and Injustice

Ideologies of language value one linguistic form or code as better or worse than another, promoting some people's voices and muzzling others'.

Iconization

A language, dialect, or feature may be taken as representative of a group of people. The association with the group is arbitrary, but iconization treats the feature as having an inherent link with the group (Irvine and Gal 2000). This scenario finds biblical expression in the use of *shibboleth* as a linguistic test in Judges chapter 12. After defeating the tribe of Ephraim, the Gileadites waited for the fleeing Ephraimites at the River Jordan:

> Whenever one of the fugitives of Ephraim said, "Let me go over," the men of Gilead would say to him, "Are you an Ephraimite?" When he said, "No," they said to him, "Then say Shibboleth," and he said, "Sibboleth," for he could not pronounce it right. Then they seized him and killed him at the fords of the Jordan. (Judg 12:5–6)

The word *shibboleth* has been carried into English to mean precisely a language feature which is stereotypical of a group.

Erasure

If what you speak is not recognized as a language, your voice may be denigrated or ignored, and you will likely be subject to linguistic injustice. In countless countries, minority-group children have been punished for speaking their home language at school, in the belief that one linguistic form or code is better or worse than another. It sounds more beautiful or more ugly, is superior or inferior, is more or less moral. This forms the basis for much linguistic injustice. We place people socially by the way they talk. As George Bernard Shaw wrote in the preface to his play *Pygmalion*, words later paraphrased into one of the songs of *My Fair Lady*:

> An Englishman's way of speaking absolutely classifies him,
> The moment he talks he makes some other Englishman despise
> him.

The saddest outcome of such denigration is when that is reflected in speakers also downgrading their own speech.

Jesus and Linguistic Discrimination

Jesus was also probably subject to linguistic denigration. We know that Galilee was regarded as a cultural backwater by the Jerusalem elite – reflected in Nathanael's rhetorical question, "Can anything good come out of Nazareth?"

(John 1:46). We also know how distinctive was the Galilean accent, because it gave Peter away as he hovered on the fringes of Jesus's trial (Matt 26:73). We can assume that Jesus had a similar accent to Peter's, so the Jerusalem rulers' hostility was probably not just to what Jesus said but to how he said it. His voice was also "despised and rejected."

Language as a Site of Struggle

The early twentieth-century Russian thinker Mikhail Bakhtin maintained that language is a site of struggle between the dynamic centrifugal forces which whirl it apart into diversity, and the hegemonic centripetal forces which strive to prescribe the way language should be. Bakhtin – a Christian – celebrates the centrifugal: the divergence, individuality, creativity, even the chaos of language variety.

Standard Languages

Language standardization through national education systems is a primary site of linguistic injustice. French is arguably the world's most standardized language, since the founding of the Académie Française in the seventeenth century. But even French encompasses a large range of variety that is ignored in defining what the standard is, to the point of excluding the idea that variety even exists.

As the sociologist Pierre Bourdieu has theorized, using the standard gives speakers linguistic capital. If speaking the standard is a social advantage, then lacking it will be a disadvantage. The unavoidable outcome of language standardization is inequity, certainly for some, often for the many. The routine companion of linguistic disadvantage is economic and social disadvantage, whether that be for Moroccans in France, northerners in England, Quechua speakers in Peru, or African Americans. If the "best people" speak in a certain way, you will not become one of the best people without their speech. Most people accept the standard as natural and normal, eliding the often conflictual socioeconomic and sociolinguistic realities.

Vernacular versus Standard

However, local and subcultural groups create and maintain countervailing linguistic norms which are defiantly oppositional to the standard. Vernaculars are immensely more variegated than the standard, and are the usual locus of linguistic innovation and creativity. Shared local networks and practices serve as vernacular maintenance mechanisms with their own powers of persuasion and conformity in the face of institutional propagation of the standard.

Babel and Pentecost

The stabilizing, centralizing impetus of linguistic standard and convention is in tension with the decentralizing, momentary, creative use of language. But the belief that monolingualism is natural and that multilingualism is a curse is deeply embedded in Western consciousness, and it is the Bible that has provided the leading image of this in the cultural memory of the West.

Babel

The story in Genesis 11 is usually interpreted as a condemnation of language diversity, and is still enormously influential and productive. But there is an alternative reading available for the narrative: that the judgment of Babel promoted the spread of humankind and the rich diversification of its languages. The fault of Babel was not pride but a refusal to disperse and "fill the earth" as mandated at creation and after the flood. In Bell (2011) I argue that Babel is a blessing rather than a curse, adopting an interpretation proposed by Walter Brueggemann. Babel is in this reading a charter for linguistic variety, a manifesto for multilingualism rather than a lament for lost monolingualism, a monument to the ultimate futility of the drive to enforce monolingualism.

Pentecost

The day of Pentecost has often been described as the reversal of Babel, but close comparison shows this is not the case. Pentecost involves not Babel's reversal but rather its redemption. Speakers did not return to speaking a single language nor hearers to hearing one language. At Pentecost speakers talked and listeners heard in a great variety of languages (Acts 2 indicates no fewer than thirteen). The languages remained different but they were understood. Peter then stood up and preached to the crowd, however, presumably in a single language, and communicated well enough for them to be "cut to the heart." The multiplicity of languages at Pentecost were not given primarily as a matter of communication, then, but of *identity*. Acts 2 characterizes the languages three times as the listeners' mother tongues – the languages they grew up in, the languages they were born in, the languages they were at home in. The coming of the Spirit was marked by an affirmation of their identities and of the diverse languages and cultures in which these "devout Jews from every nation under heaven" were at home.

An Abundance of Voices

I would suggest, with Hymes and Bakhtin, that we not only seek improvement in people's linguistic conditions but address the foundations of linguistic discrimination and inequity. Linguistic justice promotes the speaking and hearing of marginalized and stifled voices. Such commitments were often the prime drivers that motivated the founders of the field of sociolinguistics, and they have continued to spur my own and successive generations of sociolinguistic scholars – many of them Christians.

It is the role of such a sociolinguistics to "give voice." To accept someone's voice is to accept that person; to reject someone's voice is to reject that person. And if we can give voice, we can also take voice away. We can disable the voices of others through not listening to them or by drowning them out – or we can "give ear" to what the socially marginalized are saying. Such staunch and adept listenership is one hallmark of a just and Christian approach to language in society: "Those who have ears to hear, let them hear."

References and Further Reading

Bakhtin, M. M. 1986. *Speech Genres and Other Late Essays*. Austin: University of Texas Press. Bakhtin summarizes his theories on language variety, voice, and centrifugal/centripetal sociolinguistic forces.

Bell, Allan. 2007. "Style in Dialogue: Bakhtin and Sociolinguistic Theory." In *Sociolinguistic Variation: Theories, Methods and Applications*, edited by Robert Bayley and Ceil Lucas, 90–109. New York: Cambridge University Press. Overview of Bakhtin's relevance to sociolinguistics.

———. 2011. "Re-constructing Babel: Discourse Analysis, Hermeneutics and the Interpretive Arc." *Discourse Studies* 13: 519–68. Examination of Ricoeur's interpretive arc in hermeneutics and discourse analysis, illustrated with detailed interpretation of the story of Babel.

Bourdieu, Pierre. 1991. *Language and Symbolic Power*. Cambridge: Polity. Examination of language as cultural capital.

Brueggemann, Walter. 1982. *Genesis: Interpretation*. Atlanta: John Knox. Babel as blessing not curse.

Hymes, Dell. 1996. *Ethnography, Linguistics, Narrative Inequality: Toward an Understanding of Voice.* London: Taylor & Francis. Sociolinguistics' pioneering theorist on justice and voice.

Irvine, Judith T., and Susan Gal. 2000. "Language Ideology and Linguistic Differentiation." In *Regimes of Language: Ideologies, Polities, and Identities,* edited by Paul V. Kroskrity, 35–83. Sante Fe: School of American Research Press. Seminal chapter and book on the study of language ideologies, iconization, and erasure.

The Obligations of Justice for Colombia's Displaced Persons

Christopher Hays

Theology, Scholar Leaders; formerly Fundación Universitaria
Seminario Bíblico de Colombia in Medellín, Colombia[13]

I engage Prof. Wolterstorff's brief on "Justice and Rights," not in my capacity as a New Testament scholar, but from my experience working with victims of forced displacement in Colombia. Our project called Faith and Displacement fuses insights from Christian theology and the social sciences to mobilize Christian communities in an effort to foster the holistic human flourishing (shalom) of internally displaced persons (IDPs). The application of Wolterstorff's work to this specifically Colombian issue may serve as a provocative case study for scholars working in analogous fields or contexts.

Against Abuses of the Rights Discourse in Colombia: From Claimants for Justice to Agents of Justice

In Colombia, the decades-long armed conflict between guerrilla militia, paramilitary groups, the national army, and drug cartels has resulted in literally millions of documented human rights violations. In response to that grave reality, the Colombian government has made human rights a major part of the educational curriculum and public discourse for the past generation. Rights language is pervasive, and generally in what Prof. Wolterstorff dubbed a "second-order" fashion (i.e. the focus is on providing restitution to the victims of the conflict). There is a lot to celebrate in that, to be sure. But some downsides (or, in Prof. Wolterstorff's language, "abuses") have attended the prominence given to rights discourse.

1. The emphasis on rights has fostered a great deal of passivity and a certain attitude of entitlement in Colombian society.

2. The government is seen as the primary conveyer of second-order justice and restorer of violated rights, despite its lack of resources and moral capacities.

3. As a combination of 1 and 2, people in this context think very little about their own agency and responsibilities vis-à-vis either first- or

---

13. gfiweb.net/contributor/53

second-order justice; quite the contrary, the nation is marked by endemic corruption and a disheartening lack of integrity (including among Christians), and the population at large seldom considers that they have an obligation either to practice integrity or to be agents of restorative justice.

Needless to say, the confluence of these three downsides/abuses of rights discourse creates vicious social dynamics.

I was struck by the way that Prof. Wolterstorff's Preview stated that "rights are grounded in the worth (excellence, dignity) of the rights-bearer." Here in Colombia, people would ground rights in our inherent dignity (under the influence of Catholic social teaching), but not in our *excellence*. A great deal could be gained, in the Colombian context, by balancing attention to the rights you have because of your inherent dignity with an emphasis on the fact that being a person with profound dignity means that you are, by your nature, a person of excellencies, excellencies with ramifications for the way in which you are also an agent of justice (first and second order) for others. To do so might activate individuals and communities as being *agents* of justice, rather than simply being *claimants* for justice.

The Rights and Obligations of Collective Entities and Their Members

Wolterstorff picks up the distinction between being *agents* of justice and *claimants* for justice and makes two further clarifications that I believe would be salutary for correcting the passivity evident in many Colombians as a result of a distorted understanding of human rights.

Extending the Argument about Rights and Obligations

Wolterstorff affirms that *collective entities have rights as well*, and not just individuals. He further flips the script of much rights discourse and argues that *all genuine rights imply duties and obligations as their corollaries*. It follows that collectives as well as individuals have obligations. I would argue further that, if a collective has an obligation, the individuals within that collective share that obligation, whether they are leaders or members of the collective.

Relevance for the Colombian Displacement Crisis

This set of maneuvers holds promise for overcoming the individualist passivity that I have identified behind the indolence of much of Colombian civil society vis-à-vis the displacement crisis. Colombia as a nation has already agreed that forced displacement is a violation of the rights of its citizens, insofar as it entails (both directly and indirectly) a transgression of the rights to a dignified life, to safety, to liberty, and to private property (Durán García and Parra Aldana 2007). Furthermore, since the Colombian government has failed in meeting its constitutional obligations to ensure the rights of its IDP citizens, the Supreme Court of Colombia has declared the displacement crisis to be an unconstitutional state of affairs. Nonetheless, the Colombian government has expressed openly that it does not have the financial or logistical resources required to rectify these human rights violations for the entire displaced population (EFE 2014). In other words, the *leadership* of the collective has admitted that it is incapable of fulfilling its obligations to IDP citizens.

The standard Colombian reaction to this state of affairs is to decry the ineptitude or corruption of the government, or to lament the tragedy of the situation, without taking personal initiative to rectify the injustices suffered by victims of the conflict. This reaction is more apparent the closer a population is to the center of governmental power in Colombia. In the Faith and Displacement project, when working with churches in Bogotá (the capital of Colombia, where the potency of the government is most apparent and where a disproportionate amount of federal money is spent), I have encountered a high degree of resistance to the idea that members of the church should take personal action on behalf of IDPs; people are eager to participate in our training under the assumption that it is primarily theoretical and about raising awareness, but balk when it comes to engaging personally with the displaced. By contrast, church teams hailing from smaller municipalities readily embrace training for work directly with displaced populations, because they are under few illusions that the government will sweep in and make good on its obligations to IDPs.

If I am right in surmising that the members of collectives share in the obligations of their collective, then the failure of the Colombian government to respond to the violated rights of the *citizens* of Colombia becomes a failing of the citizens whose rights were *not* violated. It is therefore incumbent upon those citizens to act positively and constructively at least to ameliorate if not completely rectify violations of the rights of the displaced. Constituent members of the society are duty-bound to act at least in some degree to rectify injustice.

To what degree are they duty-bound? I suggest that the extent of one's obligation correlates *directly* with the extent of one's power (i.e. a university president has greater responsibility than an impoverished shopkeeper) and the degree of gravity of the rights violated (i.e. action is more urgent in the face of genocide than in response to price manipulation), and *inversely* with the size of the collective of which one forms a part (i.e. one has relatively less obligation to address a problem on a national scale than one does to address a problem in one's own neighborhood).

Justice and Love, and the Right(s) Thereto

Prof. Wolterstorff extended King and Lewis's exhortation "You must do something" from civil society to the academy. As a theological educator, I want to shift focus to the church and academy. That requires attention to the relationship between justice and love.

Justice as a Part of Love

Prof. Wolterstorff's brief begins by discussing, not rights, but the relationship of justice and love. Wolterstorff argues that justice is a constituent component of love. Justice is not coextensive with love, but certainly inseparable from it, such that one could not claim to be exercising love while violating justice.

In relation to my ecclesially based work with displaced people, two aspects of this argument are especially worth drawing out. First, by emphasizing "care about" others, rather than "care for" others, Wolterstorff hedges against the sort of paternalistic benevolence that so often accompanies Christian work with vulnerable populations (cf. Lupton 2011; Corbett and Fikkert 2012). Such objectifying and condescending care fails to recognize and cultivate the person's intrinsic excellences, thus potentially revictimizing the person through one's own good intentions.[14]

Second, by incorporating justice (to which people have a right) within love, Wolterstorff implies that people actually have a right to at very least *an aspect* of love. I am attracted to the notion that, within the scope of Christian theology and ethics, all people have the *right* to our love (especially given that the command to love one's neighbor as oneself is widely agreed to be a duty

---

14. In our work mobilizing churches to serve displaced people, we emphasize the power and potential of the displaced person from the very beginning. See Hays 2020; Hays, Zúñiga, and Ramos 2020; and Cadavid Valencia and Cuervo 2020.

incumbent upon all Christians). A notion that people have the right to justice *qua* a subset of love could have major ramifications for Christian ministry to vulnerable populations.

Love Is Not Optional

Within evangelical Christianities in the Americas (Colombia being no exception), Christian social action is typically understood as *supererogatory piety*, that is, morally praiseworthy action that is not strictly speaking required by the religion. We do not tend to see the downtrodden of society as having a binding claim on our love. Prof. Wolterstorff's argument, however, does seem to indicate that people have a right to our love. As such, if a person with whom I am in relationship has suffered the violation of his or her first-order rights to justice, I have a moral obligation – an obligation with "peremptory" force – to love that person by pursuing second-order justice for him or her.

The Rights of the Displaced to Love and Justice

This line of reasoning is immensely applicable to the work of Faith and Displacement in mobilizing churches to foster the recuperation of the IDPs. When training churches, I begin by introducing the concept of shalom – holistically construed in terms of spiritual, material, emotional, and relational flourishing. I then move to Luke 4:16–21, to identify how Jesus (citing Isaiah 61:1–2) construed his own ministry in multidimensional fashion, entailing justice, economic well-being, political freedom, and emotional health.[15] These opening forays reveal a good deal of theological alignment with Prof. Wolterstorff's brief.

My next move in training churches, however, is to explore the sheep and goats judgment of Matthew 25:31–46. This text commends itself to the topic of serving displaced persons because it not only speaks of the impecunious, but specifically includes the *xenoi*, foreigners or migrants. The basic argument of this passage is twofold:

1. When one acts on behalf of "the least of these," one ministers to Christ and secures eschatological reward (see especially vv. 34, 40, 45).

---

15. For a glimpse of how this is done, see Donner 2020; Hays 2020; and Hays, Zúñiga, and Ramos 2020.

2. Failing to act on behalf of "the least of these" gets one sent to hell (vv. 41, 46).

I want to zero in on that second point. The King's argument in Matthew 25 is not that one is condemned for having deprived the hungry or thirsty. Rather, the goats are condemned for having simply seen the hungry, naked, and migrant, and done nothing (Hays and Acosta 2020).

The logic of this text implies that one has an obligation to the vulnerable. It is a morally binding duty, the neglect of which merits punishment. This text is thus neatly compatible with Prof. Wolterstorff's account of justice as a right that is a part of love.[16] Interpreting Matthew 25 for the twenty-first century, it would not distort the text to construe "the least of these" as people with a right to food, water, and clothing (matters of justice) as well as to being visited in prison and welcomed as strangers (matters of love more broadly). We who see the least of these, whether as members of the body of Christ or of Colombian society, have moral duties to act justly and lovingly toward them, both in terms of our daily first-order dealings with them, and in terms of pursuing second-order justice for them when the state has failed to provide it.

Conclusion

I have taken the liberty of drawing out some points that seemed implicit in Wolterstorff's argumentation, specifically venturing that members of collectives share the moral obligations of their collective (e.g. citizens share some of the moral responsibilities of their governments) and also suggesting that (within Wolterstorff's construal of justice as a part of love) people's right to justice also implies a right to love. Beyond Colombia, I would wager that my reflections above are pertinent to any number of nations in which rights discourse is prominent and in which the church finds itself sliding into passivity in the face of injustice. Such contexts are, lamentably, not few.

In closing, allow me to venture an exhortation for seminaries. Most institutions of theological education have a strong sense that, by training church leaders, they are serving the good of society, like leaven in dough. This strikes me as true. But our efficacy is often blunted by our tendency to silo ourselves off from other academic disciplines. Faith and Displacement is one seminary's attempt to learn deeply from diverse social-scientific disciplines,

---

16. Even if the biblical author's own thinking would have been rooted, not in rights discourse, but in Old Testament, Second Temple, and apostolic Christian values about caring for the poor, the sick, the migrant, and the prisoner.

at the levels of theory, practice, and empirical verification. The Global Faculty Initiative has the potential to facilitate much the same thing, albeit in relation to a much wider range of disciplines and topics. The Faculty Initiative invites the seminary professor to contribute her or his theological knowledge to believers in other academic disciplines, as well as to receive help from those believing scholars with diverse specialties, in order to be more effective in serving the mission of the church in the world. It is an invitation to see interdisciplinary study, not as a niche endeavor for fringe theologians, but as an opportunity to speak more truly about God, if we believe that all truth is God's truth (Holmes 1977). I think we'd be foolish to pass it up.

References

Cadavid Valencia, Laura Milena, and Ivón Natalia Cuervo. 2020. *Enfoque y metodologías participativas, dar voz a las comunidades.* 2nd ed. Medellín: Publicaciones SBC.

Corbett, Steve, and Brian Fikkert. 2012. *When Helping Hurts: How to Alleviate Poverty without Hurting the Poor . . . and Yourself.* Chicago: Moody.

Donner, Saskia Alexandra, ed. 2020. *Diplomado de Fe y Desplazamiento: cuaderno de trabajo.* Medellín: Publicaciones SBC.

Durán García, David Alfonso, and Juliana Inés Parra Aldana. 2007. "Derechos de las víctimas del desplazamiento forzado: aportes desde la jurisprudencia y la doctrina." In *Desplazamiento forzado en Colombia: derechos, acceso a la justicia y reparaciones*, edited by Javier Aguirre Román, 13–59. Colombia: UNHCR.

EFE. 2014. "El Estado no tiene capacidad para atender a todas las víctimas al mismo tiempo." *El Espectador* 9 (April).

Hays, Christopher M. 2020. *El profesional cristiano y la recuperación económica de las personas en situación de desplazamiento.* 2nd ed. Medellín: Publicaciones SBC.

Hays, Christopher M., and Milton Acosta. 2020. "Jesus as Missional Migrant: Latin American Christologies, the New Testament Witness, and Twenty-First Century Migration." In *Who Do You Say I Am? On the Humanity of Jesus*, edited by George Kalantzis, David B. Capes, and Ty Kieser, 158–77. Eugene: Cascade.

Hays, Christopher M., Isaura Espitia Zúñiga, and Steban Andrés Villadiego Ramos. 2020. *La misión integral de la iglesia: cómo fortalecer o crear un ministerio a favor de personas en situación de desplazamiento: manual del facilitador.* 2nd ed. Medellín: Publicaciones SBC.

Holmes, Arthur F. 1977. *All Truth Is God's Truth.* Grand Rapids: Eerdmans.

Lupton, Robert D. 2011. *Toxic Charity: How Churches and Charities Hurt Those They Help (and How to Reverse It).* New York: HarperCollins.

3

Law and Society

Restorative Justice

Christopher D. Marshall

Restorative Justice, Emeritus

Te Herenga Waka-Victoria University of Wellington, New Zealand[1]

Introduction

Professor Wolterstorff's lucid and perceptive account of a Christian conception of justice and rights provides an excellent framework for locating the distinctive concerns of restorative justice theory and practice, as well as for helping navigate some of the current debates in the field, especially around the appropriate boundaries and scope of restorative justice. Particularly helpful is his distinction between "first-order" and "second-order" justice, for it serves to reinforce the central principle of restorative justice – namely, that justice interventions should be understood, fundamentally, as second-order attempts to *restore* first-order justice in its holistic sense, to make things right again and open up a new future for the participants. This, after all, is how divine justice typically functions in Scripture (Marshall 2001a).

By way of introduction, the term "restorative justice" typically describes a facilitated, face-to-face dialogue between victims and offenders that aims to explore the harm perpetrated by the offending and to determine what should

---

1. gfiweb.net/contributor/63

be done practically to demonstrate accountability for the harm done and to promote healing and repair. It turns on the premise, memorably expressed by John Braithwaite (2002, 80), that "because crime wounds, justice must heal, as long as justice is understood relationally." Though not intended as a theological observation (Braithwaite is a secular theorist), it is hard to miss its resonance with the key biblical texts and themes cited by Wolterstorff.

The ease with which it is possible, at least for me, to build connections between Wolterstorff's framework and restorative justice is because of the formative role biblical notions of justice and reconciliation – mediated through the beliefs and practices of the Anabaptist peace church tradition – played in the emergence of the modern restorative justice movement in the early 1970s. This theological contribution is often misunderstood, minimized, or completely elided from secular accounts of the origin and distinctive features of the movement. But it is surely significant that the earliest architects of restorative justice theory and practice were Christian peace activists intentionally striving to put their spiritual and ethical beliefs into practice in the public arena. One might even say that the biblically informed theology of peace and justice to which they subscribed served as midwife at the birth of restorative justice in the modern era and that without the influence of such core Christian values and beliefs, the central tenets of restorative theory might not have emerged with such clarity and conviction.

This is not to say that Christianity can claim exclusive proprietary rights to the restorative justice ideal. There are precedents and parallels in other cultural and religious traditions as well. Moreover, as the modern restorative justice movement has grown and spread, it has been molded by a wide array of societal concerns and disciplinary interests, giving restorative justice a dynamic or synthetic quality, which remains a singular strength. Nevertheless, the legacy of Christian influence is evident in the characteristic emphasis it places on repentance, accountability, relational repair, and human transformation.

It is also evident, I suggest, in the congruence that exists between restorative justice and indigenous ways of seeing the world. There are clear resemblances between restorative justice processes and the mechanisms used in traditional societies for addressing harm and restoring balance. This resemblance is at least partly attributable to the overt role that biblical values and beliefs played in first shaping restorative justice. In both biblical and indigenous worldviews, there is an instinctive recognition that doing justice in the face of transgression is a deeply spiritual undertaking. It is not simply a matter of assessing facts, determining blame, and allocating penalties. It is also about addressing the loss of spiritual dignity (or *mana* as Māori call it) caused by the offence, a lifting of the shame inflicted, a repairing of the rupture caused to the fabric of the community, a cleansing of the land from impurity, and a restoring of order and balance to the cosmic domain which interconnects all things. This holistic concept of justice helped inform the early development of restorative justice and has made its relational processes and priorities seem intuitively familiar to indigenous communities, especially in North America and New Zealand.

Two Orders of Justice

Wolterstorff posits a fundamental distinction between "first-order justice," which describes the type of justice that consists of agents acting justly in their ordinary affairs, and "second-order justice," which refers to just ways of responding to violations of first-order justice, whether those violations take the form of interpersonal wrongdoing or social injustice. Biblical terms for first-order justice include *righteousness*, which describes right living in its broadest sense, and peace or shalom, which describes a flourishing in all the dimensions of our relational existence. Biblical terminology for second-order justice includes the language of *judgment, justice* and *justification* (or righteousness-restoring action).

I take first-order justice to mean both (1) that second-order actions presuppose a normative understanding of how things *ought* to be in our personal and social relationships and (2) that in responding to violations of that normative order, justice responses should aspire to *restore* a just ordering of affairs and relationships. This is where restorative justice has something important and distinctive to offer.

Unlike many Christian thinkers today, Wolterstorff sees great merit in using the language of "rights" to explicate the demands of justice. He draws a basic distinction between externally *conferred rights* (including those conferred by the law) and intrinsically *nonconferred rights* (those which stem from being the sort of creature the rights-bearer is). Justice entails respecting these rights. It involves recognizing the intrinsic worth of rights-bearers and rendering them what is their rightful due. Injustice, accordingly, involves a failure to respect the dignity and morally legitimate rights of others.

In most jurisdictions today that provide an option for restorative justice, it typically operates within the constraints and protections imposed by the wider justice system. Among other things, this helps ensure that the participants' conferred legal rights are safeguarded. Some critics have alleged that restorative justice undermines due process and erodes respect for the rule of law. But there is little empirical evidence to support that claim. Indeed research in New

Zealand has shown that people who have participated in restorative justice often end up feeling more confident in the existing justice system than before. They do so precisely because the system has provided them with the opportunity to address their psychological and emotional needs in a restorative setting, in a way that is not possible within the formal processes of trial, adjudication, and punishment.

Why "Restorative" Justice?

Advocates still disagree on how best to define restorative justice, and some critics claim it comprises a hodgepodge of contradictory ideals. Yet there remains something recognizably distinctive about a *restorative* way of responding to personal and social harms, something that sets it apart from the more familiar retributive or therapeutic ways of doing so. This distinctiveness lies, in my view, in its peculiar *combination* of values, processes, and intended outcomes. This means that the most helpful way to define or capture the meaning of restorative justice is one that includes all three components in the formulation. My attempt to do so is as follows:

> Restorative justice involves a voluntary, relational process whereby those with a personal stake in an offence or conflict or injustice come together, in a safe and respectful environment, with the help of skilled facilitators, to speak truthfully about what happened and its impact on their lives, to clarify accountability for the harms that have occurred, and to resolve together how best to promote repair and bring about positive changes for all involved. (Marshall 2020, 103–4)

Each element of this definition requires further elaboration, but importantly the definition incorporates the distinctive *process* of restorative justice (a facilitated dialogue between those directly involved in harmful events), its undergirding relational *values* (including freedom of choice, respect, truthfulness, accountability, and equal concern), and the envisioned goals or *outcomes* of the practice (the clarification of what happened in the past and its human impact, and collaborative decision-making about how best to promote repair and achieve positive changes in the future for all involved). This integration of values, processes, and goals is sometimes expressed as a series of foundational principles, and while there is no unanimity on how best to define restorative justice, there is a broad agreement on its core principles.

The suitability of the label has not been without its critics, however. Many object to the adjective "restorative," since it seems to imply an attempt to recover some prior state of equilibrium or harmony, as though the clock can be turned back and the past retrieved. Others object to the perceived narrowness of the term "justice" and its binary, and often arbitrary, distinction between victims and offenders.

Despite such misgivings, the name "restorative justice" has stuck. It has resonated with people all over the world, possibly because it suggests that justice is about achieving concrete change. Justice is not about upholding abstract principles or legal doctrines or human rights standards or moral codes or metaphysical beliefs. True justice *changes* things on the ground: it *rectifies* past wrongs, *repairs* present harms, and *restores* well-being and future safety. Or, to use Wolterstorff's language, it aspires to establish or re-establish first-order justice in which people treat each other with the respect and dignity they are due, both as fellow citizens and fellow human beings.

In terms of *values*, restorative justice seeks to restore respect, dignity, and peace to relationships that have been damaged by wrongdoing. To be the object of intentional malice is often experienced by victims as a fundamental act of disrespect, a failure to value the sufferer's intrinsic worth, identity, legitimate rights, and feelings, as though these things don't really matter. Such disrespect can only be remedied by a restoration of respect, by a clear acknowledgment on the part of the person responsible for the contemptuous behavior that the victim did not deserve to be treated in that way and that the victim's rights, feelings, and interests *do* indeed matter, every bit as much as his or her own. It is often said that "respect" is the primary restorative justice value and the key to its transformative power.

In terms of *process*, restorative justice restores agency, ownership, and decision-making power to those directly affected by the harmful event – victims, offenders, their families and supporters, and the wider community. Victimization is also commonly experienced as a form of disempowerment, a loss of control over one's life and security and a disconnection from those who have failed to provide protection or care. This feeling of disempowerment is often exacerbated by participation in the criminal trial process over which victims have no control and which renders them passive spectators of their own suffering. A similar disempowerment is experienced by defendants, whose case is presented on their behalf by paid advocates and who passively await the trial's outcome of verdict and sentencing. By contrast, rather than deferring all responsibility to the state or to legal professionals, restorative justice aims to restore instrumental power to the immediate participants in resolving the harm.

In terms of *outcomes*, by striving to repair the harms caused by the crime, restorative justice seeks to restore well-being to the individuals affected *and* to restore the relationship between them to a just condition. Both goals are crucial and inseparable. Individual well-being is promoted by trying to meet the needs of moral repair, such as having one's voice heard, one's experience validated, one's story verified, one's integrity or innocence vindicated, and one's intrinsic value affirmed. Yet because human beings are irreducibly *relational* creatures, as the biblical creation stories affirm, none of this can happen apart from restoring the relationship between the parties to a just condition, that is, to a condition in which both sides recognize the rights, dignity, and legitimate interests of the other.

To speak of relational restoration in this connection does not necessarily imply the reconciliation of formerly estranged parties: the participants may not have known each other before the event occurred. Nor does it mean the advent of personal warmth or intimacy between them in the future: the two parties may agree never to see each other again. Rather it means that the nature of the relationship between them, as fellow citizens and fellow human beings, as well as co-participants in the harmful episode, is *restored to a rightful state*, that is, to one marked by equality of concern, dignity, freedom from deceit or coercion, and at least minimal social trust.

Emergence of a Movement

"It is no accident," Wolterstorff writes, "that all the great social justice movements of the twentieth century, struggling against one or another form of systemic injustice, employed the language of rights." While rights-language has not been as prominent in restorative justice discourse as, say, the language of healing, restorative justice has certainly grown from small, experimental beginnings into a global social movement for change.

Initially the concept of restorative justice was used solely with respect to criminal justice concerns, and there are still some theorists and practitioners who insist the phrase should be used only for criminalizable actions. But the reach of restorative approaches has since extended into schools, workplaces, human services providers, voluntary associations, community groups, businesses, governance bodies, and regulatory agencies. The literature now speaks of restorative *practices*, restorative *organizations*, restorative *communities*, restorative regulatory *systems*, restorative *leadership*, even of restorative *cities* and restorative *societies*. These developments may be viewed as different faces of the same diamond, different applications of the same values and principles. The restorative justice movement may therefore be seen as a project aimed at the creation of interpersonal relationships and societal institutions that conscientiously foster human dignity, equality, freedom, mutual respect, human rights, democratic participation, and collaborative governance – or first-order justice.

Arguably the comprehensiveness of this larger restorative vision was encoded in the DNA of the approach in the beginning, for it calls to mind the biblical notion of shalom that directly informed the first experiments in victim-offender reconciliation. Shalom in the Bible means more than the absence of conflict and violence. Rather it denotes the positive presence of harmony and wholeness, of health and prosperity, of integration and balance. It is a state of soundness and flourishing in all the dimensions of one's existence – in one's relationship with God, with others in society, with the wider created order, and with one's own self. Shalom is where everything is as it ought to be, a condition of "all-rightness" in every department of life. It thus combines in one concept the meaning of both justice and peace, which are inseparable ingredients of first-order justice.

In her recent assessment of the current state of the restorative justice movement, Carolyn Boyes-Watson (2019, 7–20) expresses extreme pessimism about its future as a technocratic or managerial solution to the inadequacies of the existing criminal justice system, as is typically favored by legislators and policymakers. She is much more optimistic, however, about its future in the new wave of restorative justice activism that is engaging with issues of oppression, discrimination, economic injustice, and environmental abuse. Here there is no separation between politics and ethics, between justice and spirituality, head-thinking and heart-thinking, individual transformation and societal change. The goal is not just to resolve individual conflicts over past harms but to build an all-embracing and enduring just peace.

Boyes-Watson traces this holistic aspiration back to the unifying vision of shalom and to the "essentially spiritual and ethical understandings of 'right relationship'" that Howard Zehr originally identified as the touchstones of the restorative justice paradigm, as well as to the movement's original goal of building the "beloved community," not simply of forging a more efficient and effective criminal justice system. All this, once again, invites us to see restorative justice as a set of second-order actions guided by the vision of restoring first-order justice in its richest and most inclusive sense.

References and Further Reading

Boyes-Watson, Carolyn. 2019. "Looking at the Past of Restorative Justice: Normative Reflections on Its Future." In *Routledge International Handbook of Restorative Justice*, edited by Theo Gavrielides, 7–20. London/New York: Routledge, 2019. A brief overview of where the field has come from and where it is going.

Braithwaite, John. 2002. *Restorative Justice and Responsive Regulation*. New York: Oxford University Press. A foundational theorist who extended its principles and practices into the wider regulatory sphere.

Marshall, Christopher David. 2001a. *Beyond Retribution: A New Testament Vision for Justice, Crime and Punishment*. Grand Rapids: Eerdmans. Argues that the first Christians exhibited an understanding of justice as a power that heals, restores, and reconciles, and that this understanding ought to drive a Christian contribution to criminal justice debate today.

———. 2001b. *Crowned with Glory and Honor: Human Rights in the Biblical Tradition*. Telford/Scottdale: Pandora/Herald. Despite the limited use of rights-language in traditional Christian sources, shows how the modern notion of human rights is grounded in the central themes of the biblical story.

———. 2012. *Compassionate Justice: An Interdisciplinary Dialogue with Two Gospel Parables on Law, Crime, and Restorative Justice*. Eugene: Cascade. An exploration of Jesus's two most influential parables from a restorative perspective and their continuing relevance to modern justice concerns.

———. 2020. "Restorative Justice." In *Religion Matters: The Contemporary Relevance of Religion*, edited by Paul Babie and Rick Sarre, 101–18. Singapore: Springer Nature. Explores the often-overlooked contribution of religious faith to the birth and shaping of restorative justice.

Zehr, Howard. 2002. *The Little Book of Restorative Justice*. Intercourse: Good Books. An excellent brief account by the person often called "the grandfather of restorative justice."

Justice, Judgment, and Virtue in the Law

Nicholas Aroney

Constitutional Law, University of Queensland, Australia[2]

In his Theology Brief on "Justice and Rights," Professor Nicholas Wolterstorff has offered an account of justice that distinguishes between *first-order justice*, in which individuals and institutions act justly in their everyday affairs, and *second-order justice*, which concerns the laws, sanctions, and systems that secure first-order justice.

Three Distinctives
Right Action or Personal Virtue?

Fundamental to Prof. Wolterstorff's argument is the proposition that justice, properly and biblically understood, involves an interpersonal, normative state of affairs concerning how individuals and institutions interact with each other, rather than a personal virtue or character trait. It is not entirely clear, however, how far Prof. Wolterstorff wishes to distinguish his position from virtue-ethics approaches because in several places he refers to justice as a virtue and he adopts the definition of justice proposed by the Roman jurist Ulpian, which is nothing other than a definition of the virtue of justice.[3] This is broadly consistent with the stance taken by Thomas Aquinas when he endorsed Isidore of Seville's definition of justice as the particular virtue that "makes men capable of doing just actions."[4] Wolterstorff appears to acknowledge that human beings will not act justly unless they themselves have the character and disposition to do so.

Justice and Judgment

Also fundamental to Prof. Wolterstorff's paper is the proposition that first-order justice is distinct from and more fundamental than second-order justice. In his longer study on the topic, *Justice: Rights and Wrongs*, Wolterstorff (2008b) critiques the argument advanced by Prof. Oliver O'Donovan that the biblical

---

2. gfiweb.net/contributor/31
3. Watson 1998, 1.1.10: "Justice is a steady enduring will to render to everyone his right." The Latin text is "Iustitia est constans et perpetua voluntas ius suum cuique tribuendi."
4. *Summa Theologiae* II.II Q57, Art. 1.

texts place more emphasis on "judgment" – and especially "just judgment" – than they do on "justice" conceived abstractly and generally. According to Wolterstorff, O'Donovan mistakenly considers that the key Hebrew word *mišpāṭ*, which appears hundreds of times in the Old Testament, is properly to be understood as referring to the act of "judgment," rather than the more abstract state of affairs that we call "justice." This is a controversy that I will take up further below.

Justice and Rights

A third distinctive of Prof. Wolterstorff's argument is that the essence of justice is to accord others their *rights*. He argues that the idea of natural rights has a much older and more Christian and biblical provenance than the secular philosophies of the Enlightenment. In *Justice: Rights and Wrongs*, he adopts the view of Brian Tierney (1997) that church lawyers of the twelfth century were already using the Latin term *ius* in a way that designated the particular *subjective* rights to which individuals were legally entitled and not only to refer to an *objectively* just state of affairs. However, other scholars have argued not that there was no concept of subjective right but that the right was not *subjectively grounded* in the will and desire of the isolated individual (Milbank 2012).

Practical Consequences
Human Rights and Anti-discrimination Laws

These differences of opinion have practical implications. Prof. Wolterstorff draws attention to the importance of rights-arguments for the advancement of many of the great social justice movements of the twentieth century. While these arguments were framed in the language of rights, he points out that they were directed at various forms of systemic injustice. The American Civil Rights Act of 1964, for example, prohibited discrimination on the basis of race, color, religion, or national origin in the provision of goods and services in any place of public accommodation, such as hotels, restaurants, and theaters. Similarly, the International Convention on the Elimination of All Forms of Racial Discrimination, adopted by the General Assembly of the United Nations in 1965, required signatory states to take measures to eliminate all forms of discrimination on the basis of race, color, descent, or national or ethnic origin if that discrimination had the purpose or effect of nullifying or impairing the recognition, enjoyment, or exercise, on an equal footing, of human rights and fundamental freedoms in the political, economic, social, cultural, or any other field of public life.

Since the 1960s, the scope of anti-discrimination laws has expanded tremendously. This raises significant concerns for many private associations and religious organizations because maintenance of their distinctive religious or other identity depends on their ability to adopt particular standards of membership or to employ staff who share their religious convictions. While most anti-discrimination laws include special carve-outs that run against the grain of such laws, over time the exceptions that protect religious freedom have contracted, as the underlying premises of anti-discrimination laws have been pressed to their logical conclusions.

Subjective Grounding of Rights

Why has this happened? As Milbank (2012) has argued, rights have come to be understood as essentially individual and subjective in nature, such that the individual right not to be discriminated against is considered more basic and fundamental than the right of a religious group or organization to maintain its distinctive character. Accordingly, when there is a conflict between such rights, the individual right must prevail over the collective right. This is applied even to the right to religious freedom itself, which is increasingly confined to the personal and the private, while its corporate and public dimensions are progressively restricted. There is a lot at stake, therefore, in these debates about the origin and nature of human rights (Aroney 2014, 133).

Liberal social ontologies tend to understand all social formations and cultural groups – including the state itself – as compositions of individuals (Taylor 1985; Aroney and Parkinson 2019). On this view, only individuals are ontologically real and have normative weight. Social groups exist to meet the needs and wants of individuals. Families, religious communities, and cultural groups tend to be seen as special kinds of voluntary association. They have weight in moral, political, and legal deliberation only to the extent that the state or individuals positively attribute significance to them. As a consequence, in any contest between the rights of an individual and the rights of a social group, the rights of the individual must have normative priority. The rights of individuals are regarded as more natural, basic, and fundamental than group rights. In this way, as Benjamin Berger (2015, 100) has put it, the "law shapes religion in its own ideological image and likeness and conceptually confines it to the individual, choice-centred, and private dimensions of human life."

Theological Perspectives

Subsidiarity and Sphere Sovereignty

Within Roman Catholic social thought, the term *subsidiarity* has come to refer to a principle which resists the stark duality of individual and state that is characteristic of liberal political philosophy.[5] According to Pope John Paul II, the principle of subsidiarity recognizes that

> a community of a higher order should not interfere in the internal life of a community of a lower order, depriving the latter of its functions, but rather should support it in case of need and help to coordinate its activity with the activities of the rest of society, always with a view to the common good. (John Paul 1991, 18)

Such an approach is often called *personalism,* because it seeks to affirm two important truths about humanity: first, the dignity of each individual person and, second, the embedding of each individual within a matrix of associations and communities. Human beings have inherent dignity, but this dignity does not isolate the individual from his or her social context and does not fixate, as Immanuel Kant did, on the autonomous will of the individual as the lodestar of ethical reasoning.[6]

Within Reformed Christian thought, a similar perspective is advanced under the name of *sphere sovereignty.* As Prof. Wolterstorff (2008a, 105, 109–10) has elsewhere pointed out, sphere sovereignty is the view that human life is "differentiated into distinct spheres," each with its own authority structure which is not delegated to it by some external authority but is original to it. According to its best-known advocate, Dutch theologian and politician Abraham Kuyper (1931, 79), the principle has a theological basis, namely, "the Sovereignty of the Triune God over the whole Cosmos, in all its spheres and kingdoms, visible and invisible." This "primordial Sovereignty," he argued, "eradiates in mankind in a threefold deduced supremacy": in the state, in society, and in the church. Moreover, according to Kuyper (1931, 90–91), within society there are several particular "social spheres" – including especially the family, business, science, and art – which "do not derive the law of their life from the superiority of the state," but are rather subject directly to the highest authority of God himself. It follows that the state ought to "recognize and maintain the various life spheres of family, church and culture" and should respect their independence (Bavinck 2011, 133, 160).

---

5. The best explanation of the origin and nature of the idea in Roman Catholic social teaching is Hittinger 2002.

6. I discuss the Christian theological roots of human dignity in Aroney 2021.

Simple Space or Complex Space?

Subsidiarity and sphere sovereignty have deep roots in Christian reflection on human nature and human sociality. In the thirteenth century, Thomas Aquinas modified the position taken by the Greek philosopher Aristotle by maintaining that human beings are not only *political* animals, but also *social* animals (Aroney 2007, 161, 177–79). Aquinas recognized the existence of what German historian Otto von Gierke later described as a "manifold and graduated system" of "intermediating units" (Gierke 1922, 20–21) lying between the individual on the one hand and the empire and church on the other. John Milbank (1997, 268, 276, 284) has called this sort of social arrangement *complex space*, which means that society consists of a whole array of intermediate groups and institutions, such as guilds, trade unions, religious associations, and universities, that are "not simply subordinate to the greater whole," but rather are formed into a complex network of "free associations and complex varying jurisdictions." This contrasts with what Milbank calls the *simple space* of liberal modernity, in which the only basic terms are the rights of individuals and the power of the state. In his groundbreaking work *Law and Revolution*, Harold Berman (1983) has similarly argued that the most distinctive characteristic of the Western legal tradition has been "the coexistence and competition within the same community of diverse jurisdictions and diverse legal systems," in which no particular community or institution is necessarily regarded as "sovereign" in any absolute sense.[7]

What is it about Christian faith and practice which historically gave rise to this complex space? The duality of church and state is an important part of the answer. Its roots lie in the teaching of Christ that his disciples ought to "render to Caesar the things that are Caesar's, and to God the things that are God's" (Luke 20:25 ESV). As resident aliens whose citizenship is heavenly (1 Pet 1:1; 2:11; Phil 3:20; Eph 2:12, 19), Christians are counseled to submit to the authorities, acknowledging that they are instituted by God to punish evil and praise the good (Rom 13:1–7; 1 Pet 2:13–14). However, in case of conflicting obligations, they are also required to obey God rather than human beings (Acts 4:19; 5:29), for Christians are ambassadors of the kingdom of heaven (2 Cor 5:20; Eph 6:20) and owe their highest allegiance to Jesus Christ, who alone is King of kings and Lord of lords (1 Tim 6:15; Rev 17:14; 19:16).

---

7. I discuss differing theological and legal conceptions of sovereignty in Aroney 2020.

Two Loves, Two Cities

Reflecting on these teachings, St. Augustine of Hippo (354–430) proposed that there are two cities: the earthly city characterized by love of self, and the heavenly city characterized by love of God.[8] Pope Gelasius I (492–96) taught that whereas the role of kings and the role of priests had once been combined (such as when the Roman emperors bore the title *pontifex maximus*), after Christ the two roles were separated on account of "human weakness," each operating in "its sphere of operation."[9] Consequently there were "two swords" by which the world was ruled: the consecrated authority of the priests and the royal power.[10] Especially after the investiture contest of the eleventh and twelfth centuries, the Roman concept of jurisdiction was used by civil lawyers and canon lawyers to identify the particular matters that fell within the authority of church and state. In the striking words of Étienne de Tournai (Stephen of Tournai; 1128–1203):

> In the same city under the same king there are two people. With two people there are two types of life. With two types of life there are two forms of government. From the two forms of government arise two jurisdictions, the city and the church. . . . There are two jurisdictions, divine and human justice, rights, and equity. If each is rendered its due, all things will be harmonious.[11]

According to Brian Tierney (1982, 9–13) it was this insistence on jurisdictional boundaries between popes and emperors, bishops and kings, priests and princes, that largely explains the emergence of what we today know as constitutional government. It meant, in practice, that "none of the coexisting ecclesiastical and secular legal systems that constituted the western legal tradition could claim to be entirely all-inclusive or omnicompetent" and therefore "each had to develop constitutional standards for locating and limiting sovereignty, for allocating governmental powers within such sovereignty, and for determining the basic rights and duties of members" (Berman 1983, 225).

---

8. Augustine, *The City of God* (413–426), 14.28.

9. Gelasius, *The Bond of Anathema*, reproduced in O'Donovan and O'Donovan 1999, 178.

10. Gelasius, *Letter to Emperor Anastasius*, in O'Donovan and O'Donovan 1999, 179. On the unfolding distinction between "two cities" and "two swords," see O'Donovan 2005, 193–211.

11. Stephen of Tournai, *Summa* on Gratian's *Decretum*, cited in Pennington 2019, 35, 45.

Justice, Judgment, and Virtue

The apostle Paul's teaching was that rulers were servants of God, responsible to administer just judgment against wrongdoers (Rom 13:4). This was consistent with the teaching of the Old Testament, which required kings and judges to enact just judgment (Deut 1:16; 16:18). To fulfill this task, it was necessary that the judges were capable, God-fearing, trustworthy, and averse to dishonest gain (Exod 18:13–23). In the striking language of Amos 5:24, righteous judgment is compared to a life-giving stream of water. Contrary to the argument of Prof. Wolterstorff (2008b, 73–74), the text does not separate judgment from justice. The passage literally reads: "but let run down like water judgment and righteousness like a stream enduring." The two key Hebrew terms, *mišpāṭ* and *ṣĕdāqâ*, are at the center of the grammatical construction. The same occurs earlier in the passage, where the opposite ethical evaluation is expressed using the same grammatical construction: "you who turn to wormwood judgment and righteousness in the earth cast down" (Amos 5:7). This intimate association between the masculine *mišpāṭ* (judgment) and the feminine *ṣĕdāqâ* (justice) appears many times in the Old Testament and is especially predicated of David (2 Sam 8:15; 2 Chr 18:14), Solomon (1 Kgs 10:9; 2 Chr 9:8), the ideal King-Messiah (Ps 99:4; Jer 23:5; 33:15), and fundamentally of God himself (Isa 33:5; Jer 9:24).

In New Testament times, the Caesars had increasingly asserted the prerogatives of deity, proclaiming themselves to be gods. Under the influence of Christian teaching, however, later Roman emperors "abandoned their claim to be true divinity on earth and recognized instead in God the origin of their power" (Ullman 1966, 27). From as early as the eighth century, kings and emperors were expected at their coronations to swear oaths that they would, among other things, execute justice and mercy in their judgments, and later, that they would govern in accordance with the established customs and laws of the realm.[12]

In his book *The Ways of Judgment*, Prof. O'Donovan (2005, 6–7) distinguishes between three conceptions of justice: justice-as-right, justice-as-virtue, and justice-as-judgment. Justice-as-right is a state of affairs in which persons and things are in an altogether just set of relationships. Justice-as-virtue is an ordered disposition of the powers of the soul which disposes a person to act justly. Justice-as-judgment refers to the act of moral discrimination pursuant to which a wrong act or a wrong state of affairs is effectively set right. Justice-as-right is a presupposition of justice-as-judgment, which can only be

---

12. I discuss the role of oaths of office in Aroney 2018, 195.

fully enacted by those who possess justice-as-virtue (O'Donovan 2005, 7, 31). While the original creation was entirely good and therefore exemplified a just state of affairs (Gen 1:31), the fall from this primordial goodness necessitates judgment (Gen 3:14–19) and our need to recover the virtue of justice in and through the gospel (Rom 1:16–17). This is, I think, a helpful way to think about it, consistently with the tenor of Scripture as a whole.

References

Aroney, Nicholas. 2007. "Subsidiarity, Federalism and the Best Constitution: Thomas Aquinas on City, Province and Empire." *Law and Philosophy* 26: 161–79.

———. 2014. "Freedom of Religion as an Associational Right." *University of Queensland Law Journal* 33: 153–85.

———. 2018. "The Rule of Law, Religious Authority, and Oaths of Office." *Journal of Law, Religion and State* 6: 195–212.

———. 2020. "Christianity, Sovereignty, and Global Law." In *Christianity and Global Law*, edited by Rafael Domingo and John Witte, 267–87. London: Routledge.

———. 2021. "The Rise and Fall of Human Dignity." *BYU Law Review* 46: 1211–43.

Aroney, Nicholas, and Patrick Parkinson. 2019. "Associational Freedom, Anti-Discrimination Law and the New Multiculturalism." *Australasian Journal of Legal Philosophy* 44: 1–29.

Bavinck, Herman. 2011. "The Kingdom of God, the Highest Good." *The Bavinck Review* 2: 133–70.

Berger, Benjamin L. 2015. *Law's Religion*. Toronto: University of Toronto Press.

Berman, Harold J. 1983. *Law and Revolution: The Formation of the Western Legal Tradition*. Cambridge: Harvard University Press.

Gierke, Otto von. 1922. *Political Theories of the Middle Age*. Frederic William Maitland trans. Cambridge University Press.

Hittinger, Russell. 2002. "Social Pluralism and Subsidiarity in Catholic Social Doctrine." *Annales Theologici* 16: 385–408.

John Paul II (pope). 1991. "*Centesimus Annus*: Encyclical Letter on the Hundredth Anniversary of Rerum Novarum" (1 May).

Kuyper, Abraham. 1931. *Lectures on Calvinism*. Grand Rapids: Eerdmans.

Milbank, John. 1997. "On Complex Space." In *The Word Made Strange: Theology, Language, Culture*, 268–86. London: Blackwell.

———. 2012. "Against Human Rights: Liberty in the Western Tradition." *Oxford Journal of Law and Religion* 1, issue 1 (April): 203–34. https://doi.org/10.1093/ojlr/rwr014.

O'Donovan, Oliver. 2005. *The Ways of Judgment*. Grand Rapids: Eerdmans.

O'Donovan, Oliver, and Joan Lockwood O'Donovan. 1999. *From Irenaeus to Grotius: A Sourcebook in Christian Political Thought, 100–1625*. Grand Rapids: Eerdmans.

Pennington, Kenneth. 2019. "Stephen of Tournai (Étienne de Tournai) (1128–1203)." In *Great Christian Jurists in French History*, edited by Olivier Descamps and Rafael Domingo, 35–51. Cambridge: Cambridge University Press.

Taylor, Charles. 1985. "Atomism." In *Philosophy and the Human Sciences*, 187–210. Cambridge: Cambridge University Press.

Tierney, Brian. 1982. *Religion, Law and the Growth of Constitutional Thought*. Cambridge: Cambridge University Press.

———. 1997. *The Idea of Natural Rights: Studies on Natural Rights, Natural Law and Church Law 1150–1625*. Atlanta: Scholars.

Ullmann, Walter. 1966. *Principles of Government and Politics in the Middle Ages*. 2nd ed. London: Methuen.

Watson, Alan, ed. 1998. *The Digest of Justinian*. Philadelphia: University of Pennsylvania Press.

Wolterstorff, Nicholas. 2008a. "Abraham Kuyper on the Limited Authority of Church and State." *Georgetown Journal of Law & Public Policy* 7, no. 1: 105–10.

———. 2008b. *Justice: Rights and Wrongs*. Princeton: Princeton University Press.

Being Treated Justly in Society and Politics

Karen Man Yee Lee

Law, La Trobe Law School, La Trobe University, Victoria, Australia[13]

While legal authorities are mostly concerned and deal with issues arising from second-order justice, for example of attributing legal liabilities and dispensing punishment, ordinary people may be more concerned about whether they are treated "justly," not only by the legal system, but also by the social and political systems, the ramifications of which affect almost all aspects of their lives, be it education, employment, and the exercise of various social and political rights. This is an increasingly fraught issue in Hong Kong, where a growing number of people are increasingly dissatisfied with the way they are treated by the city's undemocratic government in a highly polarized political environment.

---

13. gfiweb.net/contributor/61

Justice, Rights, and Family Relationships

Patrick Parkinson

Law, Emeritus, University of Queensland, Australia[14]

Nicholas Wolterstorff's fascinating and helpful essay on justice and rights is thought-provoking in many respects. As a lawyer, I hardly need reminding, of course, of the centrality of justice in all that I do. Without what Wolterstorff calls second-order justice (that is, the laws, sanctions, and systems that secure first-order justice), not only would I have no professional work to do, but I would also have no students to teach.

This brief response offers some thoughts about Wolterstorff's analysis in the context of my own work in family law.

The Intoxication with Rights

Wolterstorff's essay is greatly concerned with rights. That is unsurprising for two reasons. First, much of law is indeed about vindicating rights, and so the terms "rights" and "justice" necessarily go hand in hand. Second, rights-talk is ubiquitous in many international and national settings, notably in the United States which is, with respect, particularly intoxicated with "rights," for better or for worse. That is to say, rights are a hugely important part of American political discourse. A great many social arguments are fought out on the battlefield of the courtroom by reference to claims of constitutional rights.

This is a culturally specific phenomenon, and we must guard against either an assumption of its universality or a belief that a rights-oriented society is a manifestation of a lived-out Christianity. Asian societies are not at all similar. In Japan, for example, honor and good faith have traditionally been seen as important factors in maintaining relations (Haley 1998, 162–67). Japan, as it modernized, adopted a "Western" legal order; but this idea of law was largely grafted onto traditional Japanese methods of social ordering (Davis 1996; Kawashima 1963).

I was struck by the ongoing relevance of this a few years ago in a discussion with senior staff of the Ministry of Justice in Singapore. Singapore has for a long time restricted the intake of students to its law schools and has limited the number of law schools in other countries whose degrees are recognized.

---

14. gfiweb.net/contributor/141

The senior manager explained to me that the Singaporean government did not want to have many lawyers because it did not want the country to become an overly litigious society.

Of course, a society that does not have a robust legal system through which the panoply of human rights, property rights, and contractual rights are protected by an independent judiciary is gravely deficient. However, reflection on the values of other successful cultures is an important corrective to any assumption that a rights-based order of the kind that exists in some of the more litigious Western societies gives effect to Christian beliefs.

Family Law and the Maintenance of Relationships

Not every area of law involves consideration of rights. Certainly, rights-talk is not very helpful in the family law context. Yes, the right to bodily integrity, the right to dignity, and a variety of other rights could be invoked to explain why it is that we must tackle the scourge of domestic violence. However, a duty based upon *agapē* might be equally or more compelling as an explanation for why men should not beat their loved ones, whether out of rage or alcohol or drug-fueled disinhibition.

When it comes to parenting arrangements after separation, which is where most disputation occurs, rights are unhelpful. What is needed, for the most part, is cooperation and compromise when there may be no particularly good solutions. Counseling and mediation are frontline forms of assistance to help parents reach child-focused parenting arrangements. Laws have little of real value to add to the resolution of such conflicts unless a court decision is necessary.

The limitation of a rights analysis may be illustrated by the problem of relocation disputes. These are cases where the primary caregiver, almost invariably the mother, wants to relocate a long distance from the father and take the children with her. Often there are good reasons for this, such as wanting to go "home" to where there is parental or other family support, or furthering a new relationship.

Family breakdown brings two legitimate claims into conflict. The first is the claim to autonomy – the right to begin afresh and control one's own future destiny. The second is the children's right to an ongoing relationship with both their parents. Parents have obligations toward their children, and this will ordinarily involve an obligation on each parent to support and protect the children's relationship with the other. Marriage may be freely dissoluble in an era of no-fault divorce; but parenthood is not (Parkinson 2011).

The tension between the right to post-separation autonomy and the benefit to children of maintaining a close relationship with both their parents is particularly acute in relocation cases. If the father cannot move to where the mother wants to live, then very difficult decisions need to be made about where the best interests of the children lie in the circumstances, given the conflicting but legitimate desires and aspirations of each parent.

The analysis is not particularly helped by rights-talk, for if mothers or fathers assert their rights – and they do – what they mean, not infrequently, is that their interests should take precedence over the interests of the other parent or the children.

Nor is it really helpful to ask what is "just." My starting point, in thinking about what is just, is that our obligations to our children trump our rights. We have obligations to the children *and* to our former partner that put considerable restraints upon our autonomy. This is so whether we have entered into the covenant of marriage or have made an implied commitment to the sexual partner and any future child by engaging in sexual intercourse that may result in a child's birth.

This does not mean that ordinarily mothers should be restrained from taking the children away from the location where the father happens to live. Parenting after separation does not rest upon the rule in musical chairs that you need to remain wherever you happen to be when the music stops. It must always be asked whether fathers can move to where the mothers want to live, even if this is difficult. Sometimes, though, it really may be impossible. The divorced or unmarried partner may have no legal right to live and work in the other parent's country of origin.

Even if I have a prima facie view that the responsibility to protect the children's relationship with the other parent should ordinarily take precedence over personal fulfillment, I have to acknowledge that the issues are not often resolved by appeals to a preconceived idea of what is just.

My colleagues and I followed eighty parents in seventy families who had relocation disputes over some five years (Parkinson and Cashmore 2015). The circumstances of these parents were enormously varied. A few of the mothers had been subjected to serious violence. Some fathers had, from the mothers' accounts at least, a very limited sense of responsibility toward their children. Memorably, one mother described her former partner as a "hands-on parent." He always handed over the care of his young children to a woman in his life – his mother, or his latest girlfriend (Parkinson and Cashmore 2013). Yet he strongly opposed the relocation of the children's mother to a place where she had more family support. In other cases, the fathers were extraordinarily dedicated to the well-being of their children. Of course, the accounts of each of our interviewees were colored by their own perspectives. In only ten cases did we hear both parents' stories.

What was clear from the research was that where children did have a close relationship with the nonresident parent, a move a long distance from that parent was detrimental to the children's well-being (Cashmore and Parkinson 2016). Video technology and the ease of plane travel diminished children's sense of loss but did not eradicate it.

The Relationship between the First and Second Orders of Justice

This brings me to my final observation on Wolterstorff's very helpful analysis. Second-order justice is not always about rights. In the family law context, second-order justice provides a decision-maker when parents cannot agree. The family law judge must make decisions about what is in the best interests of children with little reference to rights. That it is a legal process at all may seem puzzling to the outside observer; but sometimes there are factual issues of great significance to determine, such as the extent of domestic violence or allegations of child sexual abuse. A good family law system needs to depend heavily on appropriately qualified medical or psychology-trained experts who can offer opinions on what is likely to be in the best interests of children.

Family law judges don't really seek to administer justice in parenting cases. We ask of them not that their decisions be just but that they be wise. The second-order justice is what litigants have a "right" to – a right to present their case to an independent decision-maker who will deliver Solomonic justice (but often without the benefit of Solomon's wisdom). Family law thus complicates Wolterstorff's distinction between first- and second-order justice.

Justice, Relationships, and Peacemaking

So as a Christian, what aspect of the faith is most important to me in working in this difficult area of family law? It is not Isaiah 61, pertinent as this is in so many other societal contexts. My role is to ask myself how we can resolve these difficult family law disputes in ways that are most protective of children and which reduce, as far as possible, the levels of conflict between parents.

In this respect, I believe the innovation to the Australian family law system in which I have been involved will, in the long term, prove to have been most valuable. This is the development of Family Relationship Centres across the country. These centers, almost fully funded by government, provide an early intervention strategy in the aftermath of relationship breakdown and offer an alternative to resolving parenting issues after separation through lawyers and courts (Parkinson 2013). They aim to help parents in a holistic way to navigate the transition from parenting together to parenting apart. The staff, at intake, refer parents to the range of different services that they might need in the aftermath of separation and offer free, or almost free, mediation.

Yes, as lawyers we must pursue justice and, where appropriate, seek to vindicate rights; but we should beware lest our thinking about justice be dominated by a rights paradigm. Blessed, said Jesus, are the peacemakers. In his teaching in the Sermon on the Mount he urged us at times not to pursue our rights. "If anyone wants to sue you and take your shirt, hand over your coat as well. If anyone forces you to go one mile, go with them two miles" (Matt 5:40–41 NIV). Relationships may matter more than rights in certain situations. Loving our enemies may be better than suing them. It is not that a focus on rights, particularly the rights of others, is misplaced – not at all – but in Jesus's teaching, justice is contextualized within a broader ethical and relational framework.

References

Cashmore, J., and P. Parkinson. 2016. "Children's 'Wishes and Feelings' in Relocation Disputes." *Child and Family Law Quarterly* 28: 151–73.

Davis, J. 1996. *Dispute Resolution in Japan*. Den Haag: Kluwer Law International.

Haley, J. 1998. *The Spirit of Japanese Law*. Athens/London: University of Georgia Press.

Kawashima, T. 1963. "Dispute Resolution in Contemporary Japan." In *Law in Japan: The Legal Order in a Changing Society*, edited by A. Taylor von Mehren, 41–72. Cambridge: Harvard University Press.

Parkinson, P. 2011. *Family Law and the Indissolubility of Parenthood*. New York: Cambridge University Press.

———. 2013. "The Idea of Family Relationship Centres." *Family Court Review* 51: 195–213.

Parkinson, P., and J. Cashmore. 2013. "When Mothers Stay: Adjusting to Loss after Relocation Disputes." *Family Law Quarterly* 47: 65–96.

———. 2015. "Reforming Relocation Law – An Evidence-Based Approach." *Family Court Review* 53: 23–39.

Sexual Violence and Sexual Dignity

Anna High

Law, University of Otago, New Zealand[15]

In his Theology Brief "Justice and Rights," Professor Wolterstorff explores the idea of *first-order justice* from a Christian perspective, including the place of considerations of justice in disciplinary subject matter. Wolterstorff rejects the term "distributive justice" for the type of justice which consists of agents acting justly in their ordinary affairs. However, although such justice can often be seen in terms of ways benefits and/or burdens are distributed, that is not always the case. Consider rape, which Wolterstorff characterizes as "a profound violation of justice, a profound wrong. But what fundamentally makes it wrong is not that benefits and burdens have been mal-distributed – though they have been. What makes it wrong is that the victim has been violated, *treated with indignity*" (emphasis added).

Dignity as a Legal Norm

In an article in the *Yale Journal of Law & Feminism* (High 2021), I explore this idea at quite some length – that dignity is an organizing principle or idea underpinning the crime of rape. My starting point is the observation that dignity has been deployed by judges, in jurisdictions from America to Zimbabwe, to do both expressive work (e.g. as a normatively powerful value which is useful for condemning the multiplicity of rape's harms) and doctrinal work (e.g. to ground arguments about how the doctrines of rape law should evolve) in relation to the criminalization of sexual violence. As Professor Wolterstorff notes, dignity has achieved the status of an assumed norm in international human rights. Christopher McCrudden (2008) has mapped the emergence of human dignity as the hallmark of international human rights law since the second half of the twentieth century, in resilement from the horrors of World War II. The atrocities committed in that war by their nature denied the inherent equal excellence and worth of various people groups. "Dignity" as a political and legal value affirms the equal inalienable worth of all people (McCrudden refers to this as dignity's "ontological claim") and the resulting "relational claims" as to how people can and cannot be treated.

---

15. gfiweb.net/contributor/55

"Dignity talk" is now prevalent in law, not only in jurisdictions such as Germany, Israel, and South Africa which have enacted dignity as a constitutional norm of the highest order, but also in jurisdictions whose constitutions make no direct reference to dignity. For example, in the United States, some of the Supreme Court's most seminal decisions – relating to abortion, same-sex marriage, capital punishment – turn on dignity.

In my work, I trace the permeation of dignity talk into the legal subdiscipline of sexual violence. My work is "bottom up," in that I seek to understand how and why judges use dignity in case law. To establish a framework for that analysis, I first map the broad contours of a feminist understanding of "sexual dignity" in sexual violence theory; in that body of work, it is possible to identify an emerging consensus on the meaning of dignity as a thick, multidimensional concept, capacious enough to express the multiplicity of rape's wrongs. That feminist theory of sexual dignity is then applied to review the use of dignity in sexual violence case law from multiple jurisdictions.

Diminishment of Dignity and Degradation

One key point I explore is the distinction made by Jean Hampton between diminishment of dignity and degradation. Hampton is cited by Wolterstorff as explicating quite clearly the wrongfulness of dignity-defying acts: "A person wrongs another, treats that person as he or she has a right not to be treated, 'if and only if (while acting as a responsible agent) she treats him in a way that is objectively . . . demeaning, that is disrespectful of [that person's] worth.'" Importantly, Hampton has elsewhere argued that there is an important distinction between "diminishment (the mere portrayal of someone as lower) and degradation (the actual lowering of a person's value)" (Hampton 1999, 138). The distinction is important, argues Hampton, because

> we need a way of understanding when sex can be wrong, even while holding to the idea that its wrongfulness is never something that can lessen a woman's worth as a person, no matter what her society (or her psychologists) might tell her (or do to her) in the aftermath of the experience. The point of distinguishing between diminishment . . . and degradation . . . , then linking wrongdoing only with diminishment, is that we are able to affirm that the value of the victim always persists after the crime. (Hampton 1999, 135)

Diminishment may be subjectively experienced as degradation; indeed, rape is "a kind of event that seeks to make that diminished status a reality. The woman is used as though she is an object, and so she is thought to be one" (Hampton 1999, 135). But importantly, dignity as it is understood in secular Western law and philosophy is assumed to be permanent, a point that the diminishment/degradation highlights well.

Feminist and Christian Resonances on Dignity

For Christians a sacred conception of dignity premised on *imago Dei* is even more fundamentally understood as inalienable and permanent. Because our dignity derives from being made in God's image, it cannot be taken away, even by the most harmful of acts. It can only be denied. This can, of course, be subjectively experienced by the rape victim as an actual degradation of selfhood or the "cessation of selfhood" (West 1999, 109); but her dignity-bearing self, her *imago Dei* self, endures.

Professor Wolterstorff's brief centers justice in dignity. This brief has elaborated by highlighting one way in which a feminist understanding of sexual dignity – a key concept underpinning the criminal justice response to sexual violence – resonates with a Christian understanding of the *imago Dei*-derived dignity of all humankind as permanent and inalienable. Human dignity may be denied but it cannot be extinguished.

References and Further Reading

Hampton, Jean. 1999. "Defining Wrong and Defining Rape." In *A Most Detestable Crime: New Philosophical Essays on Rape*, edited by Keith Burgess-Jackson, 118–56. Oxford: Oxford University Press. Uses the concepts of diminishment and degradation to understand morally wrongful sex.

High, Anna. 2021. "Sexual Dignity in Rape Law." *Yale Journal of Law & Feminism* 33, no. 2. 33 pages. http://hdl.handle.net/10523/12056. Explores the idea of sexual dignity in feminist legal theory and comparative case law on sexual violence.

McCrudden, Christopher. 2008. "Human Dignity and Judicial Interpretation of Human Rights." *European Journal of International Law* 19, no. 4: 655–724. For discussion of the emergence, meaning, and function of human dignity as a legal value in international and comparative human rights law.

West, Robin. 1999. *Caring for Justice*. New York: New York University Press. For a feminist account of the harms to selfhood involved in being treated as a sexual object.

Justice and Economic and Social Rights
Karen Kong
Law, University of Hong Kong, Hong Kong[16]

My research on social and economic rights looks at how resources should be fairly distributed in the society based on human rights norms. "Render to each what is his [or her] right" can be applied to social and economic rights as well, as each person has a moral claim to basic necessities in this world. Treating each person in ways that show due respect for that person's worth should include respecting his or her dignity and ensuring that he or she is not deprived of basic needs such as food, water, shelter, primary health care, and basic education.

The following are human rights and justice issues: Should migrants, nonnationals, and refugees be given the same rights as citizens? Should grounds of discrimination be limited to personal characteristics listed in the international human rights instruments, such as race, color, sex, and religion? When there are discrepancies between human rights norms and the Bible, how should they be dealt with by academics?

---

16. gfiweb.net/contributor/59

Market Failures and Government Agency Rulemaking

Alex Lee
Law, Northwestern University, USA[17]

Law is the chief institution through which second-order justice is administered. We live in a liberal society where everything is permitted unless specifically prohibited. But Scripture tells us that we are fallen creatures. Lawmaking, therefore, must play a critical role in shaping second-order justice, in Wolterstorff's terms, and it is important to ensure that our governments make laws that are just and righteous, as we strive toward first-order justice.

Administrative Rulemaking

One area of my research is looking into the mechanisms of administrative rulemaking. Administrative rulemaking is the process by which government agencies adopt rules that have the force of law. In the US we typically think of lawmaking as an act of Congress, carried out by elected officials in their representative capacity. But in today's administrative state in the US, and in many other democratic societies and advanced economies, many rules that have far-reaching economic and social impacts – including efficiency and distributive consequences – are adopted at the agency level by appointed officials or civil servants. This is considered constitutional as long as each agency acts within its lawfully delegated authority from Congress.

The basic rulemaking process in the US is governed by the Administrative Procedure Act of 1946. The most common process includes (1) an agency's issuance of a notice of proposed rulemaking, (2) a thirty-day period during which the general public can submit comments and views on the proposed rule, and (3) the agency's adoption of the final rule after giving a careful consideration of the submitted comments and views. Once a rule is adopted, those citizens or interest groups who desire to challenge the rule can seek judicial review and have the court examine whether the agency followed a proper procedure and acted within its statutory authority in adopting the rule.

---

17. gfiweb.net/contributor/184

Market Failure as an Obstacle to First-Order Justice

The traditional basis for government regulation is a market failure. In economic terms, a market failure is a situation in which the allocation of goods and services by an unregulated market fails to achieve efficiency. Typical examples include natural monopoly, public goods, information asymmetry, and externalities. For economists, the main problem with a market failure is that society is leaving money on the table, and valuable resources or opportunities are being wasted due to transaction costs.

Under Wolterstorff's framework, however, a market failure can also be seen as hindering first-order justice in the economy. Market participants often fail to practice first-order justice because their incentives are misaligned or because they lack information. As a result, agency rules that can effectively address market failures, coupled with enforcement actions, can help, guide, or compel individuals and institutions to render to others what is due to them. Accordingly, improving the government's process of administrative rulemaking can lead to a better administration of second-order justice and render greater first-order justice in our economy.

How Second-Order Justice Can Be Thwarted

My research agenda seeks to broadly identify innovative mechanisms by which we can promote more transparent, empirically informed, and fair rulemaking in a world where agencies often have to operate on the basis of less than perfect information. Innovation is necessary in this area because, in practice, there are a number of ways in which administrative rulemaking may be misguided.

First, a well-intentioned agency head can design and adopt a rule based on incomplete or biased information. In such instances, an agency may have correctly identified the relevant market failure, but it may end up adopting a rule that comes short of addressing it appropriately.

Second, a well-intentioned agency head can face opposition by powerful and well-funded interest groups that may have their own agenda. Those groups can seek judicial review of an agency's rule once it is adopted. In some instances, an agency can lose the legal challenge and the reviewing court may vacate what could have been an efficient rule. This can happen, for example, if the court finds that the agency did not sufficiently analyze the rule's benefits and its costs on the economy.

Third, an agency head herself may strive to adopt a rule that will have a very particular political outcome. In so doing, she may turn a blind eye to how the rule may bring about other consequences. In such instances, a rule adopted by the agency can have a mix of good and bad effects. It may also come with significant distribution concerns. In all these instances, second-order justice is thwarted, and unfair outcomes may result.

Justice in SEC Rulemaking

My special interest lies at the intersection of securities regulation (a body of law that regulates the market for capital) and administrative law (a body of law that regulates the administration of government agencies). Between 2007 and 2012, I had the privilege of working at the US Securities and Exchange Commission (SEC). The SEC is a federal government agency whose mission is to protect investors, maintain fair, orderly, and efficient markets, and facilitate capital formation. The agency routinely adopts corporate disclosure rules to provide greater transparency for investors and brings enforcement actions against those who violate the law.

During my first three years at the agency, I was an Economic Fellow and helped the Commission analyze the costs and benefits of various rules the agency sought to adopt. One challenge facing a regulatory agency such as the SEC is that it must at times adopt a rule to address a clear market failure, but without a large amount of relevant data. Without data, quantifying benefits and costs will be nearly impossible and the agency will have to resort to qualitative reasoning to justify its rule. During the last two years, I worked as an attorney advisor in the Division of Economic and Risk Analysis and worked closely with the Office of the General Counsel when the Commission had to defend its rules from legal challenges by various petitioners who argued that the agency's economic analysis was faulty or otherwise insufficient.

Throughout my time at the SEC, I was preoccupied with the administrative rulemaking process. The basic process posed two difficulties. First, it was easy for powerful interest groups, intent on opposing a proposed rule, to hijack the process by submitting voluminous technical comments with a vast lot of information that might be one-sided. Second, there was insufficient transparency in the way the agency staff or the commenters communicated their own reservations, uncertainties, or risks about a rule. I began thinking about ways to make modest and implementable reforms to address these difficulties – including *ex post* and *ex ante* mechanisms to bring more data to the process and analytical frameworks for considering the economic and distributive effects of a rule in a more comprehensive manner.

Eventually, I joined legal academia with the hope that my research in this area could contribute to promoting more transparent and productive regulatory dialogues in rulemaking and lead to agency rules that are both efficient and effective. There is much work to be done in this area. In an increasingly complex world, challenges to designing an optimal rule will be formidable. But these are challenges, I believe, worth tackling.

References and Further Reading

Lee, Yoon-Ho. 2013. "An Options-Approach to Agency Rulemaking." *Administrative Law Review* 65: 881–941. Discusses the advantage of a real-option approach to agency rulemaking in the presence of uncertainty.

———. 2015a. "The Efficiency Criterion for Securities Regulation: Investor Welfare or Total Surplus?" *Arizona Law Review* 57: 85–128. Discusses the significance of articulating a clear cost-benefit analysis framework in agency rulemaking.

———. 2015b. "SEC Rules, Stakeholder Interests, and Cost-Benefit Analysis." *Capital Markets Law Journal* 10: 31–28. Compares and contrasts two different frameworks of cost-benefit analysis in the context of SEC rules.

———. 2016. "Beyond Agency Core Mission." *Administrative Law Review* 68: 551–603. Discusses the necessity of departing from the core-mission model.

———. 2019. "Incorporating Market Reactions into Agency Rulemaking." *Wake Forest Law Review* 54: 1361–98. Suggests ways to incorporate stock market reactions into the administrative rulemaking process.

———. 2021. "A Model of Stock-Market-Based Rulemaking." *American Law & Economics Review* 23: 1–55. Presents a game-theoretic model of stock-market-based rulemaking.

On Justice in Land Use
Philip Bess
Architecture, University of Notre Dame, USA[18]

Justice in Ulpian's and Wolterstorff's sense (as well as environmental stewardship, which seems to me related to justice but also distinguishable) is central to my interest in the laws that govern land use and how we make contemporary human settlements.

---

18. gfiweb.net/contributor/35

4

International and Global Justice

Climate Change Justice

Donald Hay

Economics, Emeritus, Jesus College, University of Oxford, UK[1]

and

Gordon Menzies

Economics, University of Technology Sydney, Australia[2]

The call for climate *justice* has emerged from many environmental campaigners in recent months, not least from the lips of Greta Thunberg and her young followers. It is less evident in the vocabulary of environmental economists, but a type of "justice" is implicit in the analysis that economists present and the policy solutions that they propose. This Disciplinary Brief looks for engagement between the analysis of justice that Wolterstorff has presented, and that of mainstream environmental economics.

The Science and Economics of the Problem

To set it in context, we must briefly review the main scientific and economic elements of the problem (see Hepburn 2019 and Perman et al. 2011).

First, climate change is an example of an economic "externality," that is, an economic consequence of decisions by a consumer or a producer of goods

---

1. gfiweb.net/contributor/21
2. gfiweb.net/contributor/66

and services that is not accounted for in markets and therefore is not taken into account by them. If the consumer or producer uses energy derived from a fossil fuel, the result is an emission of CO_2 or some other greenhouse gas. Emissions add to the stock of greenhouse gases in the atmosphere. The effects of multiple private decisions on the stock, when compounded, have devastating effects, generating costs for everyone. Hepburn (2019, 4) outlines some of the more salient ones. It is evident that these effects have important consequences for human flourishing.

Second, implicit in financial markets is a discounting future events, whether good or bad. Thus a cost of $100 arising fifty years from now has a current cost of approximately only $23 if, for example, the interest rate is 3 percent. Hence economic actors, if motivated *solely* by economic rationality, should not be too bothered about costs that will be incurred by their grandchildren and great-grandchildren. (This is *not*, unsurprisingly, a judgment with which we personally concur.) And, of course, their grandchildren may not yet be born, so they are unable to express any preferences about the future state of the world.

Third, a key feature of markets is the anonymity of those involved. Markets do not distinguish between an impact on a rich person and on a poor person. A rise in sea level due to global warming may flood both the Mar-a-Lago estate in Florida and a small inhabited island in the Pacific. It might be thought that the owner of the estate can take the financial hit, but it will be utterly catastrophic for the islanders as it will destroy their homes and livelihoods. These are not morally equivalent.

An insurance framework reinforces this moral point. Action on global warming can be justified even in the face of high uncertainty over future impacts. Suppose that the anticipated effects of warming and adverse weather events by the second half of the twenty-first century had only a 50 percent probability (virtually all scientists would regard this as implausibly low). Even in this case, the damage associated would justify paying for "insurance" in the form of slowing or halting warming. Policy actions being considered and implemented by the governments of the world display a moral imperative common to all insurance. That is, insurance is a blessing for the under-resourced and marginalized. The well-off, such as the resident of Mar-a-Lago, can insure themselves by, say, buying a property elsewhere. The islanders cannot, and instead face not only economic devastation but also the extinction of their community and culture.

Implications for Economic Policy on Climate Change

What implications for economic policy follow from these three elements? The standard economic prescription to deal with externalities is to ensure that they are priced, so that decisions taken by households and firms take them into account. In the case of climate change arising from CO_2 emissions, the proposed price is either a tax on carbon that reflects the costs fully, or the requirement to purchase a "right to pollute" permit. The ruling authorities are responsible for adjusting the tax rates, or the scale of the market for permits, to arrive at a sensible level of emissions. This in turn depends on the costs to society of ongoing emissions. Yet estimating these costs is a formidable challenge.

Evaluate Costs

First, we need to evaluate the economic costs of the consequences of global warming listed above. Recall that many of these costs will be incurred in the future, maybe not before the end of this century. Moreover, the likely changes in technologies between now and then have to be considered: the world is unlikely to sit back and watch the unfolding catastrophe without trying to do something about it. In assessing the economic impact we should also take account of where those costs fall: it might be right to weight the costs for poorer people more highly than those for the rich.

Fixing a Discount Rate

Second, we need to specify an appropriate discount rate to convert future costs into current values. As noted above, the choice of discount rate has a major consequence for current values, so identifying the right value is critically important. Economists tend to go back to first principles in deriving a rate. They note three elements:

1. The phenomenon of pure time preference: people prefer "jam today to jam tomorrow." Quite why that should be is much discussed, but it is a human trait which is hard to dismiss.

2. There are potential catastrophes which threaten the existence of humankind (for example, nuclear war, asteroid strikes, and global pandemics). Consideration of such eventualities could lead to a myopic orientation toward the present, and some climate change economists have used this as a justification for a positive discount rate privileging the present generation over future generations. The

doctrine of providence might make a Christian thinker pause before uncritically accepting this logic: consider the Noahic covenant in Genesis 9:8–17, with its unconditional promise to sustain the natural order.

3. The experience of economies is that incomes rise over time: future generations will be richer than us, and so we should be less concerned about future costs they will be better able to bear.

There is no consensus on what discount rate should emerge from these elements: the Stern Review came up with 2.2 percent per annum, but was criticized for being too kind to future (wealthier?) generations. Other economists dismiss all this as "back of the envelope," and argue for the use of market discount rates, which tend to be rather higher, implicitly discounting the costs to be incurred by future generations.

First-Order Justice in Environmental Economics

What concept of justice is implicit in the approach of environmental economists? The underlying utilitarian presumption is that the costs of climate change should be assigned across generations: if, *ceteris paribus*, a particular economic activity will bring equal benefits to current and future generations, then the "pain" should be shared between them. Note, however, that this is a judgment that is made by the current generation, since future generations are not present to exercise their voice. It is far from evident that the evaluation of future generations will be the same as that of their predecessors: they have been deprived of their right to express their preferences.

What "rights" might we assign to future generations, to relate this discussion to Wolterstorff's treatment of rights as fundamental to justice? He puts it like this: "All instances of first-order justice are cases of an agent rendering to another what is the other's right or due: all instances of first-order injustice are cases of an agent not rendering to another what is the other's right or due." In his analysis of climate change, Caney (2006) appeals to the 1972 Stockholm Declaration of the UN Conference on Human Environment: "Man has the fundamental right to freedom, equality and adequate conditions of life, in an environment that permits a life of dignity and well-being, and he bears a solemn responsibility to protect and improve the environment for present and future generations." If this is correct then the present generation *in toto* has to render to future generations an environment that is not despoiled or irreversibly degraded. Discounting the future does not come into the analysis of this right and our obligation. There is no good reason for diminishing the rights of future generations just because they happen to have been born after us.

It was also claimed above that pricing "rights to pollute" through permits or taxes was a good way of deciding which units (individuals or businesses) would be the ones to reduce emissions. But although rationing through price allows the continuance of many worthwhile activities, it is a crude solution. The problem is that some units (individuals or businesses) may not have the resources to pay for worthwhile emissions, so their "right to pollute" cannot be exercised. This is an example of a more general problem of using prices and markets to allocate goods.

The discussion so far has assumed an anthropocentric understanding of the moral implications of climate change. But that is only a part of the Christian understanding. No doubt humankind is given the created order to provide for human flourishing. But humankind is also enjoined (in the Genesis account) to exercise covenantal responsibility. It is God's creation, which he sees as "very good"; we have the responsibility to steward it carefully. The language of dominion ("rule over") is used in the OT on the responsibility of kingship, and the ideal of kingship is that of the shepherd, who has a particular concern for the poor and disadvantaged.

Economic analysis works with a thin doctrine of the "rights" of future generations. It is morally indefensible to allow ourselves greater consumption now, and to transfer the environmental costs and consequences to our children and grandchildren who have no voice. They have as much right as we do to a world that is not irretrievably damaged. To employ the insurance argument again, although it has been the historic experience of the last two centuries that forebears are poorer than their progeny, this state of affairs may not continue – an eventuality which current generations can insure against by good stewardship and greenhouse gas abatement. Most importantly, God has commanded us to care for his created order, even as we are permitted to use it for human flourishing. We have no right to despoil it.

Second-Order Justice in Environmental Economics

Our discussion would be incomplete if we did not address what Wolterstorff terms "second-order justice." Our focus so far has been on "first-order justice": agents (individuals, households, firms, institutions, authorities) treating others as their rights require. "Second-order justice" is what is needed to put right injustices that have been perpetrated when first-order justice has been violated. This can involve a range of measures, but in the climate change context these might most naturally include compensation for costs inflicted on others, and action to reverse the environmental damage that has been caused.

Compensation for Costs

Much of the accumulation of CO_2 in the atmosphere is historic, arising from the Industrial Revolution in Europe and later in North America. The call from many poorer countries for financial assistance to deal with the consequences of climate change should be seen as putting right a historic injustice.

Action to Reverse

Perhaps the rich economies of the West should be required to invest heavily in carbon capture, not just to offset current emissions, but also to deal with the CO_2 build-up for which they were responsible. Reversing environmental damage is probably best addressed by programs not only to preserve what remains from exploitation, but also to restore it. Deforestation is a global problem. We not only need to stop destruction of tropical rainforests, but we also need projects to replant wherever this is feasible. More speculatively, we should perhaps think of second-order justice in relation to God himself. If we have not been responsible in exercising our stewardship of his world, then Christians at least must consider what they might do to redress some of the damage caused in the past. Conservation and restoration should become a part of Christian discipleship, not just the calling of a few environmentally committed Christians.

References

Caney, C. 2006. "Cosmopolitan Justice, Rights and Global Climate Change." *Canadian Journal of Law and Jurisprudence* 19: 255–78.

Hepburn, C. 2019. *Common Climate Questions and Answers.* Oxford: Smith School of Enterprise and the Environment.

Kapic, Kelly M. 2022. *You're Only Human: How Your Limits Reflect God's Design and Why That's Good News.* Grand Rapids: Brazos.

Perman, R., Y. Ma, M. Common, D. Maddison, and J. McGilvray. 2011. *Natural Resource and Environmental Economics.* 4th ed. London: Pearson.

Stern, N. H. 2007. *The Economics of Climate Change: The Stern Review.* Cambridge: Cambridge University Press.

Atrocities, Accountability, and Reconciliation: The Pursuit of Justice in International Relations

Cecilia Jacob

International Relations, Coral Bell School of Asia and the
Pacific, Australian National University, Australia[3]

I found the Theology Brief "Justice and Rights" stimulating, in particular the attention paid to the relationship between justice and love, righteousness, and rights as action-oriented. I approach this response to the brief through the lens of my own research focus, namely, the governance of human protection at the global level, including policy-oriented research on atrocity prevention and hate speech. In the area of global governance of human protection in situations of conflict and atrocities, power structures in key institutions, such as the United Nations Security Council, and in the foreign policy practices of states, have perpetuated deep structural injustices between the powerful states and those most vulnerable in international society. The ongoing repression of Uyghur populations in China, democracy protesters in Myanmar, or Tigrayans in Ethiopia fails to garner meaningful international protection responses because the decision-making processes and structure at the global level subordinate these crises to political and material interest.

The conviction that the international community has certain obligations and a responsibility to *respond to* atrocities against civilian populations ("first-order" injustices) operates as a mode of "second-order" justice, as defined by Wolterstorff. Efforts to advance justice at the international level have progressed through the creation of international legal standards, normative doctrines, and institutions to protect the world's most vulnerable from systematic abuse. Yet inconsistent and inadequate application of these standards leads to the fundamental research problem that I address here, which relates to injustice expressed through ineffective protection outcomes for the vulnerable.

Accountability

The first thematic area that I am addressing in my current research relates to the rise of accountability in the global governance of human protection. A proliferation of judicial and institutional accountability mechanisms seeks to

---

3. gfiweb.net/contributor/56

prevent, protect, and prosecute mass violations of human rights, serving both a normative goal of enhancing global justice, and a practical purpose of deterring and providing remedy for major human rights violations and atrocities.

Trends in Human Protection

From empirical research that I have conducted over the past few years, I see several trends emerging in the field of human protection:

- *The geopolitical context has become much more volatile* due to heightened competition between major and rising powers.
- Heightened geopolitical tensions have emboldened many state actors to *push back on fundamental liberal values* within multilateral institutions and other forms of global interactions, and *human rights have been undermined in many quarters.*
- The global backlash on human rights in global governance institutions has *undermined the protection of populations facing systematic human rights abuse and atrocities.* As my research shows, efforts by powerful governments to break the link between human rights protection and conflict prevention during recent processes of reform within the United Nations have undermined the capacity of that international organization to protect populations in local contexts where they operate (Jacob 2020; Jacob 2021), impeding international community efforts toward second-order justice.
- Numerous governments committed to human rights have sought to overcome the impasse through the pursuit of judicial and human rights accountability mechanisms for perpetrators of mass violence, conceptually linking the ability to *hold perpetrators to account* with more "just" outcomes for those populations. Examples include North Korea, Syria, and Myanmar.

Mechanisms for Pursuing Accountability

Examples of mechanisms for pursuing accountability at the international level are the Special Procedures and Commissions of Inquiry in the United Nations Human Rights Council to investigate and provide recommendations on allegations of systematic human rights violations. Judicial prosecution occurs at the international level through international criminal tribunals and courts such as the International Criminal Court or International Court of

Justice, and within the domestic court system of third-party states through the application of universal jurisdiction. Prosecutions (or the threat thereof) are warranted to apply pressure to high-level decision-makers responsible for instigating and abetting major atrocities. However, *problems that remain* include the following:

- Limited evidence that prosecutions will reduce violence and injustices for populations being protected (based on my own interviews and current literature in this field), or that they serve as an effective deterrent to prevent future cycles of atrocity violence.
- Perpetuating a *retributive/punitive understanding* of accountability, a thin justice, that holds offenders to account without adequate attention or resourcing provided for restorative modes of justice aimed at repairing harms at the societal level.
- Lack of priority and resources for reparations and *local-level justice mechanisms* have meant that the few prosecutions that have taken place have done little to intercept cycles of impunity, repression, and systematic violence.

I find, therefore, that an emergent consequence of the accountability turn has been a tendency for international actors to employ the language and framework of accountability as an *alternative* that permits the international community to default on its wider obligations to mitigate or halt violence and provide tangible protection for populations on the ground in situations where major states (the decision-makers) are unable to cooperate.

Problematizing the Accountability Turn

I conclude, then, that there is a need to problematize the accountability turn in the governance of human protection crises to push beyond prosecutions, "naming and shaming," and other forms of sanctioning/retribution of perpetrators to promote meaningful protection outcomes for vulnerable populations in the pursuit of "second-order" justice. It is crucial to bring powerful actors to account for the atrocities they have orchestrated; however, I question whether the tendency to substitute (rather than complement) human protection practices with accountability through judicial solutions leads toward "just" outcomes for vulnerable populations.

Accountability is fundamental to justice, assigning blame for injustices committed in the past to pave the way for reparations and reconciliation, deterring recurrence of violations looking to the future, and reinforcing the legitimacy of relevant systems/institutions of responsibility. The relationship between accountability and justice is a theme that merits further thinking from a Christian perspective given the centrality of reconciliation and restoration in the gospel message. This theme was not directly addressed in Wolterstorff's Theology Brief. However, the framework of justice as shalom – a broader framework of being at peace with God, in a state of reconciliation and completeness – is one avenue opened in the Theology Brief to further reflect on these questions.

Reconciliation and Restorative Justice

Within the peace-building literature, the act of reconciliation between conflicting parties is fundamental to achieving restorative justice outcomes. To this end, reconciliation is a process of making peace between parties in conflict, and to be reconciled is to be in a state of right relationship. In other words, the reconciled relationship is a just relationship, if we are to employ Wolterstorff's understanding of first-order justice.

Wolterstorff's definition of justice as "rendering to others what is their right" or their "due" (p. 9) is employed as the foundation for first-order justice, which is then extended to more complex modes of social and institutional injustices. My own research places a stronger emphasis on understanding how to promote reconciliation in order to ensure that conflicted relationships are reconciled to prevent the continuation of injustices for future generations. *The emphasis, I think, needs to shift from meeting individual rights/dues to promoting a relational understanding of justice – justice as being in a state of right relationship.* A relational ontology of justice does not negate a rights-oriented account of justice but situates those rights and the context for their fulfillment within the broader social context that individuals occupy.

Christian Scholarly Practice and Mass Violations of Human Rights

There are practical implications for pursuing both accountability and reconciliation when responding to the injustices of mass violations of human rights that are evident in my own more policy-oriented research.

How to Prevent Mass Atrocity Crimes

I am co-chairing the Asia-Pacific Study Group of the global network Global Action Against Mass Atrocity Crimes (GAAMAC). GAAMAC is the largest global network of government, academia, and civil society members that works toward the prevention of mass atrocities. Our report *Preventing Hate Speech, Incitement, and Discrimination* (Jacob and Morada, 2021), commissioned and funded through this state-led initiative, supported by the Swiss Ministry of Foreign Affairs, and disseminated at both global and regional meetings, is an example of the type of work that bridges the values of restorative justice in social contexts of intergroup conflict and violence.

The report covers six countries in the Asia-Pacific region and points to systematic patterns that foster hate speech and incitement to violence in these countries:

- Legacies of mass violence that remain unaddressed with cultures of impunity persisting at the highest levels of authority;
- The absence of meaningful processes of local justice or reconciliation between ethnonationalist or religious minorities in these societies;
- Language/speech that draws on historical narratives of injustice and stereotyping that is used to dehumanize populations (denying population groups recognition of their inherent worth/dignity) as a process that legitimizes the incitement of, and acts of violence against, these population groups.

The theme of justice is integral to every case study and the recommendations produced by this report for steering policy actors, civil society, and faith communities toward just outcomes. This project illustrates the potential for Christian scholars (within a secular institution and disciplinary field or research) to interact with academic, civil society, and government actors in an area of fundamental injustice in international relations that align with a biblical understanding of justice. The report draws on scholarly research into the problem of hate speech and mass atrocities and identifies sources of first- and second-order injustices that produce the social context for hate speech and atrocities to thrive. These are grounded in historical grievances between ethnic and/or religious communities, often compounded by other historical injustices (such as colonialism, civil conflict, and majority rule) for which there has been absence of meaningful accountability and reconciliation.

Promising Sites for Prevention of Mass Violence and Injustice

This study points to numerous sites through which the pursuit of justice is instrumental to prevent future cycles of violence and injustice. Examples include intercommunity reconciliation processes (acknowledgment of past atrocities and meaningful efforts to provide apology, reparation, and peace-building), legal reform (such as repealing discriminatory laws and introducing new legislation to provide for greater protection of targeted groups), and reforms in governance, judiciary, and security institutions that have institutionalized and perpetuated discriminatory practices and impunity for perpetrators. We also identify a significant role for religious leaders, civil society groups, and the media for transforming relationships between communities that can pave the way for healing of past grievances and reconciliation.

In sum, this case study demonstrates the crucial importance of both first-order and second-order justice (often hard to separate in the area of human rights violations and atrocities that have both a direct interpersonal and a structural dimension to their persistence) in Christian orientations toward social injustice writ large. The pursuit of justice informs/motivates this research, but processes/mechanisms of justice and accountability are also the substantive empirical focus of the research. Engaging with justice is a crucial entry point for Christian scholars into research topics that are being extensively developed in the secular literature and have significant bearing on the "subjects" of our research who are subjected to gross acts of injustice.

References and Further Reading

Jacob, Cecilia. 2020. "A Christian Response to Global Conflict: Realism and Reconciliation." *International Journal of Public Theology* 14, no. 4: 438–55. Explores a Christian worldview of justice in international relations and draws on Christian realism and political reconciliation.

———. 2021. "Institutionalizing Prevention at the UN: International Organization Reform as a Site of Norm Contestation." *Global Governance* 27, no. 2: 179–201. Argues that human rights are being actively eroded in processes to reform the United Nations' capacity to protect civilians and prevent conflict.

Jacob, Cecilia, and Noel M. Morada, eds. 2021. *Preventing Hate Speech, Incitement, and Discrimination: Lessons on Promoting Tolerance and Respect for Diversity in the Asia Pacific*. Geneva: Global Action Against Mass Atrocity Crimes and Federal Department of Foreign Affairs, Government of Switzerland. Studies hate speech and violence in six countries, and provides recommendations to governments and community-based actors.

Philpott, Daniel. 2012. *Just and Unjust Peace: An Ethic of Political Reconciliation*. New York: Oxford University Press. A theory of political reconciliation, drawing on Christianity, Judaism, and Islamic understandings of justice, mercy, and peace as a corrective to secular models of peace-building.

Justice in Transnational Legal Orders

Terence C. Halliday

Sociology, Emeritus, American Bar Foundation; Northwestern University, USA;
Australian National University, Australia[4]

The world confronts enormous problems that very often, perhaps always, require responses beyond the capacity of single national governments or states. Indeed, in my view, we can no longer think about the solution of any vexing problem of any magnitude entirely within the bounds of a single state. Invariably the actors (individuals, organizations, governments) which seek solutions to problems do so through the mechanisms of law.

These laws come in bewildering varieties. Contrast laws promulgated by international organizations, such as UN treaties or the Inter-American Court of Human Rights, with laws produced by national institutions, such as India's parliament or Brazil's administrative agencies, or state laws and municipal ordnances authorized by subnational or local bodies, such as Nigeria's state governments or the Jakarta city council.

Increasingly these laws are woven together into transnational legal orders (TLOs). These orders penetrate deeply into our national and local everyday lives. Wolterstorff's Theology Brief on "Justice and Rights" (hereafter NWTB) has stimulated me to revisit my work on TLOs through the fresh theological lens he offers. I seek to apply to TLOs his distinction between first-order justice, which characterizes the everyday and ordinary affairs of our lives, and second-order justice, which responds to violations of first-order justice. I shall offer three propositions about justice and TLOs, each of which raises several questions.

TLOs Deserve Theological Engagement
Why TLOs?

A transnational legal order (TLO) can arise when individuals or industries or states or nonprofit organizations or international organizations or any other kind of social actor seeks to solve problems that span national borders by legal means. These problems are as wide as the human condition: *violence against women in civil conflicts* (cf. International Criminal Tribunal for the Former

---

4. gfiweb.net/contributor/392

Yugoslavia, International Criminal Court); *failing businesses* (cf. the Legislative Guide on Insolvency produced by the UN Commission on International Trade Law [UNCITRAL]); *pandemics* (cf. the policy guidance issued by the World Health Organization). In practice, a TLO can be the response to any social, economic, or political issue that actors or norm entrepreneurs can successfully frame as a "problem" to be solved in whole or in part by law.

What Is a TLO?

TLOs emerge when entrepreneurial actors (e.g. individuals, industry groups, religious organizations, international NGOs) identify a problem. To solve the problem they offer solutions that rely on law and legal institutions.

A TLO has three elements (Halliday and Shaffer 2015, 5):

- A TLO is *transnational*: that is, it seeks to bring orderly relationships sometimes across the borders of states, sometimes across entire regions, sometimes across the world (cf. UNCITRAL's Rotterdam Rules on carrying goods across the world's oceans; Block-Lieb and Halliday 2017).
- A TLO is *legal*: it includes *hard law*, such as treaties between and among states, and *soft law*, which ranges from legislative guides and model laws to standards, guides, best practices, principles, and codes of conduct.
- A TLO is constructed to produce *order*: a TLO is fully established when there is substantial concordance of laws between transnational bodies and national and local institutions. Such an order is intended to guide behavior in predictable ways that are observable in patterns of behavior.

Why TLOs Now?

My colleagues in international relations at the Australian National University[5] express the view that a liberal international order has been dominant in the world since a new architecture of institutions and laws emerged from the ashes of World War II. That architecture led to international institutions (the UN, World Bank, International Monetary Fund, World Health Organization, among

---

5. I express my appreciation for the insights and mutual support of Benjamin Day, Luke Glanville, and Cecilia Jacob, in our Scholarly Circle (https://brill.com/view/journals/ijpt/14/4/article-p389_2.xml) at the Australian National University.

hundreds of others) which created and propagated a kind of international rule of law with courts and tribunals to arbitrate among conflicting parties in international disputes, such as the rights that China, Vietnam, the Philippines, and other states have in the South China Sea. Both the architecture and the institutions were led and dominated by the victors of World War II and their ways of thinking.

At present, there is something of a revolt against this international order. Most confrontationally it is led by China, which chafes at standards and practices of the international community, for example on rule of law or human rights, which lead to criticism and condemnation of its domestic behavior (Halliday, Zilberstein, and Espeland 2021). Yet there is another line of critique that converges with the theological ethics proposed in NWTB. There is some justice in the charge that the rules of the international order were ordered and overdetermined by powerful states in the international political economy – the US, the G7, and the thirty-eight rich countries in the Organization for Economic Cooperation and Development (OECD).

TLOs Warrant Theological Appraisal in Terms of Justice and Rights

If TLOs are widespread, then they should be the focus of theological ethics. NWTB opens up that prospect, beginning with the Old Testament imperative to do "social (systemic) justice" (pp. 3 and 10). Where NWTB opens the door to social institutions within the state, we may widen the scale of social institutions to those beyond the state – the international and the global.

What is this field of institutions? It includes international organizations of states (e.g. UN, EU, OECD, or Mercator, the South American trade bloc); international nongovernmental organizations (INGOs); international industry and professional associations; international religious groups; international bodies of indigenous or dominated peoples (e.g. World Uyghur Congress, International Campaign for Tibet); and international media, among others. The list is almost endless and it grows geometrically, given the vibrancy of international civil society and the interdependency of states in the twenty-first century.

NWTB's pairing of the Isaiah 61 and Luke 4 passages opens up the prospect that justice orientations to the institutions, actors, processes, and products of TLOs must not only embrace individuals and classes of people within states, but extend to "poor" peoples and first-nation tribes and weak states in the international economic and political orders; "captives" in political prisons in despotic regimes or refugee camps in Bangladesh or Gaza; "oppressed" peoples, such as the Uyghurs in concentration camps in Xinjiang, China, or the billions suffering under repressive rulers; and the "brokenhearted" refugees in Europe or South East Asia who are losing their families, languages, culture, and customs.

Ideals of First-Order Justice Should Be Applied to TLOs

NWTB writes of first-order justice. To a considerable extent, TLOs provide the legal skeleton and muscle of first-order justice. If the shape of first-order institutions is molded by TLOs, then TLOs themselves should be subject, NWTB implies, to the theological ethics of justice and rights.

I have elsewhere argued that a justice orientation derived from the logics of Isaiah 61 and Luke 4 warrants particular attention to *weak* actors in TLOs (Halliday 2021). Two ethical standards of justice illustrate how common ground can be found for Christian ethics and sociological analysis. I apply both here to the process of creating laws for the world, as building blocks of TLOs, in international organizations.

Participation

In his writings on the "global common good," Roman Catholic theologian David Hollenbach (2002) critiques "global political institutions" for excluding the voices of many of the world's peoples from the creation of rules that will influence their lives. He proposes four ways that I find useful to better understand the meaning of my own research on global lawmaking: (1) they need to be sitting at the lawmaking table; (2) they need to be able to "voice" their views; (3) they need to be drawn into dialog where their views are discussed; and (4) they need to be casting votes and exercising influence when decisions are made.

If we take these four ways as Christian ethical ideals for the construction of a just TLO, then a social scientist can readily translate them into empirical research questions (Block-Lieb and Halliday 2017, ch. 12), such as:

- What actors (states, organizations) are aware of lawmaking efforts?
- Who is invited to participate?
- Who gets to set the lawmaking agenda?
- Who attends the lawmaking sessions?
- Who gets to participate in the informal dialogs that always characterize international negotiations?

- Who is heard?
- Who has impact, and how?

In all these ways the dignity of the weak, the voices of the marginal, the excellences of the supposedly peripheral can be addressed in two ways. TLOs can be *appraised* – do actual practices fall short of the Christian ideal of participation? They can also be *corrected* – are international organizations changing their practices of lawmaking, of constructing and adapting TLOs in ways that accord with Wolterstorff's ideals of justice and rights as they are specified more empirically in global forums?

Creativity

In response to his question "Can globalization be shaped?," theologian Miroslav Volf (2015) argues for freely exercising "initiative and creativity" in defending the weakest across the world. Similar notes are struck by others – Max Stackhouse in his call for nurture and release of our God-given abilities to pursue the universal common good, and Pope John Paul II for living out, in the global domain, "the creativity which is the distinguishing mark of the human person." (Stackhouse 1987, 137–38)

The transnational and global lawmaking that is an essential part of a TLO invariably requires creativity.[6] Oddly, this is not much studied by social scientists. However, if theologians press social scientists to imagine how global lawmaking might be seen through a theological lens of creativity it opens up several vistas where views may be shared.

For instance, in my reflections on weak global actors in global lawmaking, the institutions conforming to ideals of a first-order justice might enhance creativity in several ways: (1) imagining new forums or the adaptations of current lawmaking forums to draw out the creativities of weak actors; (2) listening to the views of weak actors on which kinds of law (e.g. treaties, model laws, guidelines) are more likely to be accepted by their governments and society; (3) recognizing that weak actors, such as emerging economies, may have particular problems that require attention less relevant to advanced economies; and (4) acknowledging the special areas of expertise of government leaders, lawmakers, and law implementers, in what will or will not work in their special circumstances (Block-Lieb and Halliday 2017, 389–420).

---

6. See Block-Lieb and Halliday 2017, ch. 6.

For me, Wolterstorff's term "excellences" creates a kind of mental shift. It affirms dignity and acknowledges the giftedness of God's grace given to delegates and delegations too often thought of as deprived or unsophisticated or to be treated as law-takers and not law-makers. It demands a theologically inspired reorientation toward the architects and builders of TLOs.

Theological Ethics for TLOs

Wolterstorff frames his Theology Brief in terms which enable its extrapolation in two ways that are highly relevant for my research on TLOs.

First, he points to the several levels of social behavior where justice and rights are salient. While he uses interactions between persons, dyads, as his idiomatic mainstay, he notes that the logic of his argument applies to all social institutions within a society. For those of us who work on international institutions and global politics and society, we would take a step farther and explore more thoughtfully what justice ethics and Christian conceptions of rights can be brought to bear on the international sphere.

Second, we should bolster our theological understanding of first-order justice by examining how those "first-order institutions" are permeated by TLOs beyond the state, by the state, within the state. For all laws within a TLO NWTB calls upon us to bring a theological standard both at the highest levels of giving others "their due" and recognizing their rights and "excellences," and at more empirically observable levels of such theological ethics as the enhancement of decision-making participation and affirmations of diverse creativities.

I conclude with two questions. How can we expand this conversation between theologians and social scientists to help Christians and persons of faith to think beyond the personal or the local and relational to institutions and states? Even further, in a world of global interdependence and global rivalry, how may we carry further our Christian theological ethics into international organizations and transnational and global orders?

I might also ask: Does a theological ethics of justice and rights exert a special calling on Christian scholars of global governance? What does it ask of me as I study TLOs, global norms and who makes them, how they are made, what opportunities and creativities they open up for those whose voices are marginalized, and how effective they are in bringing justice to the poor, imprisoned, oppressed, and heartbroken?

References and Further Reading

Block-Lieb, Susan, and Terence C. Halliday. 2017. *Global Lawmaking: International Organizations in the Crafting of World Markets.* Cambridge: Cambridge University Press. Presents empirical sociolegal research on international lawmaking for global commerce.

Cartledge, Mark J. 2016. "Public Theology and Empirical Research: Developing an Agenda." *International Journal of Political Theology* 10: 15–66. Calls for closer relationships between social scientists and theologians.

Halliday, Terence C. 2021. "Public Theology and Global Governance: Weak Actors in Lawmaking for the World Economy." *International Journal of Public Theology* 14: 415–37.

Halliday, Terence C., and Gregory Shaffer, eds. 2015. *Transnational Legal Orders.* New York: Cambridge University Press. On the theory of transnational legal orders (TLOs) with empirical studies of TLOs in commerce, business and finance, human rights, and climate change.

Halliday, Terence C., Shira Zilberstein, and Wendy Espeland. 2021. "Protecting Basic Legal Freedoms: International Legal Complexes, Accountability Devices, and the Deviant Case of China." *Annual Review of Law and Social Science* 17: 159–80.

Hollenbach, David. 2002. *The Common Good and Christian Ethics.* Cambridge: Cambridge University Press.

Stackhouse, Max L. 1987. *Public Theology and Political Economy.* Grand Rapids: Eerdmans.

Volf, Miroslav. 2015. *Flourishing: Why We Need Religion in a Globalized World.* New Haven: Yale University Press.

5

Justice in Biological, Physical, and Medical Sciences

Doing Justice to Nature in Science

Ian H. Hutchinson

Nuclear Science and Engineering, Emeritus, Massachusetts Institute of Technology (MIT), USA[1]

This is a brief, speculative, and exploratory response from the perspective of a physicist to the understanding of justice proposed by Nicholas Wolterstorff in his Theology Brief for the Global Faculty Initiative. His key points may be summarized as follows:

- First-order justice concerns agents, individuals, and institutions acting justly; and is best understood as each rendering to others their right or due.
- Second-order justice concerns the laws, sanctions, and systems that secure first-order justice.
- A right (due) is a morally legitimate claim to something, an entitlement.
- Conferred rights are attached to a position, promise, law, or social practice.

---

1. gfiweb.net/contributor/13

- Nonconferred rights are grounded in the excellence (goodness, worth, dignity, praiseworthiness) of the rights-bearer, such as natural rights and human rights.
- Justice and attention to rights should play a pervasive role in the university.

Objectivity and Morality

The content of natural science concerns itself with what is – not what ought to be. Natural science is experimental and observational. It studies the repeatable, and what appear to be the unchanging and normally inescapable principles that govern the working of the natural world. Its theoretical explanations are required to observe intellectual standards of clarity, self-consistency, logic, and mathematical rigor, some of which are common to nonscience disciplines too. But natural science is founded on the authority of nature: of reproducible experiment and observation, to which theoretical speculations must ultimately conform if they are to be accepted. Moreover, science's whole approach to explanation is to set aside intentionality, and personality, instead seeking explanations in terms of efficient causes.

Superficially, then, what science finds out does not appear to demand an assessment of worth, or goodness, beyond the material and pragmatic. It is not prima facie about human or any other personal value. And that has led to a view that its contents (though not its institutions) are free from ideological or religious bias: that its knowledge is purely detached and factual. Postmodern critiques aside, most scientists do regard science's findings as objective.

That does not mean all scientists view their discipline as lacking in wider, or perhaps even transcendent significance; nor are they necessarily unemotional; nor are aesthetic or ethical considerations excluded from their thinking or practice. But it does mean that when scientists discuss justice in their discipline they mostly focus on scientific social practice and applications, not on the content of scientific knowledge. This social perspective has become even more obvious recently as professional scientific societies have responded to critiques from minority groups about inequity and bias. Social diversity, equity, and inclusion have become a major preoccupation in professional societies. And it shows up when the application of science, especially its commercial application, is seen as its main justifying rationale. The underlying ethical principles and values on which such discussions proceed come from outside science, whether scientists realize it or not. Here I want instead (or perhaps in addition) to suggest that natural science has priorities, which can reasonably be considered matters of justice, that derive from nature itself. Doing justice to nature is something both science and all of human endeavor should take as a priority.

Justice in Science

If, as Wolterstorff says, first-order justice derives from excellence (goodness, worth, dignity, praiseworthiness), are there not aspects of the natural world that possess this sort of excellence, and are there not important features of the very content of science that call for just recognition?

The Christian and Jewish Scriptures, in countless places, celebrate the natural world (e.g. Gen 1:31; Pss 8; 96:1–6), its goodness, wonder, majesty, power, and beauty; and they also praise it as the ongoing gift and creation of God (Pss 65:9–13; 95:4–5; 104). Are these excellences the foundation of what constitutes justice in respect of nature? And are they perhaps even a major part of what undergirds the just practice of science?

Even the most secular of scientists and science commentators are unashamed to celebrate the awesome character of the universe, the wonder and mystery of what governs quantum and subatomic physics, and the intricacies of the biosphere. When doing so, are they recognizing something that truly goes beyond the impersonal and pragmatic, or are they just being led by their inescapable humanity into a spurious emotionalism? Christian teaching is that the awesome character of the universe is in fact attributable to the will and wisdom of a personal Creator, and that in engaging scientifically with nature we are engaging with the excellences of a creation.

As a Christian, I see my professional science as engaging with the natural world in a way that does justice to its excellence, worth, and dignity, which is a reflection of the character of God. In doing so, I stand in a historic tradition of people of religious faith who have seen intrinsic worth in knowing and understanding the working principles of nature. Such abstract knowledge is not in conflict with a call to practicality; indeed it can be argued that Francis Bacon's call to knowledge "for the relief of man's estate" was a vital stimulus to abandon purely speculative knowledge, and focus for charity's sake on reproducible experimental demonstration, which undergirds modern science. However, there is, in a society dominated by the technological application of science, a vital need to balance practical and commercial interests with the call to do justice to nature not just in the employment of technology in human society, but also in our valuing of the excellence and worth of the natural world. Thus, pure science is valuable foundationally because of the excellence, worth, dignity, and praiseworthiness of the creation, recognizable by all regardless of theology, but recognized by the faithful as a part of their spiritual understanding.

Since natural science is concerned with the reproducible and unambiguous aspects of the world, its successful pursuit demands, and eventually rewards, certain practices that have a moral character. Perhaps foremost among these is truthfulness. Of all the virtues, truth is perhaps the one most explicitly attributed to Jesus (John 1:14 "the Word became flesh and dwelt among us . . . full of grace and truth" [ESV]; John 14:6 "I am the way, and the truth, and the life," etc.) and enjoined on Christians (1 Cor 5:8; 2 Cor 6:7; Eph 4:25, etc.). Science demands truthful observing and reporting. This is a discipline that requires a certain unselfish honesty, and echoes biblical calls that serious Christians take seriously. Perhaps that is one reason for the very influential role played by Christians in the development of modern science. Personal discipline, important though it is, has never been sufficient on its own; and science has also institutional practices that seek to enforce truthfulness and uncover error or (self-)deception. It was once relatively straightforward for observational or experimental reports to be checked and reproduced by other natural philosophers, and for scientific discoveries to be quickly confirmed or dismissed. Moreover, when science was predominantly a pastime for enthusiastic amateurs rather than a source of wealth, the only personal benefit to be obtained from it was reputation. Today it is far more difficult to detect incompetence, error, or deception because of science's complexity. And the potential personal advantages are considerably more tempting. Truth has recently become more difficult to establish and less practically compelling, with regrettable consequences. In many scientific fields there is a crisis of reproducibility, and in virtually all of science there is a glut of unreliable and incorrect journal articles, fed by the now negligible cost of publication and dissemination. These are injustices, I suggest, not merely because of the cost, trouble, or suffering that they impose on others, but also because they fail to render to nature the truth that is its due.

Just Treatment of Nature

"Environmental justice" is a phrase widely invoked today that seems to suggest that there is such a thing as justice toward nature. A major discussion thread that often dominates the development of what environmental justice means is equitable human sharing of natural resources. Wolterstorff has argued that this sort of "distributive justice," while important, is just one facet of first-order justice. Nevertheless he speaks almost entirely of "agents" (including social entities) as being the givers and receivers of justice. Beyond that, I want to propose that there is a meaningful sense in which the relationship of humans to the natural world calls us not only to do justice to our fellow humans, but also to do justice to nature. If so, then it would be too narrow a characterization to say that justice concerns rendering to other *agents* their right or due. Instead, unconscious or even inanimate features of creation are owed their just due. And these "rights" might well compete with the desires or "rights" of people or other agents.[2]

This also is a profoundly biblical idea, encapsulated in the Old Testament primacy of Sabbath (Deut 5:12–14) and Jubilee (Lev 25:8–22). As one of the Ten Commandments, observing the Sabbath is certainly in part about justice toward employees and servants, and in part about acting justly toward God in worship. But it is also about rest for the land, for animals, and for nature. Rest for the land is, of course, a recognition by the religious instruction of the Hebrews that an agricultural society's flourishing depends on the health of fields, which is promoted by avoiding overutilization. But it is also a recognition of what we justly owe to the care and stewardship of creation, because of its intrinsic worth. Creation care is a duty for humans, not just for reasons of self-interest, but also for justice toward nature.

What, as a consequence, do we owe to the study of nature? What moral and ethical priorities does science demand? And do those priorities (those "rights") moderate, constrain, or conflict with other rights claims?

It is perhaps obvious that, when investigating the biology of humans, ethical constraints on what is acceptable experimental practice should be enforced. It is uncontroversial to see these as a matter of justice. But the puzzles seem to me considerably more difficult when it comes to the justice of animal experiments. Do animals have rights, and if so which animals, and what rights? Beyond the animal kingdom, does the environment, the oceans, the atmosphere, the landscape, the planet have rights? Is there a question of justice in recognizing their excellence and worthiness? Is it justice that is violated by pollution, excessive consumption, or other environmental exploitation?

Here is where utilitarianism most obviously falls short of providing properly grounded ethics. It can presume some value or values based on human survival or prosperity, but it cannot justify any value, worth, or dignity derived from the character of nonhuman nature. It can cash in the emotional

---

2. Wolterstorff's discussion of justice does not address what seems to me a crucial difficulty in a "rights" perspective, which is that different rights often do compete; so an absolute assertion that a right trumps other considerations is impractical.

or aesthetic appreciation that many people feel toward the natural world, but it cannot attribute an intrinsic value or excellence to nature, possessed independently of humans. Christian teaching does attribute high worth to humans – because God loves us. But, rightly understood, that worth does not override the worth of the rest of creation, because God loves it too. Nature deserves to be valued by us humans. And science is a discipline that places high value on understanding it. Perhaps, then, justice toward nature, based on its excellence and praiseworthiness, is a compelling, and Christ-worthy, ethical priority.

When the flourishing of humans and of nature seem to be in conflict with one another, I believe that a proper balance can be greatly facilitated by seeing *both* priorities as being about justice based on what is due. Natural science at its best can foster this understanding.

Justice in Biomedicine and Biotechnology
Jeff Hardin
Biology, University of Wisconsin-Madison, USA[3]

Wolterstorff raises some key issues related to *bioethics*. I found myself asking several profound questions as a result: (1) How is "value" or "worth" defined? Is it defined as a set of characters encapsulating "excellence"? Christian thinkers have more often than not been uncomfortable with this approach. If, instead, value is intrinsic, how can biblical conceptions be applied in a way and using language that "secular" bioethicists and society at large will be drawn toward? (2) How does "value" or "worth" apply to embryos? (3) How do our answers to (1) and (2) influence our policies toward technological manipulation of human embryos or embryo-like beings at the genetic and cellular levels?

---

3. gfiweb.net/contributor/51

Justice of Space-Based Communication Architectures

Daniel Hastings

Aeronautics and Astronautics, Massachusetts Institute of Technology (MIT), USA[4]

My research is on the design and development of large-scale satellite architectures. Two examples relevant to this discussion are the Global Positioning System (GPS) and the current development of global space-based systems to provide worldwide internet access. There are several currently in development and deployment with the three which are furthest along being Starlink by SpaceX (backed by Elon Musk), OneWeb (backed by a consortium including SoftBank and the UK Government), and Kuiper from Amazon (backed by Jeff Bezos).

From a Government-Supported Public Good

GPS was developed by the US Air Force, an arm of the US Government, fundamentally for military purposes, namely, to guide nuclear bombers to their targets. Initially it had an open "civilian" signal and an encrypted "military" signal. The civilian signal gave a degraded position and timing signal while the military signal was very accurate. After the Soviet shooting down of KAL007, the US Government declassified the system and said anyone could use the civilian signal. In 1997, the US Government removed the encryption from the military signal and said anyone in the world could use it. The existence of a highly accurate position and timing signal is now estimated to be worth over a billion dollars a day in economic return underwritten by the US Government. The contributions of this system to justice are manifest in that it enables anybody in the world to accurately map land, to accurately show the position of resources, and of course to guide cars through apps all over the world. It has become a global commodity that being free to the world enhances the provision of justice.

To a For-Profit Private Commodity

In contrast, the systems now under development and deployment that will provide worldwide internet access are being put up by commercial companies

---

4. gfiweb.net/contributor/97

that will charge a price for access to this service. While people in cities will have access to the internet through abundant cellular service, this same access will not be true of people in rural areas or the poor all over the world. This access will be provided by the for-profit satellite networks.

Justice and Fairness in Internet Communications

A fundamental question is whether access to the internet can and should be thought of as a right or a privilege. The internet allows access to information, good and bad, from around the world. It also allows terrorists to communicate and coordinate and for hate speech to spread quickly. However, as a question of distribution, it seems unfair for some to have easy access and for others, the poor, not to have access.

Perhaps the just and fair thing would be for the global networks to provide a basic level of network access for all for free and then to charge an amount for faster speeds to make a profit. This is the strategy that the Europeans have decided upon for their Global Positioning System (called Galileo). Everyone gets access to basic services for free, but if you want more then you have to pay. This allows justice and fairness to be balanced.

Justice and Public Health

Tyler VanderWeele

Public Health, Harvard University, USA[5]

Public health has been defined as "the art and science of preventing disease, prolonging life and promoting health through the organized efforts of society" (Acheson 1988; WHO 1946). The term "public health" might thus concern the *study* of preventing disease, prolonging life, and promoting health, or the actual *practice* of doing so through the organized efforts of society. The term can also denote the actual state of affairs concerning the health of the public, that is, the health of a certain population. Health arises in part as a natural state through the operation of normal biological processes, but is shaped in part by access to resources that allow for the promotion and maintenance of health and to resources that allow for the restoration of health. Health itself is constitutive of well-being but also is important instrumentally in the capacity to attain other goods and ends.

Considerations of justice within public health arise in part in the context of human subjects research, in part because various resources are advantageous in the maintenance and restoration of health, and in part because health is both intrinsically and instrumentally related to well-being. With regard to research, the *Belmont Report* (National Commission for the Protection of Human Subjects of Biomedical and Behavioral Research 1979) put forward justice, along with beneficence and respect for persons, as one of three ethical principles to guide human subjects research. However, perhaps more profoundly, justice is relevant within public health because of considerations regarding the *distribution* of health and health-related resources, which often, in public health contexts, fall under the rubric of "social justice." Because health is shaped in part by access to resources, and because health itself affects our capacity to attain various goods and ends, and because public health involves the organized efforts of society to bring about health, public health must fundamentally be concerned with justice.

As discussed by Wolterstorff in his Theology Brief, considerations of justice and of the pursuit of justice are also fundamental to the Christian faith. How, then, might a Christian understanding of justice overlap with, be in tension with, and potentially extend beyond understandings of justice within public

---

5. gfiweb.net/contributor/135

health? In this essay, I will briefly consider the concept of justice as it relates to health and public health efforts, and will relate Christian teachings on justice to notions of justice and rights that are commonly held within public health. I will focus mainly on the principles put forward in the World Health Organization's Constitution (WHO 1946).

The Concept of Justice

In his Theology Brief Wolterstorff considers various accounts of justice. His favored notion, from the Roman jurist Ulpian, is that justice "is a steady and enduring will to render to each what is his or her right, or due." He argues against the notion, found in Aristotle and elsewhere, that justice consists of the equitable or fair distribution of benefits and burdens. However, if those benefits and burdens are themselves understood as respect for rights then the two definitions are effectively equivalent (see also Aquinas 1274/1948 2.2.Q58.1; 2.2.Q57.1). Understood thus, justice may pertain to a *state of affairs* in which each has received his or her due; an *act*, one which respects rights, or renders to each his or her due; a *virtue*, the habit of acting with a steady and enduring will to render to each his or her due; or potentially the *acts or restitutions* required to return to the state of affairs in which each receives his or her due after such a state of affairs has somehow been disrupted.

Justice has sometimes been understood as fairness within the public health context (Daniels 2008). If fairness is again understood as fairness or equality *with respect to rights*, then this may indeed be a reasonable conception. Justice with respect to health cannot involve perfect equality of health, which not only would be practically unobtainable but could also lead to perverse attempts at reduction to the lowest common attainable standard (Parfit 1998; Kass et al. 2015). Wolterstorff, in his Theology Brief, relatedly comments that equity alone does not make distributions just or unjust. However, once again, if justice with respect to health is understood to concern equal respect with regard to rights, then this might be a reasonable way to conceive of justice in the public health context.

Rights to the "Highest Attainable Standard of Health"
Principles of the WHO

The World Health Organization (WHO) 1946 Constitution puts forward the principle that "the enjoyment of the highest attainable standard of health is one of the fundamental rights of every human being without distinction of race, religion, political belief, economic or social condition." The notion of the "highest attainable standard of health" may be interpreted in a way that recognizes that perfect health, and perfect equality of health, may not be attainable. What is "attainable" respects the constraints of nature. Moreover, what is "attainable" may also be understood in a way that respects the freedom of individuals to potentially act in ways that may be contrary to their health, thereby altering what is attainable. What is attainable may also be relative to the resources that are available (Hunt et al. 2015) and indeed the United Nations Committee on Economic, Social and Cultural Rights has subsequently gone some way in specifying what the right to the "highest attainable standard of health" might be understood, in practice, to entail (UNCESCR 2000). However, even with these caveats, "highest attainable standard of health [for a given individual]" is a relatively high bar. The notion that the enjoyment of such a standard of health is a *right* is thus one that needs careful consideration.

Intrinsic and Instrumental Goals of Health

Nevertheless, because of not only the intrinsic but also the instrumental role of health in well-being, a commitment to the highest attainable standard of health for all is a laudable goal, one which the Constitution declares is "basic to the happiness, harmonious relations and security of all peoples." Health is not only a good that requires justice in its distribution, but one that has implications for justice in the distribution of other goods. The Constitution goes on to state,

> The health of all peoples is fundamental to the attainment of peace and security and is dependent upon the fullest co-operation of individuals and States. The achievement of any State in the promotion and protection of health is of value to all. Unequal development in different countries in the promotion of health and control of disease, especially communicable disease, is a common danger.

The Constitution further notes the importance of the "healthy development of the child," perhaps implicitly acknowledging the role of the family in ensuring this right to the highest attainable standard of health, and goes on to emphasize the dissemination of health-related knowledge to all people, active cooperation on the part of the public, and the responsibility of governments.

The Constitution itself establishes the World Health Organization and states as its objective "the attainment by all people of the highest possible level of health."

It is not entirely clear from the Constitution itself what the grounds are for this purported right. In the terms employed by Wolterstorff, it is unclear from the Constitution whether the right to "the highest attainable standard of health" is being viewed as a nonconferred human right, or is being proposed as a positive right for states to adopt, or is being put into place as a conferred right that the World Health Organization is itself establishing and taking responsibility for.

Whose Responsibility for Rights to Health?

As noted by Wolterstorff, rights also entail duties or responsibilities. One interpretation as to what is being envisioned is that this right to "the highest attainable standard of health" is to arise from some combination of both nonconferred and positive rights. The World Health Organization's constitution seems to recognize that the responsibility for attaining the "highest attainable standard of health" lies in part with the individual but also with the broader community, and communities perhaps ranging from the family to the public health community, to the state, to the World Health Organization itself (cf. Hunt et al., 2015). Each person arguably has the natural right, barring instances of another's rights being violated, to not be intentionally harmed by other individuals. Parents have both rights and responsibilities to care for their children. A well-functioning state will arguably establish positive rights to various health-related resources. As noted above, the World Health Organization's Constitution seems to use language that effectively establishes rights conferred by agreement of the World Health Organization and member states. The combination of these might be taken then as establishing a right to the "highest attainable standard of health" that is itself constituted by various natural rights, positive rights, and conferred rights.

Health as Wholeness

Having considered the notion of rights, let us now turn to the notion of health. How is health itself to be understood? The Constitution's first principle is in fact, "Health is a state of complete physical, mental and social well-being and not merely the absence of disease or infirmity." From a Christian standpoint, and from that of many other world religious traditions, that definition should perhaps be extended to "Health is a state of complete physical, mental, social and *spiritual* well-being" (Larson 1996; Cloninger et al. 2010; VanderWeele 2017b). Understood thus, health might be conceived of as wholeness *of a person*, effectively synonymous with flourishing (VanderWeele 2017a; VanderWeele et al. 2019a). This might be contrasted with a narrow conception of health involving the *health of the body* (VanderWeele et al. 2019b) or wholeness of the body. Both the broader and the narrower conceptions are arguably found in ordinary language.

The broader conception of health as a state of complete physical, mental, social, and spiritual well-being might be viewed within a Christian biblical understanding as that of shalom (Wolterstorff's Theology Brief). The complete health or wholeness of the person is life lived according to God's intent. Such a broad conception, inclusive of social well-being, arguably entails also a well-functioning community, one that is just. Justice is thus needed to help ensure that a right to the highest attainable standard of health or well-being is realized, but justice (concerning health and other matters) is in fact also constitutive of the health or wholeness of a person, and of his or her community, of shalom.

Shared and Divergent Goals with the Public Health Community
Shared Goals

Many of the goals and principles of the public health community are in strong alignment with Christian principles. Goals of child development, prevention of disease, promotion of physical and mental health, harmonious relations, and security of all people are arguably goals shared in common by the international public health community and Christian churches. Likewise, principles such as special attention and care for those who are worst off, and respect for the freedom of people, would likewise be shared by these communities (Pontifical Council of Justice and Peace 2004). Both sets of communities are concerned with justice and there is notable overlap in how justice is understood.

Divergent Goals

Nevertheless, the set of ends pursued by these communities and the relative weight or importance given to each do vary. The ends of public health organizations do not typically extend to spiritual well-being, whereas religious communities will characteristically prioritize spiritual well-being over other goods, and over physical health. Public health organizations can recognize the spiritual ends sought by religious communities, without necessarily actively advancing them, by respecting and ensuring religious liberty. Nevertheless, tensions between public health organizations and religious communities can arise when these ends of the health of the body and of spiritual or religious well-being potentially come into conflict.

An ongoing tension within public health ethics is the extent to which individual freedoms or autonomy can be compromised for the sake of community health (Kass et al. 2015), an issue considered also further below. Justice understood as the state of affairs in which each has been rendered his or her due, or in which the rights of all have been respected, would include respect not only for a right to "the highest attainable standard of health" but also for all other rights, including the right to the free practice of religion.

Bearers of Rights and Christian Tensions within Public Health

An area of substantial tension between public health communities and traditional Christian teaching concerns abortion. The majority view within the international public health community is that individual rights for women entail "reproductive rights" which are often understood to include access to safe abortion. The present position of the World Health Organization concerning abortion is that

> every individual has the right to decide freely and responsibly – without discrimination, coercion and violence – the number, spacing and timing of their children, and to have the information and means to do so, and the right to attain the highest standard of sexual and reproductive health. . . . Access to legal, safe and comprehensive abortion care, including post-abortion care, is essential for the attainment of the highest possible level of sexual and reproductive health. (WHO 2021)

Such an understanding of rights is in strong tension with the vast majority of Christian tradition and teaching on abortion (May 2008), much of which has emphasized the respect for life from the moment of conception until natural death. Under this understanding, the embryo is a human person in development and, as such, has rights, the most fundamental of which is the right to life. Such a right to life would obviously contradict the notion that reproductive rights include a right to abortion.

Of course, central to this dispute is who is a bearer of rights and, even more fundamentally, what is a human person? This is arguably first a metaphysical question and second an ethical question. It is not one that can be settled on scientific grounds. Most of the Christian tradition has insisted that from the time of conception, the embryo is a human person in development and the bearer of rights and thus in almost all circumstances it is wrong – unjust – to intentionally put an end to this life. This human person in development likewise has a right to the "enjoyment of the highest attainable standard of health," and health itself presupposes life.

However, if both the mother and the embryo or fetus has the right to the enjoyment of the highest attainable standard of health, this itself creates responsibilities for the community – for the public health community, for the state, for the father, for friends, for the extended family. All are to work to attain the highest attainable standard of health for both the mother and the baby. Justice – respecting the rights of all – requires work to make such health possible.

Individual Rights versus the Common Good in Public Health

In the case of abortion, tensions concerning rights and justice potentially arise because of differing metaphysical and ethical positions concerning the notion of persons and the bearers of rights. However, other tensions concerning rights and justice arise within public health and concern individual rights, freedoms, and interests weighed against community interests. A fundamental question that arises in this regard is whether and the extent to which individual rights can be set aside or are suspended for community interests (Lappe 1986; Kass et al. 2015).

One idea that has been put forward to navigate this question is that of "proportionality" (Faden and Faden 1978): the idea that the burden posed by (particularly nonvoluntary) interventions should be low and benefits high. This idea has been used to argue that incentives should be favored over disincentives, education favored over manipulative messages, and government intervention ought not to occur without considerable evidence about effectiveness. While some have subsequently advocated for voluntary approaches being the only acceptable approaches, counter-arguments have been put forward that since other outside influences can encourage people to alter their preferences unknowingly, coercive measures or potentially manipulative messages are sometimes needed to counter these in the interest of public health (Kass et al. 2015). Personal interconnectedness and the mutual influence that people have on one another, both in general in thought and behavior, but also concerning contagion and infectious disease, complicate these matters yet further. These issues have of course been evident in discussions over balancing individual rights with the common good in the recent COVID-19 pandemic.

These questions of course come down to questions of the rights of individuals and what is owed to individuals by the government both with regard to freedoms but also with regard to preservation of the common good. These are questions of justice. The answers to these questions are not always easy to discern, but they are central to matters of the promotion of public health and the freedom of people to pursue other goods and ends that may themselves perhaps be viewed as constitutive of health in its broader sense.

Love and Justice in Public Health

Justice Alone Will Not Suffice

If public health is ultimately aimed at achieving the "highest attainable standard of health" for all, then it is in fact not clear that a focus on justice alone will suffice. A person acts justly by acting so as to render to each what is his or her due. This will inevitably entail not intentionally doing harm to another, and doing what is within one's reasonable ability to help others in one's community. Attaining health for all will require justice, both so as not to harm the well-being of others and as a constitutive part of what is entailed by the wholeness or well-being of a person and of a community. However, there is only so much an individual can do to promote the "highest attainable standard of health" for another.

Any chance of achieving this will require the action of communities and institutions. As noted above, the right to the "highest attainable standard of health" might be viewed as arising out of some combination of human rights, the positive rights granted by governments, and the rights conferred by institutions. However, if health is to be understood as "a state of complete physical, mental and social [and spiritual] well-being," then it is not clear that even just actions of individuals and well-intentioned policies and interventions of institutions will suffice. If health includes social well-being, more than this may be needed.

Health and Wholeness Require Love

Social relationships are arguably most powerfully and adequately formed out of love, out of a disposition to desire the good for the other and union with the other (Aquinas 1274/1948, I.II.Q26.4; Stump 2006). Likewise, from a Christian understanding, attaining spiritual well-being requires charity – a love for God – along with the presence of God's grace and love, characteristically mediated in and through the church community. Health, understood as the wholeness of the person, requires love.

Love for another will entail justice (cf. Wolterstorff 2015). One does not properly love the other, or God, if one does not respect the other person's rights. But love entails more than justice; it entails a disposition toward willing the other's good, and to being with him or her, resulting also in an affirmation of the goodness of the other's being (Pieper 1974). It is what almost all persons seek; it is the fabric of social well-being. It is the foundation of spiritual well-being. It is for this reason that the New Testament and Christian teaching put love – love of God and love of neighbor – at the foundation of all of the law, of all of ethics (Matt 22:37–40; Rom 13:9–10). The wholeness of persons requires justice, but it requires more than justice. It requires love.

Relationships Profoundly Contribute to Health

Love – love of neighbor and love of God – is also needed for health because it is arguably a powerful resource for physical and mental well-being as well. There is now ample empirical evidence that social relationships themselves and participation in religious community (i.e. social and spiritual well-being) profoundly contribute to both physical health and mental health (Holt-Lunstad et al. 2015; VanderWeele 2017b). Social and spiritual well-being are perhaps among the most powerful, but neglected, forces for attaining physical and mental health. If we are committed to trying to achieve the "highest attainable standard of health" for all, this will require love. It will require love because love is the foundation of social and spiritual well-being and it will require love because this also powerfully shapes physical and mental well-being. The only way to adequately attempt to preserve and support the partially conferred right to the "enjoyment of the highest attainable standard of health" is to look beyond rights and beyond justice – it is to look to love. We must seek a just society – yes – but we must also seek to create a civilization of love (Pontifical Council of Justice and Peace 2004).

Wholeness Requires Healing from Injustice

Finally, the wholeness of persons and of communities also requires love because we, as individuals and as communities, are in need of healing. We are in need of healing because there are injustices; there are wrongs; there are hurts. From a Christian understanding, we are in need of healing because there is sin. The administration of justice understood as the acts of punishment or restitutions required to return to the state of affairs that is just can go some way; but it does not fully heal. It alone is often not sufficient to restore a person to wholeness; it often does not heal the relationship or the community. For that we also need forgiveness, understood as the replacing of ill will toward the offender with goodwill, and thus itself a form of love (Stump 2006). It is in such forgiveness that we are released from the offense and the offender, that healing can occur, and that relationships can, when appropriate, be restored. Forgiveness is not incompatible with justice or with punishment; one can forgive and desire the ultimate well-being of the offender, and yet still seek a just outcome. But forgiveness frees the victim, promotes his or her mental health (as now demonstrated by ample empirical evidence; cf. Toussaint et al. 2015; Long et al. 2020), and opens the way for a restoration of wholeness to the individual and the community. In our fallen world, forgiveness is needed for the attainment of health and well-being, and is needed for the restoration of relationships with one another. It is part of Christian teaching that forgiveness is also what is ultimately needed for spiritual well-being, for a restored relationship with God, for a restoration to wholeness as God intended. It is a restoration mysteriously accomplished, and in accord with God's justice, through the life, death, and resurrection of Jesus Christ. Our love is needed to bring about physical, mental, social, and spiritual well-being. But God's love and forgiveness are needed to bring about this complete restoration to wholeness as well. The highest attainable standard of health cannot be brought about without love.

Summary: The End of Health Requires Justice and Love

Justice is constituted by the state of affairs in which each is rendered his or her due. Justice is relevant in considerations of health both with respect to the resources that sustain health, and also with regard to health itself being instrumental in the attaining of other goods and ends. Acknowledging a right to the "highest attainable standard of health" involves a combination of natural rights, positive rights, and conferred rights. If health is to be understood as wholeness of the person – as a state of complete physical, mental, social, and spiritual well-being – then this will require the practice and pursuit of justice so as to avoid harm, preserve and promote health, and create a well-functioning community. However, the end of health – understood as the wholeness of a person – requires more than justice; it requires love. Love does not neglect justice, and is compatible with justice, but it extends beyond justice to affirm the goodness of being of the other, to foster social and spiritual well-being, to enable physical and mental health, and to promote the wholeness of the person and of the community according to God's intent.

References

Acheson, D. 1988. *Public Health in England: The Report of the Committee of Inquiry into the Future Development of the Public Health Function.* London: The Stationery Office.

Aquinas, T. 1274/1948. *Summa Theologica.* Complete English translation in five volumes. Notre Dame: Ave Maria Press.

Cloninger, C. R., A. H. Zohar, and K. M. Cloninger. 2010. "Promotion of Well-Being in Person-Centered Mental Health Care." *Focus* 8, no. 2: 165–79.

Daniels, N. 2008. *Just Health: Meeting Health Needs Fairly.* New York: Cambridge University Press.

Faden, R. R., and A. I. Faden. 1978. "The Ethics of Health Education as Public Policy." *Health Education Monographs* 6, no. 2: 180–97.

Holt-Lunstad, J., T. B. Smith, M. Baker, T. Harris, and D. Stephenson. 2015. "Loneliness and Social Isolation as Risk Factors for Mortality: A Meta-Analytic Review." *Perspectives on Psychological Science* 10, no. 2: 227–37.

Hunt, P., G. Backman, J. B. de Mesquita, L. Finer, R. Khosla, D. Korljan, and L. Oldring. 2015. "The Right to the Highest Attainable Standard of Health." In *Oxford Textbook of Global Public Health*, edited by Roger Detels, Martin Gulliford, Quarraisha Abdool Karim, and Chorh Chuan Tan, 277–92. 6th ed. Oxford: Oxford University Press. https://doi.org/10.1093/med/9780199661756.003.0018.

Kass, N., A. Paul, and A. Siege. 2015. "Ethical Principles and Ethical Issues in Public Health." In *Oxford Textbook of Global Public Health*, edited by Roger Detels, Martin Gulliford, Quarraisha Abdool Karim, and Chorh Chuan Tan, 267–76. 6th ed. Oxford: Oxford University Press. https://doi.org/10.1093/med/9780199661756.003.0017.

Lappe, M. 1986. "Ethics and Public Health." In *Maxcy-Rosenau Public Health and Preventive Medicine*, edited by J. M. Last, 1867–77. 12th ed. Norwalk: Appleton-Century-Crofts.

Larson, James S. 1996. "The World Health Organization's Definition of Health: Social versus Spiritual Health." *Social Indicators Research* 28, no. 2 (June), 181–92.

Long, K. N., E. L. Worthington, T. J. VanderWeele, and Y. Chen. 2020. "Forgiveness of Others and Subsequent Health and Well-Being in Mid-life: A Longitudinal Study on Female Nurses." *BMC Psychology* 8, no. 1: 1–11.

May, W. 2008. *Catholic Bioethics and the Gift of Human Life.* Huntington: Our Sunday Visitor.

National Commission for the Protection of Human Subjects of Biomedical and Behavioral Research. 1979. *The Belmont Report: Ethical Principles and Guidelines for the Protection of Human Subjects of Research*. Washington, DC: Government Printing Office.

Parfit, D. 1998. "Equality and Priority." In *Ideals of Equality*, edited by A. Mason, 21–36. Oxford: Blackwell.

Pieper, J. 1974. *About Love*. Translated by R. Winston and C. Winston. Chicago: Franciscan Herald Press.

Pontifical Council of Justice and Peace. 2004. *Compendium of the Social Doctrine of the Church*. USCCB Publishing.

Stump, E. 2006. "Love, by All Accounts." *Proceedings and Addresses of the American Philosophical Association* 80, no. 2: 25–43.

Toussaint, L. L., E. L. J. Worthington, and D. R. Williams. 2015. *Forgiveness and Health: Scientific Evidence and Theories Relating Forgiveness to Better Health*. Dordrecht/ New York: Springer.

UNCESCR (United Nations Committee on Economic, Social and Cultural Rights). 2000. "The Right to the Highest Attainable Standard of Health." General Comment No. 14 (Twenty Second Session). UN Document E/C.12/2000/4. Geneva: UN.

VanderWeele, T. J. 2017a. "On the Promotion of Human Flourishing." *Proceedings of the National Academy of Sciences* 114, no. 31: 8148–56.

———. 2017b. "Religion and Health: A Synthesis." In *Spirituality and Religion within the Culture of Medicine: From Evidence to Practice*, edited by M. J. Balboni and J. R. Peteet, 357–401. New York: Oxford University Press.

VanderWeele, T. J., E. McNeely, and H. K. Koh. 2019a. "Reimagining Health – Flourishing." *JAMA* 321, no. 17: 1667–68.

———. 2019b. "Flourishing as a Definition of Health – Reply." *JAMA* 322, no. 10: 981–82.

WHO (World Health Organization). 1946. "Constitution of the World Health Organization." Adopted by the International Health Conference, New York, 19 June–22 July 1946, and signed on 22 July 1946. Geneva: WHO.

———. 2021. "Abortion." https://www.who.int/health-topics/abortion#tab=tab_1.

Wolterstorff, N. 2015. *Justice in Love*. Grand Rapids: Eerdmans.

Being Just in Mental Health Care
John Peteet, M.D.
Psychiatry, Harvard Medical School, USA[6]

Justice may at first seem peripheral to the therapeutic enterprise, with its emphases on nonjudgmental acceptance and individual growth. But first-order justice is often central to the goals of treatment, the clinician's approach, and the delivery of care.

Many patients bring to treatment the impacts of trauma, including, as Judith Herman points out, a shattered worldview (Herman 1992, 36). An important task of their therapy is coming to terms with injustice. A therapist needs to give patients what they are due, and by acting justly to foster trust in the therapeutic frame, faith in a just order, and hope for living.

Patients are sometimes also perpetrators of injustice. A goal of their therapy may be to become fairer to others and to themselves, both treating themselves and others as having intrinsic dignity and welcoming their accountability to others.

Many patients also struggle in treatment with how to honor their commitments to justice. Should they insist on their rights, forego these to achieve a larger goal, forgive repeated offenses? When should they rely on procedural justice, or insist on restorative justice?

The COVID-19 pandemic has made clearer how inequitable access to quality mental health treatment has become. Clinicians honoring justice as a cardinal principle of bioethics will work for more just access, for example by accepting what insurance pays. They will also be alert to the generational impacts of systemic injustice, and of their own racial and other biases on their work. Those informed by a Christian vision will be inspired by grace to go beyond what simple justice requires: "Heal the sick. . . . Freely you have received; freely give" (Matt 10:8 NIV).

Further Reading

Herman, J. L. 1992. *Trauma and Recovery*. New York Basic Books.

Peteet, J. R. 2004. *Doing the Right Thing: An Approach to Moral Issues in Mental Health Treatment.* Washington, DC: American Psychiatric Publishing. For a framework for dealing with patients' moral concerns, and the clinician's role as a moral agent.

Peteet, J. R., ed. 2022. *The Virtues in Psychiatric Practice.* New York: Oxford University Press. For a discussion of the nature and clinical implications of virtues of self-control (accountability, humility, and equanimity), benevolence (forgiveness, compassion, and love), intelligence (defiance and phronesis, or practical wisdom), and positivity (gratitude, self-transcendence, and hope).

Peteet, J. R., H. S. Moffic, A. Hankir, and H. G. Koenig, eds. 2021. *Christianity and Psychiatry.* New York: Springer. For diverse perspectives on the role of the patient's Christian faith in treatment, including ways to enlist the resources of his or her faith.

Mercy, Not Justice, in Medicine
Lydia Dugdale, M.D.
Medicine, Columbia University, USA[7]

I am struck that the modern practice of medicine often challenges Wolterstorff's treatment of justice ("rendering to each what is his or her right, or due") in two key ways. First, the regnant principle in medicine is respect for autonomy, which means that treatment for patients often becomes mere wish fulfillment (which may in fact be unjust). And second, inherent to the practice of medicine is a sort of mercy that overlooks culpability on the patient's part. The smoker thus receives treatment for his lung cancer, and the intravenous drug user treatment for her hepatitis C, despite their own complicity in becoming sick – again, a matter of mercy, not justice.

---

7. gfiweb.net/contributor/46

Vaccine Nationalism During COVID-19

Benjamin Day

International Relations, Australian National University, Australia[8]

What Is Justice?

Nicholas Wolterstorff's Theology Brief on justice illustrates how the notion of justice pervades virtually every element of human existence. I focus here on how matters of justice intersect with my own work on international development within the discipline of international relations. Timothy Keller offers a straightforward definition of justice: "giving humans their due as people in the image of God" (Scharold 2010). I like this definition, as does Wolterstorff (p. 29). In the reflections below, I highlight two precepts that flow from this conception of justice. First, notions of justice are unavoidably political. And second, efforts to "do" justice require constant recalibration and readjustment.

Justice in International Relations

At the outset of his classic article "Justice and International Relations," the political theorist Charles Beitz (1975, 360) posed the following question: "Do citizens of relatively affluent countries have obligations founded on justice to share their wealth with poorer people elsewhere?" This question increasingly guides my own attempts to "think Christianly" about how states provide development aid (see Day 2020). For me, the most basic answer to this question is settled: Yes, citizens of affluent countries *do* have such obligations. Yet the more difficult and pressing question is how we – as both individuals *and* members of political communities – should most effectively discharge these obligations in a rapidly changing global environment.

Who Does Justice?

International relations (IR) primarily considers interactions between *states*, the most macro-level institutionalized communities of global politics. For a range of historical, disciplinary, and theoretical reasons, IR scholars have

---

8. gfiweb.net/contributor/114

focused predominantly on the most powerful states and conceptualized them as unitary actors. This "billiard ball" model of states, which "black boxes" internal dynamics influencing behavior, reduces interstate relations to an arena governed by materialistic laws derived from the relative economic and military might of its constituent units. This conceptualization is problematic in myriad ways, not least in dissolving the space for individual responsibility and agency. We see this in the way our language often ascribes agency to a state, rather than its decision-makers (for example, newspapers report how "Australia refused to sign," or "The United States imposed sanctions"). Yet, as Valerie Hudson (2005, 2) has argued, "States are not agents because states are abstractions and thus have no agency."

This theoretical discussion has serious practical implications because it ultimately concerns a decisive question: Who *does* justice? Is it individuals, or is it states? Or is it some combination of the two? In addition, how are we, as individuals, responsible for the actions of the states to which we belong? Getting even more practical, consider the question of redressing unequal development. Is the provision of bilateral (i.e. state-to-state) international development assistance (foreign aid) something the *state* does? Or is the state acting on behalf of its citizens? Or does a leader exercise agency on behalf of the citizens of a state?

Nationalists versus Globalists

These questions are the remit of political theory. In his book *Political Theory and International Relations*, Bietz (1979) essentially translates John Rawls's theory of justice from the domestic sphere to the international one. At issue is where – and how – to draw boundaries around political communities, especially as they relate to responsibilities to do justice to individuals outside these boundaries. These age-old questions have resurfaced in the debate pitting "Nationalists" against "Globalists," most notably in the USA but also in the UK and elsewhere in the West (albeit often employing slightly different terminology).

In my observation, scholars of IR, as well as many Christians, are inclined to draw boundaries of moral responsibility too narrowly and too neatly. In both cases, this can lead to a tendency to excise obligations for individuals and states to do justice in part because of the ease of hiding behind neat and politically convenient international boundaries. To be clear, I am not suggesting that states and their leaders do not have primary obligations ("special duties") to their own citizens. Rather, I am arguing that the balance between the way states approach "doing justice" to those inside their borders versus those outside them needs active tending.

This tension will always be challenging to navigate. Nonetheless, I am of the view that this "insider-outsider" tension has recently been resolved too far in favor of the insider, at least in the rich Western states with which I am most familiar. Against the backdrop of a changing and uncertain global order, there is a mood among Western states to circumscribe their international justice-doing activities. This tendency is evident in policies relating to immigration, climate change, and development assistance, for example. As elaborated below, it is also evident in the global response to the COVID-19 pandemic.

Why Christians Should Widen Their Horizons

First, for most of us, the nature of our practical engagement with each other across the globe makes national-international distinctions virtually obsolete in important domains. This is especially the case when it comes to financial markets. Beitz's critique of Rawls turns on this notion (1975, 374). He argues that because the borders of states do not, in practice, demarcate where social interactions stop, then neither should they demarcate where social obligations stop. The dramatic expansion of international capital flows, people flows, information flows, and trade since Beitz made this argument only makes it more compelling.

Second, the rules and institutions that govern these cross-border flows are themselves often a source of injustice, not least because the rules are typically written (and underwritten) by the most powerful states. In other words, many of our shortcomings in doing justice beyond borders relate to not seeing (or being *unwilling* to see) how our own behaviors are contributing to the perpetration of injustice elsewhere. Expressed in more technical language, we are typically much more aware of our failures to uphold "positive duties" (obligations that we should undertake to help others) than our failures to uphold our "negative duties" (obligations not to inadvertently harm others through our actions). For example, rapid recent changes in global financial flows now mean that, more than ever before, what a state gives on the one hand through the provision of development aid (complying with a positive duty) can easily be taken away with the other, through the pursuit of non-aid policies that harm poorer countries (violating negative duties). Examples include unfair laws and practices concerning trade, arms transfers, agricultural and fishing subsidies, intellectual property laws, and remittances (see Day 2020).

Third, while we are quick to identify the limits of our obligations, very often advocating that they diminish at the border of our state, we rarely treat the benefits we accrue from outside our state in the same manner. For example, citizens of rich states obtain multitudes of cheap goods manufactured overseas that they use every day.

COVID-19 and Vaccine Nationalism

The global response to the COVID-19 pandemic usefully illustrates the "insider-outsider" tension mentioned earlier. Since viruses do not respect national boundaries, the most effective global response would also be supranational. In practice, however, it was clear early in the pandemic that states were focused almost exclusively on meeting their own needs – a stance that, while politically understandable, would ultimately be counterproductive. Thomas Bollyky and Chad Bown (2020) were among those warning that vaccine nationalism would prolong the pandemic. They advised that "distributing scarce early vaccine supplies to the settings and populations where they can do the most good is the most efficient way to bring this pandemic under control. Doing so would also speed the global economic recovery and avoid unnecessary geopolitical conflict."

Inequalities in Vaccine Allocation

In practice, the inverse occurred. By late 2020, "nations representing just one-seventh of the world's population [had] reserved more than half of all the promising vaccine supplies" (Bollyky and Bown 2020). In stark contrast, COVAX, the multilateral entity established to provide vaccines to lower-income countries, was struggling to acquire supplies. According to Olivier Wouters and his coauthors (2021, 1031), "the widespread disregard for a global approach to vaccine allocation shown by national governments misses an opportunity to maximise the common good by reducing the global death toll, supporting widespread economic recovery, and mitigating supply chain disruptions." Meanwhile, a less visible form of injustice was proceeding, in the form of rich countries violating negative duties that made it more difficult for poor states to respond to COVID-19.

Impacts on Poor Countries

Consider the impact that just one domain of global injustice had on the ability of poor countries to respond to the pandemic: the lack of access to global credit markets. Homi Kharas (2021, 3) recognized how "advanced economy governments have the exorbitant privilege of borrowing in their own currencies, while development countries cannot." This reality had important flow-on effects. First, the inability of poor countries to borrow is a large part of why they found themselves at the end of the vaccine queue. The risk of preordering prospective vaccines was simply too high.

Second, while rich states borrowed cheaply to finance huge stimulus spending, poor states had little capacity to mount a fiscal response. In my own region, for example, Australia's initial fiscal response was to leverage additional expenditure in response to COVID-19 equivalent to 9.5 percent of GDP. This compared with a stimulus of 0.6 percent of GDP in Papua New Guinea (PNG) and 0.8 percent of GDP in Fiji, the Pacific Island region's two biggest economies (Howes and Surandiran 2020). The differences in these headline figures are stark enough, but must be further contextualized by understanding that PNG's economy, for example, is around sixty times smaller than Australia's to begin with.

Third, the labor force in low-income economies is overwhelmingly employed in the informal sector. Such workers have their livelihoods withdrawn during lockdowns, unable to work from home via an online connection. Many workers therefore faced the double bind of being unable to access credit markets at the personal level, as well as living in a state that was unable to access credit markets for social spending.

Beyond Reductionism

In his brief, Wolterstorff voices concern that scholars working across many academic disciplines, even those that "deal directly with interactions among human beings and social entities," can become so beholden to reductionism that they do not bring justice "into the picture." In this brief, I have tried to illustrate how scholars of international relations are prone to this. The discipline has normalized a form of reductionism that reduces states to abstractions. The attendant risk is that, in the service of theoretical parsimony (or political expediency), people are squeezed out of the conceptual and analytical frame. Conceptualizing states as mechanistic and deterministic entities tends to obscure how doing justice – or not doing justice – is always ultimately a choice, made by people.

References and Further Reading

Beitz, Charles R. 1975. "Justice and International Relations." *Philosophy & Public Affairs* 4, no. 4: 360–89. Asks whether citizens of relatively affluent countries have obligations to share their wealth with poorer people elsewhere.

———. 1979. *Political Theory and International Relations*. Princeton: Princeton University Press. Translates John Rawls's theory of justice to the international sphere.

Bollyky, Thomas J., and Chad P. Bown. 2020. "Vaccine Nationalism Will Prolong the Pandemic." *Foreign Affairs*, 29 December 2020. https://www.foreignaffairs.com/articles/world/2020-12-29/vaccine-nationalism-will-prolong-pandemic. A plea, issued early in the COVID-19 pandemic, for states to cooperate in the distribution of vaccines.

Day, Benjamin. 2020. "Amos and the Beyond Aid Agenda: The 0.7% Target, COVID-19, and Reimagining International Development." *International Journal of Public Theology* 14, no. 4: 475–98. How to "think Christianly" about how states can improve the lives of the poor beyond their borders.

Howes, Stephen, and Sherman Surandiran. 2020. "COVID-19 Spending across the Pacific: The Self-Funded, the Aid-Financed, and the Constrained." *DevpolicyBlog* (blog), 20 August 2020. https://devpolicy.org/covid-19-spending-across-the-pacific-20200820/. Compares government fiscal responses to COVID-19 across the Pacific.

Hudson, Valerie M. 2005. "Foreign Policy Analysis: Actor-Specific Theory and the Ground of International Relations." *Foreign Policy Analysis* 1, no. 1: 1–30. A foundational article charting the key tenets of foreign policy analysis, a subdiscipline of international relations.

Kharas, Homi. 2021. "Global Development Cooperation in a COVID-19 World." Global Working Paper 150. Washington, DC: Brookings Institution. https://www.brookings.edu/wp-content/uploads/2021/01/Global-Development-Cooperation-COVID-19-World.pdf. Contemplates how the COVID-19 pandemic will shape the future of development cooperation.

Scharold, Kristen. 2010. "Tim Keller: What We Owe the Poor." *Christianity Today*, 6 December 2010. https://www.christianitytoday.com/ct/2010/december/10.69.html. The late pastor and theologian Tim Keller shares his views on caring for the poor in an interview with *Christianity Today*.

Wouters, Olivier J., Kenneth C. Shadlen, Maximilian Salcher-Konrad, Andrew J. Pollard, Heidi J. Larson, Yot Teerawattananon, and Mark Jit. 2021. "Challenges in Ensuring Global Access to COVID-19 Vaccines: Production, Affordability, Allocation, and Deployment." *The Lancet* 397, no. 10278: 1023–34. A "live" appraisal of the challenges of ensuring global access to COVID-19 vaccines.

6

Justice and the Academy

Justice in Academic Publishing and the Academic Calling: A Perspective from the Global South

Dinesha Samararatne

Law, University of Colombo, Sri Lanka[1]

Wolterstorff's brief on "Justice and Rights" clarifies the central role of justice in the academy (writ large). I find his distinction between first- and second-order justice to be useful in organizing my own thinking on the matter. The brief has provoked me to reflect on two aspects of academia which have been areas of struggle and frustration for me. They both involve academia from a global perspective and the relationship between justice and the production of knowledge, and involve first-order justice. One is that of publishing in academia and the barriers encountered by academics in academic publishing. The other is that of determining the role of an academic. Both aspects implicate several issues of first-order justice when one approaches them from a Global South perspective, and that is a perspective that is often missing. However, I do think that these questions require a global approach and response as well.

---

1. gfiweb.net/contributor/78

Academic Publishing

The inequality in the distribution of intellectual, financial, and social resources has resulted in unjust conditions for academic publishing. It is near impossible for an academic in the Global South (however understood) to publish in leading journals in his or her discipline, except as a matter of exception. Those exceptions are often personal to the academic; it is rarely a matter of institutional support. The exceptional circumstances almost always involve supportive colleagues located elsewhere in the academy, often in well-supported universities in the Global North. These allies play a supportive role by way of offering invaluable feedback on draft work and extending invitations to academic events where one can get useful feedback on work in progress. Their support also involves the sharing of material that the academic in the Global South is unable to access. Equally, and perhaps more importantly, such allies support and encourage academics in the Global South at a personal and emotional level too.

Due to the issues surrounding academic publication, the production of knowledge is incomplete in many fields and the development of theory is inadequate. To frame it in a provocative way: the production of knowledge is captured by elite actors, speaking to a limited audience that has access to that knowledge. Access has to be understood not only in terms of accessing expensive databases or subscriptions, but also in terms of the relatability of the knowledge that is being produced. To give a simple example, Wolterstorff references several books in his brief. I cannot afford to buy those books (my monthly income is approximately 2,000 USD and we are now a single-income family). Even if I could afford them, I would have to wait indefinitely to receive the books. Instead, I would have to rely on the goodwill of colleagues overseas to share PDF versions of specific chapters or the whole book. This is the daily reality of an academic in the Global South. Is this just? What obligations do academics in other contexts have in order to address this situation? What is the responsibility of individual institutions and networks? Do they have any responsibilities beyond what they have already accepted in terms of scholarship schemes and so on?

Academic Work and Societal Activism

The academic is required to engage in the pursuit of truth through the production and dissemination of knowledge. Activism, if and when an academic engages in it, is deemed optional and a matter of secondary value. I find this demarcation of the role of an academic to be meaningful and useful as a matter of principle. However, again, as a scholar in the Global

South, I find it unhelpful in navigating the daily challenges I face. Almost on a daily basis, I face a choice between lending my knowledge and other skills to a matter of political and social significance which requires support, on the one hand, and lending that knowledge and those skills to my academic work (more traditionally understood) on the other (for a recent example of my contribution, see the footnote[2]). When I do choose to devote my time to academic work at the expense of responding to the call of activism, I feel guilty and irresponsible. In a context where resources are severely limited, ethical commitments to activism are limited to the elite, and saying "no" to activism can sometimes mean that no one else will actually make the intervention that you could have made. Even when you do choose to intervene, sometimes you do so at personal risk. All of this consumes intellectual, emotional, and physical energy too.

Epistemological and First-Order Justice

Others before me have written about these challenges. I do think that these debates must continue to remain alive and be recognized for what they are. They are issues of epistemological justice. They are issues of first-order justice. There are examples of how individuals, institutions, and systems have sought to address these injustices. I, for instance, have benefited from the Fulbright scholarship program, a tuition waiver from Harvard University, and an Australia Awards Fellowship. At the Melbourne Law School, where I was a postdoctoral fellow, I thrived in an intellectual environment in which I was supported to reach the highest levels of academic publishing and I forged excellent collaborations which I now continue. These are experiences of how systems can work well to address the first-order injustices that I highlight here.

The question I ask myself is, is this enough? What more ought to be done, particularly to address injustice in the development of theory and in meeting the dilemmas of having to choose between activism and academic work? Finally, in studying these issues from a Global South perspective, what insights does this offer to academia in the Global North and then to academia from a global perspective? My intuition, at the moment, is that asking these questions from the perspective of the Global South will offer us useful insights that we can build upon in perhaps even rethinking epistemic justice at a global scale.

---

2. Dinesha Samararatne, "The Port City Bill: Legislative Carving Out from a Constitutional Democracy?," Groundviews, https://groundviews.org/2021/04/18/the-port-city-bill-legislative-carving-out-from-a-constitutional-democracy/.

Two Thoughts on Justice, Rights, and the Academy

Luke Glanville

International Relations, Australian National University, Australia[3]

Are Rights Enough?

Wolterstorff talks about justice in the language of rights. Fair enough. He has done this to great effect in earlier work, too (Wolterstorff 2010). Some, including myself, might like to see greater acknowledgment not only of the corollary relationship between rights and duties but also of the fact that, historically, duties-talk long preceded and only belatedly birthed rights-talk, and also greater justification for why rights-talk is to be preferred to duties-talk. But this is well-trodden ground by now.[4]

Contemporary Rights-Talk Is Not Enough

Something that does seem worth raising, though, is the question of what might be gained if this discussion of justice and rights was to be brought into conversation with recent debates about the political construction of rights-talk and the vital implications of this political construction for matters of justice. As Samuel Moyn (2018) and others have argued recently, insofar as human rights has been primarily defined in recent decades in terms of sufficientist understandings of basic rights and the need to protect people from atrocities and other violations of physical well-being, such rights-talk is "not enough." By sidelining questions of distributive justice, material equality, and reparations for past injustices, prevailing constructions of human rights offer only a partial vision of global justice.

Thinking with the Parable of the Good Samaritan

I think we can usefully "think with" the parable of the good Samaritan to explore this idea. While Wolterstorff may be right to suggest that human rights

---

3. gfiweb.net/contributor/49

4. See, for example, the forum on Wolterstorff's "Justice" in *Journal of Religious Ethics* 37, no. 2 (2009).

should be defined more broadly, the fact is that they are often defined politically in narrow terms of the right of beaten men lying half dead by the side of the road to be (1) not beaten in the first place and (2) upon being beaten, to be cared for by good Samaritans.

A broader vision of justice needs also to reckon with how individual people and also collectives such as sovereign states so often not only fail to behave as good Samaritans, but often behave as priests and Levites, crossing to the other side of the road to avoid encountering the vulnerable, or even in complicity with the robbers, acting in unjust ways, directly or systemically, past or present, that in one way or another amount to a degree of culpability for the vulnerability and suffering of others.

Justice for Refugees

I have tried to "think with" the parable in this way in a recent book, cowritten with my theologian brother, Mark Glanville, which considers how to think through questions of justice with respect to refugees (Glanville 2020; Glanville and Glanville 2021). Writing for a Western Christian audience, we argue that we need to understand how wealthy Western states don't simply fail to act like the good Samaritan in failing to do more to care for refugees. Rather, they act like the priest and the Levite in the parable, going out of their way to keep refugees at a distance, detaining them, deterring them, and containing them in poorer regions of the world. And they also even act like the robbers, contributing historically and today to the vulnerability and suffering and displacement of so many people.

From the wars and conquests, dispossession and eradication of indigenous peoples, the mass migration of people out of Europe, and the inflow of natural resources into Europe that attended European imperialism, to the reckless wars, exploitative economic regulations, and environmental destruction of the postcolonial era, Western states have accrued and continue to maintain territories and riches via practices that sustain the poverty, instability, and vulnerability of others, and contribute to the generation of situations that produce their displacement. Wealthy Western states thus owe obligations to displaced people as a matter of justice. Certainly, such a broader vision of justice can be articulated in terms of rights. But it is useful to recognize that prevailing discourses of rights actually often occlude such a broader vision.

How Should States Prioritize?

One further potential limit to relying on rights-talk to provide a full vision of justice, and one that I'm presently exploring in a different coauthored book project with political theorist James Pattison, is the question of how states should prioritize among multiple threats or acts of rights violations globally when thinking about where they should direct their attention and resources.[5] Think of the competing needs to respond to global poverty, mass atrocities, global pandemics, and climate change, among many global threats and crises. Confronted with a plurality of competing demands, I think we need more than mere rights-talk to help us discern the requirements of justice. Questions about the allocation of responsibilities among multiple states and the prioritization of a single state's multiple responsibilities become much more central and indispensable.

On the Scholarly Pursuit of Justice

The final part of Wolterstorff's brief turns to "the role of justice in and by and for the academy, and to the importance of being alert to that role." I am entirely in agreement with his emphasis on the importance of being alert to the role of justice in scholarly research. However, I have serious reservations about his characterizations of the tasks of various academic disciplines. While for a range of reasons my own research interests have shifted in recent years such that they are very much in alignment with the kinds of concerns for justice that Wolterstorff recommends, I think an individual Christian scholar working in disciplines that he names on page 4 – "economics, political theory, business and management, sociology and social work, health care, and gender studies" – can and often does usefully pursue a range of vital research questions that do not speak directly or explicitly to issues of justice, and we should not discourage this.

Justice Grounded in Understanding

Wolterstorff criticizes scholars in these disciplines who, instead of focusing on what is just and unjust, focus on "utilitarian considerations of power, efficiency, cost, preference, and so on." But surely so much of our understanding of what is just and unjust relies on our understanding of these very things: for example,

---

5. We lay out some of the contours of this project in Glanville and Pattison 2021. The project builds on recent work by Pattison and me, such as Glanville 2021; Pattison 2020.

(1) what are the possibilities and limits and hazards of power, (2) what options among many can be pursued with efficiency or inefficiency and with what cost, and (3) to what extent do the preferences of relevant actors shape the possibilities, limits, and hazards of certain courses of action?

Consider, for example, the question of military intervention in response to atrocities. Before we confidently argue about the justice or injustice of intervention, we surely need careful research on the practice of intervention and whether and under what conditions it might be able to succeed in saving lives, and that will necessarily involve giving attention to considerations of such things as "power, efficiency, cost, preference, and so on."[6]

So much of what we take for granted about what is just and unjust relies on certain assumptions and prevailing understandings of such things, and Christian scholars in these disciplines will often usefully take on the task of clarifying and improving such understandings. Those Christian scholars may then choose to take on the additional task of addressing their findings directly and explicitly to questions of justice in a scholarly manner, but there will often be good reasons for them to leave it to others to do this – perhaps because they have not been trained or are not adept at such things, or they lack the time or resources to do so.

History Should Inform Policy Too

Relatedly, I would question the distinction that Wolterstorff draws between the disciplines that he first lists – "economics, political theory, business and management, sociology and social work, health care, and gender studies" – and the discipline of history. Indeed, I think the basis of his argument here further reveals the justification for my previous reservation. Wolterstorff suggests that the field of history is different in that it does not make policy suggestions. I would respond that there are plenty of important research questions that Christian scholars can and do pursue in the earlier list of disciplines that also do not lead directly to policy suggestions. Often the task of offering a policy suggestion requires that scholars take an additional step of explicitly considering policy implications which, as I noted with respect to considerations of justice above, may not be best done by the same scholar who does the initial research. And at the same time, there is plenty of scope for historians to take the additional step of arguing for policy implications that follow from

---

6. For an example of such analysis undertaken for the explicit purpose of drawing better conclusions about matters of justice, see Glanville 2021, 82–87.

their *historical* research (or from the research of other historians), if they are capable of doing so. Indeed, historians often publicly lament that they have vital, policy-relevant things to say and that they try to say them publicly, but that their opinions are ignored and that it is economists instead who today have the ears of policymakers – to often-disastrous effect.[7]

References

Glanville, Luke. 2020. "The Refugee and the Sovereign State." *International Journal of Public Theology* 14, no. 4: 456–74.

———. 2021. *Sharing Responsibility: The History and Future of Protection from Atrocities.* Princeton: Princeton University Press.

Glanville, Luke, and James Pattison. 2021. "Where to Protect: Prioritization and the Responsibility to Protect." *Ethics & International Affairs* 35, no. 2: 213–25.

Glanville, Mark R., and Luke Glanville. 2021. *Refuge Reimagined: Biblical Kinship in Global Politics.* Downers Grove: InterVarsity Press.

Moyn, Samuel. 2018. *Not Enough: Human Rights in an Unequal World.* Cambridge: Harvard University Press.

Pattison, James. 2020. "Opportunity Costs Pacifism." *Law and Philosophy* 39: 545–76.

Wolterstorff, Nicholas. 2010. *Justice: Rights and Wrongs.* Princeton: Princeton University Press.

Perversions of Just Relations in the University
Ross McKenzie
Physics, University of Queensland, Australia[8]

On just relations being "pervasively violated" in the university I find it quite disturbing the way universities (and some of my colleagues) exploit international students, postdocs, and visiting scholars. Some labs are like "sweat shops." Adjunct faculty is another issue . . .

Research priorities are also skewed. Here is a good example of medical research. From the abstract: "Most studies on global health inequality consider unequal health care and socio-economic

---

7. See, for example, David Armitage, "Why Politicians Need Historians," *The Guardian*, 7 October 2014.

8. gfiweb.net/contributor/65

conditions but neglect inequality in the production of health knowledge relevant to addressing disease burden. Accordingly, conditions common to developed countries garnered more clinical research than those common to less developed countries. Many of the health needs in less developed countries do not attract attention among developed country researchers who produce the vast majority of global health knowledge—including clinical trials—in response to their own local needs." (Evans et al. 2014)

Reference

Evans, James A., Jae-Mahn Shim, John P. A. Ioannidis. 2014. "Attention to Local Health Burden and the Global Disparity of Health Research." *PLoS ONE* 9 [April 1]: https://e90147. doi:10.1371/journal.pone.0090147

Epistemic Injustice

Carlos Miguel Goméz

School of Human Sciences, University of Rosario, Bogotá, Colombia[9]

Wolterstorff's aim of bringing to light and demanding attention to the role of justice in the academy should represent a fundamental commitment for all of us. This requires a constant effort to identify and fight against subtle forms of injustice, hidden behind academic practices or institutionalized in well-established forms. To evoke a basic insight of liberation theology, sin has a social dimension: it takes form in institutions and social relationships; it has the face of certain taken-for-granted economic and cultural systems.

Besides the manifold forms that first-order injustice may take in academia, in multicultural and pluralistic societies there is a kind of injustice related not primarily to forms of interaction among agents, but to recognition and the willingness to listen and enter into dialogue with forms of knowledge coming from traditions that have been neglected, invisibilized, deformed, or eradicated. This may be called epistemic injustice. The very constitution of the university implies a certain form of understating of knowledge, science, and scholarship based on a problematic claim to universality.

Traditional Knowledge

In Latin American universities, to offer an example that has important analogies in other parts of the globe, traditional knowing systems are never included as sources of valid knowledge that may enrich and contribute to the search for a larger, more comprehensive understanding of reality. If they do attract attention, they are taken only as objects to be studied, by one or another discipline of the social sciences. Given that a practice such as traditional indigenous medicine is based on a view of reality that conflicts with many of the presuppositions of Western science, it is assumed that instead of being a legitimate interlocutor in, for instance, health research, it needs to be explained as merely a cultural, social, or historical phenomenon. Even worse, "their knowledge," usually taken as primitive, mythical, or infantile, tends to be regarded merely as an indicator of possible new resources to be exploited by modern science, technology, and industry: this is the case, for example, of ethnobotanical medicines which,

---

9. gfiweb.net/contributor/111

abstracted from the belief system and form of life in which they are understood and lived by in community, are reduced to pharmaceutical assets. But it is precisely this lived understanding proper to a worldview that should be brought into dialogue to enlarge and enrich our view of reality.

The deficiency to take the truth claims of others seriously is the heart of epistemic injustice. Even if it has consequences in the forms by which we interact with people from other traditions, it takes place before those interactions. It belongs to our fore-understanding of reality and to our basic ontological commitments. Or more precisely, it is embedded in our ways of relating to what we take for granted.

Promoting Epistemic Justice

How could we open ourselves to the truth claims of others? What does this openness require and how would it transform our research and pedagogical practices? What shape should an intercultural university take? These are some fundamental questions oriented to promote epistemic justice. An attitude of self-inquiry regarding one's own presuppositions, the disposition to listen to and learn from others, and epistemic humility, that is, the recognition that reality cannot be fully apprehended in any theory or thought system, are key values to be cultivated in an interculturally just university. Building such institutions would be a decisive way "to bring good news to the oppressed" (Isa 61:1).

Further Reading

De Sousa Santos, Boaventura. 2009. *Una epistemología del sur*. Buenos Aires: Siglo Veintiuno y CLACASO. A classic dedicated to the search for epistemological criteria to appraise forms of knowledge proper to marginalized communities.

Estermann, Josef. 2009. *Filosofía Andina: Sabiduría indígena para un mundo nuevo*. La Paz: ISEAT. An exercise in intercultural dialogue in philosophy which attempts to bring to light the principles of indigenous thought.

Gómez, Carlos Miguel. 2012. *Interculturality, Rationality and Dialogue: In Search for Intercultural Argumentative Criteria for Latin America*. Würzburg: Echter. An exploration of the conditions of possibility for intercultural dialogue, understood as criteria to evaluate arguments formulated and justified according to heterogeneous forms of rationality.

Guzy, Lidia, and James Kapaló, eds. 2017. *Marginalised and Endangered Worldviews*. Berlin: LIT. A collection of papers dealing with different aspects relevant to the study of traditional and indigenous forms of knowledge from a global perspective.

Are Students Treated Unjustly?
Thomas Chacko
Earth and Atmospheric Sciences, University of Alberta, Canada[10]

I'm not sure I agree with Dr. Wolterstorff that the call to *treat our students justly* is "pervasively" violated in academia. From my experience the large majority of supervisors treat their students justly or at least in a reasonable way. Having said that, I suspect all of us could do better. Christians in particular have a higher calling to envision graduate students and senior undergraduate students whom they supervise as their academic children rather than as a means to achieving their research goals. I have found that I need to be continually reminded to strive for this ideal in my supervision, particularly when the pressures of research tempt me to view my students in a utilitarian way.

---

10. gfiweb.net/contributor/43

Justice and Trust in Interdisciplinary Research

Claudia Vanney

Philosophy and Physics, Universidad Austral, Argentina[11]

In his Theology Brief "Justice and Rights," Prof. Nicholas Wolterstorff indicates that first-order justice pertains to how agents engage each other, how they interact. This assertion is true; however, deep interpersonal relationships require more than mere justice. In my opinion, they can only develop in a climate of trust.

This has important implications for academic work. In recent years, I have directed several interdisciplinary research projects. Through them, we have tried different ways to foster collaborative work between scholars with diverse academic backgrounds. I understand interdisciplinary research as a practice that, without denying the individual identity of the disciplines involved, results in the production of innovative knowledge with insights from different fields. In interdisciplinary research, experts from diverse disciplines work in a joint, not independent, manner on a common problem, engaging in a creative pluralism that requires them to share the way of thinking of others, and not only to learn new content from different fields.

Nevertheless, interdisciplinary research faces a series of challenges related, mainly, to the interaction between specialists and the reciprocal evaluation of their different points of view. In particular, collaborations between philosophy/theology and sciences are challenging because each researcher is used to working within the framework of a theoretical doctrine and following his or her own methods and procedures. Therefore, the lack of knowledge of many empirical details challenges the philosophers, while the sophistication of the underlying philosophical discussions challenges the scientists. Furthermore, since many terms change their meaning depending on the disciplinary context, the problem of communicating correctly challenges everyone. As interdisciplinary research involves a greater effort than that required by an exclusively disciplinary approach, the willingness of the researchers is necessary to carry the investigation through to the end.

Consequently, interdisciplinary research demands a very particular and deep type of interaction between academics. Collaborative intellectual work requires a mutual appreciation and respect among the members of the research

---

11. gfiweb.net/contributor/178

team to promote among them an attitude of openness that consolidates the desire to learn from others. These attitudes can only be developed in a climate of trust.

First-order justice is a founding pillar of trust. When there has been a violation of first-order justice, trust between people is broken. Although second-order justice is a fair way of responding to that violation, second-order justice hardly restores trust. Since a climate of trust is essential in collaborative teams, and since situations of injustice among team members could alter this climate, transparent relationships of fairness and justice among investigators should be a concern when conducting collaborative research.

The first step in developing trust among members of the research team is a fair recognition of the contributions of others, since both empirical developments and bibliographic studies or conceptual analyses all contribute equally to clarify the object of study in an interdisciplinary research. The next step could be achieved through the concerted effort to produce a joint publication. Publishing the results in coauthored articles is a deeper manifestation of trust and mutual recognition among researchers. However, as the practice of coauthorship does not follow the same rules in all disciplines, a fair authorship policy must be established. Another important aspect is transparency and equity in the management of research funding, because an unbiased distribution of the resources obtained also consolidates the trust of the researchers. In this sense, a climate of deep trust among interdisciplinary researchers can be achieved only to the extent that all of them are open to learn from each other and are firmly committed to the effort of understanding and respecting the characteristics of those epistemic fields in which they are not specialists.

Further Reading

Vanney, Claudia E. 2021. "Virtudes intelectuales para la investigación en ciencia y filosofía." In *Ciencia y filosofía: estudios en homenaje a Juan Arana*, edited by Francisco Rodríguez Valls and Juan José Padial, 501–12. Sevilla: Thématha.

Vanney, Claudia E., and Ignacio Aguinalde. 2021. "Second-Person Perspective in Interdisciplinary Research: A Cognitive Approach for Understanding and Improving the Dynamics of Collaborative Research Teams." *Scientia et Fides* 9, no. 2: 155–78.

Part IV

Postscript

Justice

Nicholas Wolterstorff

Philosophical Theology, Emeritus, Yale University; Institute for Advanced Studies in Culture, University of Virginia, USA; Australian Catholic University, Australia [1]

I found the twenty-six Disciplinary Briefs in response to my Theology Brief "Justice and Rights" perceptive, inspiring, gratifying – and sometimes surprising. What I found perceptive and inspiring was the amazing variety of ways in which these scholars employ considerations of justice in their work. What I found gratifying was the fact that so many of them found my analysis helpful, and that several of them expanded on what, in my essay, were just brief remarks. (The excellent discussion of restorative justice by Chris Marshall is a good example of this last point.)

As for what I found surprising, let me mention just two things. I was surprised – amazed, actually – by the wide range of justice issues highlighted by Allan Bell in his essay "Just Language." Before reading his essay, when thinking about justice and speech I would immediately focus my thoughts on the legal right to free speech; I doubt that I was peculiar in that regard. I now realize what a blinkered view of the matter that was. Bell's essay opened my eyes to the presence of justice and injustice in who is allowed to speak, and when and where, and what they are allowed to say, to the presence of justice and injustice in which language a group is allowed to use, to the presence of justice and injustice in whose accent is deemed estimable and whose is deemed inferior – and so forth, on and on.

Another thing that surprised me was a comment by Christopher Hays in his essay "The Obligations of Justice for Colombia's Displaced Persons." After noting that "rights language is pervasive" in Colombia, Hays writes: "The emphasis on rights has fostered a great deal of passivity." He explains that "government is seen as the primary . . . restorer of violated rights" – in spite of the fact that the government of Colombia is incapable of doing so – and that individuals exercise little agency in the matter. Hays's comment jolted me into realizing that, before reading his essay, I had rather thoughtlessly assumed that a group's recognition that its rights are being violated is a spur to action – as

---

1. gfiweb.net/contributor/9

it was, for example, in the American Civil Rights Movement. I now see that it might instead motivate the opposite response, passivity. "It's not up to us to correct the situation; we'll just put up with it." The passivity might or might not be accompanied by a sense of grievance, or by sly sullen resistance.

In this essay I propose responding to a number of the questions raised and points made in the responses to my Theology Brief, mainly to the extended responses, but also to some of the earlier brief responses. I propose doing six things. First, I will correct something I said in my Theology Brief about the origins in antiquity of our way of thinking about justice. Second, I will address the question, posed by a couple of respondents, whether there is a distinct biblical concept of justice. Third, I will address concerns about my single-minded focus on justice, to the ignoring of other components of the moral and good life. Fourth, I will address the uneasiness about rights-talk felt by some respondents. Fifth, I will respond to questions of several respondents about rights by amplifying what I said about the nature of rights and the relation of rights to duties. And finally, I will call attention to a recent publication on the history of the idea of natural rights.

A Correction

In my Theology Brief I wrote the following:

> Coming down to us from antiquity are two fundamentally different accounts of what justice is. One comes from Aristotle who . . . explained justice as equity (fairness) in the distribution of benefits and/or burdens. The other comes from the Roman jurist Ulpian. . . . Referring to the virtue of being just, Ulpian says that justice . . . is a steady and enduring will to render to each his or her *ius*.

The standard translations of *ius* are "right" or "due." In my brief, what followed the passage just quoted were reasons for preferring Ulpian's account to Aristotle's.

I now think that what I said was incorrect. Antiquity did not bequeath to us two distinct accounts of what justice is. Aristotle, in his discussion of justice in the *Nicomachean Ethics*, does not say what justice *is*; he does not say what *constitutes* justice. What he does, instead, is offer a general characterization of those situations in which justice is present: justice is present, he says, when benefits and/or burdens (goods and/or harms) are distributed equitably. That general characterization is compatible with Ulpian's account of what justice *is*.

One might hold that, in general, what persons have a right to is that they be treated equitably in the distribution of benefits and/or burdens.

In interpreting, as I now do, the relation between what Aristotle and Ulpian said about justice, I am following in the footsteps of Thomas Aquinas. Aquinas was, of course, profoundly influenced in his thought by Aristotle. Given that fact, and given that Aristotle nowhere says or suggests that justice consists of being rendered what is one's right or due, one wonders whether, perhaps, the Ulpian account of justice is missing in Aquinas. It is not. Aquinas remarks that "justice denotes a kind of equality" (*Summa Theologiae* II-II 57, 1; see also II-II 58, 2 and 59, 2). But it's clear that he did not regard that as an explanation of what justice is. For when he asks, in *Summa Theologiae* II-I, 58, 1, "what is justice," how "justice is fittingly defined," his answer is that justice is "rendering to each his right. . . . A man is said to be just because he respects the rights [*iura*] of others." Aquinas goes on to say that justice can also be defined as rendering to each "what is his" or "what is due to him" (*Summa Theologiae* II-II 58, 11).

Shortly after Justinian became ruler of the Byzantine Empire in 527 CE, he ordered the preparation of three compilations of Roman law: the *Codex*, which collected the legal pronouncements of the Roman emperors, the *Institutes*, a beginning student's handbook, and the *Digest*, which culled and organized everything of value from earlier Roman law. The *Digest* opened with Ulpian's definition of "justice."

The *Digest* was the largest of the three texts, and proved to be by far the most influential. Its influence on the subsequent legal tradition of Christendom was enormous; it became its fundamental legal text. In offering Ulpian's explanation of what justice is, Aquinas was reflecting the influence of Justinian's *Digest*.

I know of no writers who explicitly contest Ulpian's account of justice in terms of rendering to one's fellows their right or due. Some of those who write about justice pay no attention to the connection between justice and rights. Some argue that there are no natural rights, only conferred rights – that is, rights conferred on us by some action, such as a promise performed by an individual, or a legislative act performed by an authority.[2] And some hold that thought and talk about rights is so seriously abused in the modern world that we should forego such thought and talk. But to the best of my knowledge, no one explicitly contests Ulpian's thought that justice – in contrast, say, to

---

2. Those who argue that there are no natural rights typically do not think of them as nonconferred rights – which I judge is how we ought to think of them. They think of them, for example, as rights that we would have in a Lockean state of nature. They then argue that there can be no such thing as a state of nature.

benevolence – consists of rendering to others their right, what they have a right to, what is due to them, what would wrong them if they were denied it.

A parenthetical note: it's unfortunate that English does not enable us to translate Ulpian's maxim with a pair of nouns like the Latin pair *iustitia* and *ius*; we have to translate *ius* with terms that have no linguistic relation to the term "justice," such as "right" and "due." The closest we can come in English to the linguistic pairing available in Latin is this: "justice is rendering to each what is justly his or hers."

The Biblical Understanding of Justice

In my Theology Brief, after an all-too-brief presentation of what the biblical writers say about justice, I wrote this:

> The biblical writers do not explain what justice is; they assume we know what they are talking about when they speak of justice. They do not offer a "theory" of justice. For an explanation of what justice is, a theory, we have to turn to philosophers.

I then launched into my discussion of Aristotle and Ulpian.

Some respondents found this transition problematic. When I said that the biblical writers do not offer a theory of justice, I had, in the back of my mind, an observation by the Old Testament scholar Walter Brueggemann, that the dominant overarching character of "Israel's speech about God is that of testimony" (Brueggemann 2012, 119). Testimony is obviously different from theory.

None of the respondents argued, to the contrary, that the biblical writers do offer a theory of justice. But the passage gave some the impression of suggesting that, for the purpose of understanding justice, we can leave Scripture behind and turn to philosophers. They found this suggestion problematic – rightly so.

I don't think there is a distinct *concept* of justice in Scripture – not, at least, if one understands the term "concept" as philosophers understand it, namely, as the sort of thing one would find in a dictionary's definition of the term. But there is a distinct *understanding* of justice in Scripture, a distinct *way of thinking about* justice. So let me now flesh out that understanding beyond the little I said in the brief, identifying what I see as salient features of the biblical understanding of justice. There are other understandings of justice that share some of the features of the biblical understanding; but when we put all the features of the biblical understanding together, the result is highly distinctive.

1. Fundamental to the biblical understanding of justice is the declaration that God is just and loves justice, and enjoins human beings to imitate God in doing and seeking justice.[3]

"I the LORD love justice," writes the prophet Isaiah (61:8). And in a well-known passage the prophet Micah writes:

> [The LORD] has told you, O mortal, what is good;
> and what does the LORD require of you
> but to do justice, and to love kindness,
> and to walk humbly with your God? (6:8)

Plato's *Republic* is an extended dialogue on justice; Aristotle's *Nicomachean Ethics* includes an extended discourse on justice. In neither of these is there any mention of divinity; the accounts offered are purely secular. The biblical understanding of justice is an intrinsically theological understanding. God is upfront and center.

2. Equally fundamental to the biblical understanding of justice is that love for one's neighbors requires treating them justly and that one is to treat them justly out of love.

As Osam Temple notes in his response, "there can be justice without love. . . . You can do justice not out of conviction but out of the fear of the law and punishment." On the biblical understanding of justice, doing justice is both required by love and to be an exercise of love.

The English word "love" denotes a rather wide variety of different phenomena (see chapter 1 of my *United in Love*). The love of neighbor that Jesus enjoins on us – *agapē* – consists of seeking the good of the neighbor. Being treated justly is, obviously, a good in one's life. Though agapic love of neighbor often goes beyond doing what justice requires, it never falls short of doing what justice requires. It never perpetrates injustice.

In my Theology Brief I noted that, in his influential 1930s publication *Agape and Eros*, the Swedish Lutheran bishop Anders Nygren argued that the love command of Jesus supplants and supersedes the injunction of the Hebrew prophets to act justly. In chapters 4 and 5 of my *Justice: Rights and Wrongs*, I argued at some length against this supersessionist interpretation of the relation

---

3. In his response titled "The Justice of God" (pp. 56–60 in this volume), Brendan Case very perceptively analyzes some puzzles concerning the justice of God.

The Hebrew Bible / Old Testament book of Joshua is often cited as a prime example of the injustice of Israel's God. In my essay "Reading Joshua" I argued that when the genre of Joshua is rightly understood, the book is not a (purported) record of God's instructing Israel to engage in the genocide of the Palestinians. (The essay is published in Wolterstorff 2011.)

between the two Testaments. The Testaments are united in teaching that love incorporates acting justly and that we are to act justly out of love.

It is not only theologians and biblical scholars who have pitted love and justice against each other. In the intellectual culture of the West there is a long tradition of doing so. The tradition continues. In her response to the Theology Brief, Eleonore Stump notes that "in the view of some [contemporary] feminist philosophers . . . ethics based on justice needs to be supplemented, or even supplanted, by an 'ethics of care.'" I hold that caring about someone necessarily includes treating that person justly, and doing what one can to see that others do so as well.

3. Another distinctive feature of how justice figures in the Hebrew Bible/Old Testament is that, over and over, the writers connect justice with what they call, in Hebrew, *shalom* (for example, Isa 32:16–17). Shalom, often rendered as "peace" in English translations, is better translated as "well-being" or "flourishing." Shalom consists of flourishing in all dimensions of one's existence: in one's relation to God, to one's fellow human beings, to the natural world, to human artifacts, to oneself. The thought of the writers was that insofar as one is a victim of injustice, one is not fully flourishing – even if, for some reason, one is content with one's condition. Though true and full shalom goes beyond what justice requires – a just community might suffer from famine caused by drought, and thus not experience shalom – justice is a condition of shalom. Justice is, as it were, the ground floor of shalom.

4. In the biblical understanding of justice, justice is an intrinsic component of what the New Testament writers call "the kingdom of God." Luke writes that shortly after Jesus began speaking in public, he attended the synagogue in Nazareth on a Sabbath and was invited to read Scripture and comment on what he had read. He was handed the scroll of the prophet Isaiah, unrolled it, and read the following:

> The Spirit of the Lord is upon me,
>> because he has anointed me
>> to bring good news to the poor.
> He has sent me to proclaim release to the captives
>> and recovery of sight to the blind,
>> to let the oppressed go free,
> to proclaim the year of the Lord's favor. (Luke 4:18–19)

Luke reports that Jesus then "rolled up the scroll, gave it back to the attendant, and sat down. The eyes of all in the synagogue were fixed on him," writes Luke, expecting him to offer some commentary on what he had read. Jesus then said, "Today this scripture has been fulfilled in your hearing."

What Luke reported Jesus as reading was an adaptation of the opening verses of Isaiah 61, a passage that is a close parallel of one a few chapters earlier in which the prophet spoke explicitly of God's call for justice:

> Is not this the fast that I choose:
> > to loose the bonds of injustice,
> > to undo the thongs of the yoke,
> > to let the oppressed go free,
> > and to break every yoke? (Isa 58:6)

The import of Jesus's declaration "Today this scripture has been fulfilled in your hearing" is unmistakable: Jesus identified himself as the one anointed by the Spirit of the Lord to proclaim the coming of justice in the year of the Lord's favor (the Year of Jubilee).

In Matthew's gospel, Jesus has already been teaching and healing for some time when the gospel writer intrudes himself into the narrative to offer his interpretation of Jesus's identity – the same interpretation as that which Jesus himself offered in the synagogue. Jesus is "to fulfill what had been spoken through the prophet Isaiah," namely,

> I will put my Spirit upon him,
> > and he will proclaim justice [*krisis*] to the Gentiles.
> . . .
> He will not break a bruised reed
> > or quench a smoldering wick
> until he brings justice [*krisis*] to victory. (Matt 12:18–20)

5. When the biblical writers speak of justice and injustice, it is almost always social (systemic) justice and injustice that they have in mind – that is, justice and injustice in the laws and social practices of Israel. When condemning injustice, they seldom mention individual wrongdoers. The prophet Micah is typical:

> The official and the judge ask for a bribe,
> > and the powerful dictate what they desire;
> thus they pervert justice. (Mic 7:3)

6. No mention of names: A striking feature of what the biblical writers say about social justice and injustice in Israel is their emphasis on the condition of the widows, the orphans, the sojourners, and the

impoverished – call them "the quartet of the vulnerable." So striking is this that one is compelled to ask "Why? What does it mean?"

A number of South American theologians, writing in the 1960s and 1970s, suggested that the emphasis on the quartet of the vulnerable has theological significance; it is, they said, an indication of what they called "God's preferential option for the poor."

This suggestion did not sit well with a good many North American Christians: "Doesn't God love everybody alike, rich as well as poor?" The answer, surely, is yes; God loves all those who bear God's image, rich and poor alike. But why then is it the case, as it clearly is in the biblical testimony, that God has a preferential option for the poor – or more precisely, for the vulnerable?

Nowhere in Plato's long dialogue about justice in the *Republic* does he make reference to the vulnerable in Athens. The reason he does not is that he is articulating principles of justice for an ideal society.[4] The biblical writers held out the hope for a messianic age; that is the form the ideal society took for them. But when they speak about justice, their eye is seldom on justice in the messianic age; almost always it is on justice and injustice in this present, far-from-ideal age. They represent God as working to redeem humankind, and the cosmos in general, from fallenness, and as calling us to share in this cause.

Those who seek the undoing of social injustice must set priorities. No doubt the wealthy and the powerful in Israel were sometimes victims of injustice, as they are in our present-day society – victims of *episodes* of injustice. The injustice experienced by the widows, the orphans, the sojourners, and the impoverished in ancient Israel was not *episodes* of injustice but *the daily condition* of injustice. It's because the biblical God is a redeeming God that there is, in God, a preferential option for the vulnerable – an option that we are to imitate.

The vulnerable today include many more than the biblical quartet – prisoners, for example. In his response, Terence Halliday forcefully reminds us that they also include refugees and asylum seekers. I write these words two weeks after Russia invaded Ukraine. Today's edition of the *New York Times* reports that already more than 2 million Ukrainians have fled as refugees to neighboring countries.

---

4. The highly influential book of the contemporary political philosopher John Rawls, *A Theory of Justice* (1999), is also a theory of justice for an ideal society.

7. In the biblical understanding of justice, securing justice in society is central to the God-given task of government. The opening verses of Psalm 72 present a picture of the good king.

> Give the king your justice, O God,
>   and your [doing right] to a king's son.
> May he judge your people [rightly],
>   and your poor with justice. . . .
> May he defend the cause of the poor of the people,
>   give deliverance to the needy,
>   and crush the oppressor.[5]

In the thirteenth chapter of his letter to the Romans, Paul repeats this understanding of the task of government, though less expansively: "the governing [authority] . . . is God's servant for your good. . . . It is the servant of God to execute wrath on the wrongdoer" (Rom 13:1, 4).

In his book *Republican Theology: The Civil Religion of American Evangelicals*, Benjamin T. Lynerd 2014 shows, with impressive documentation, that over the past century the dominant view among American evangelicals was that the main task of government is to secure individual liberty. In the writings that he quotes, there is rarely any mention of justice. This is a sharp departure from the biblical understanding. Securing justice does often require securing individual liberty; but they are not the same. Liberty without justice is freedom for the lions and eagles of the world to seek their prey.

8. In the biblical understanding of justice, to worship God is to render to God what is due to God – to render to God what justice requires. The psalmist says:

> Ascribe to the LORD, O families of the peoples,
>   ascribe to the LORD glory and strength.
> Ascribe to the LORD the glory due his name. (Ps 96:7–8)

And in another passage:

> Praise is due to you,
>   O God, in Zion,
> and to you shall vows be performed. (Ps 65:1)

---

5. Where I have "doing right" and "rightly," the NRSV has "righteousness." The prayer is not that the king and his son have the character trait of righteousness, but that they do the right thing.

This theme is echoed in many Christian liturgies. To cite just one example: in the Holy Eucharist: Rite One of the Episcopal Church, the Great Thanksgiving begins with the following words, spoken by the celebrant:

> It is very meet, right, and our bounden duty, that we should at all times, and in all places, give thanks unto Thee, O Lord, holy Father, almighty, everlasting God.[6]

As I mentioned at the beginning of this section, some of the features salient in the biblical understanding of justice can also be found in other understandings of justice. But nowhere else is there anything like the complete biblical understanding. It is unique.

Justice in Context

Several scholars expressed uneasiness with the Theology Brief's almost exclusive focus on justice; they heard in it a *justice-is-everything* tone. They argued that justice is but one component in a good and moral life, an indispensable component, indeed, but not the whole, and that it is important to locate it within that larger context. (See especially the responses by Nicholas Aroney, pp. 103–111, and Patrick Parkinson, pp. 113–116 in this volume.)

These respondents are correct in noting that, apart from a short discussion of the relation between justice and love, the brief did not place justice within the context of the good and moral life generally; they are also correct in claiming that not doing so runs the danger of encouraging a myopic concern with justice. So let me now make some remarks on the relation of justice to other components of the good and moral life.

Ulpian's formula, from which I took my lead, was a definition of the virtue *iustitia*: *iustitia* is a steady and enduring will to render to each their *ius*. In my brief I focused my attention not on that virtue but on the action which the virtue actualizes. I asked, what constitutes *rendering to each his or her ius*? What constitutes *acting justly*? The action has explanatory priority over the virtue: to explain what the virtue is, one has to know what the action is.

The virtue is obviously important, however. If there were not, in the members of society, the virtue of a "steady and enduring will" to treat each other justly, just action would be, at best, a haphazard and fortuitous thing.

---

6. Many additional examples can be found in the Eucharistic prayers collected by Lucien Deiss 1979 in *The Springtime of the Liturgy* and in those collected by Jasper and Cuming 1980 in *Prayers of the Eucharist: Early and Reformed*.

The English term "justice," unlike the Latin *iustitia*, does not name a virtue. It's the term "being just" that names the virtue. For justice to prevail in society, the virtue of *being just* must prevail.

The virtue of being just cannot be exercised all by itself, however; it requires the exercise of a range of other virtues. It requires, above all, a certain kind of humility, a humility which takes the form of decentering, of being attentive to the dignity, the praiseworthiness, of the other person. Typically such decentering requires a willingness to listen to the other person, to listen to his or her story. Being just also requires the virtues of empathy and anger: empathy with victims of injustice, anger at the perpetrators. And very often it requires the virtue of having overcome prejudices of various sorts: prejudice against members of another race, against members of another religion, against members of another political party, against speakers of another language, against persons who are obese, and on and on.

Not only does exercising the virtue of being just require the exercise of many other virtues. Sometimes just action *consists of* exercising some other virtue. For example, sometimes treating the other person justly requires telling him or her the truth; the person who is not in the habit of truth-telling will often act unjustly. Sometimes treating the other person justly does not just *require* listening to him or her but *consists of* listening to him or her.

And sometimes the exercise of some other virtue, or the pursuit of some other value, requires exercising the virtue of being just. Friendship is a good example of the point. Though friendship, obviously, does not consist of treating each other justly it certainly requires doing so.

The example of friendship suggests a general point. Not only is it important to note the intricate intertwinement of being just and acting justly with other virtues and values. Acting justly and being treated justly are but two of the innumerable multiplicity of things that are of value in our human existence: a home of one's own, surroundings in which one can take aesthetic delight, awe before the unfathomable intricacy and immensity of God's creation, gratitude. The list has no end.

Uneasiness with Thought and Talk about Rights

Some of the respondents expressed uneasiness with the prominence of rights in my discussion. In my brief I observed that uneasiness with, and hostility toward, rights-talk is widespread, and I addressed what I saw as the root of this uneasiness or hostility. This is part of what I wrote:

This hostility has many roots, the most common being, so it appears to me, the conviction that rights-talk is made to order for expressing one of the most pervasive and malignant diseases of modern society – namely, the mentality of possessive individualism. It's made to order, so it is said, for an "entitlement society," such as ours in which individuals place themselves at the center of the moral universe, focusing on their own entitlements to the neglect of . . . the cultivation of those virtues that are indispensable for the flourishing of our lives together. . . . The theologian Joan Lockwood O'Donovan puts the point crisply: "the modern liberal concept of rights belongs to the socially atomistic and disintegrative philosophy of possessive individualism."

I went on to argue that the preoccupation of the possessive individualist with claiming his or her own rights is an abuse of rights-talk. When I am in the presence of another, not only do I have rights vis-à-vis the other person; he or she has rights vis-à-vis me. All components of our moral vocabulary are subject to abuse. When confronted with such abuse, one does not argue for the elimination of that component of our moral vocabulary; one does what one can to combat the abuse.

I now think that this response, though not mistaken, is not entirely adequate. It appears to me that not all of those who feel uneasy with, or hostile to, rights-talk have their eye on the malign influence of the "philosophy of possessive individualism." They do not all have their eye on the abuse of rights-talk by possessive individualists. Rather, so it appears to me, a good many of them, when thinking of rights, think primarily of *claiming rights*; and they are convinced that claiming rights – whether the claim is made by oneself or another person – is incompatible with, and intrinsically morally inferior to, the "being-for-the-other" (Karl Barth's words) which Jesus enjoined in his second love command – and also incompatible with, and morally inferior to, attending to one's responsibilities toward the other.

Part of my response to this analysis is similar to my response to the previous analysis: just as it is a mistake to focus just on the abuse of rights-talk by possessive individualists, so also it is a mistake, when thinking of rights, to think primarily of *claiming* rights. Rights are not only to be *claimed*, they are also to be *acknowledged*. Rights-talk is not only for claiming rights but also for acknowledging rights.

Let me take the argument a step further. Jesus's second love command was not "Love your neighbor." It was "Love your neighbor as yourself" (quoting

Lev 19:18). It was, to adapt Barth, "Be for the other as you are for yourself." The command implies the moral propriety of well-ordered self-regard – the moral propriety of well-ordered self-love. Speaking up for one's own rights, claiming them, out of well-ordered self-regard, is not intrinsically inferior morally to acknowledging the rights of others.

It's true that to forego claiming certain of one's rights, to forego speaking up for them, is sometimes the right thing to do. But the person who thinks she has no right to claim her own rights – worse yet, the person who thinks she has no rights – is morally defective in a deep and profound way, perhaps through no fault of her own. She fails to recognize that she too has dignity, that she too has worth that calls to be honored. In my brief I remarked that all the great social justice movements of the twentieth century employed the language of rights. In doing so, the members of those movements were giving voice to their recognition that they too had dignity.

Of course, it remains the case that not all rights-claims are true; a good many are false. But the same is the case for duty-claims; many of those too are false. The husband who tells his abused wife that she has a duty to submit is speaking falsehood.

Amplifying What Was Said Concerning the Nature of Rights and Their Relation to Duties

Responding to some questions raised about rights requires that I expand on what I said in the brief about the nature of rights and the relation of rights to duties.

A number of scholars noted that rights sometimes conflict, and asked what we are to make of that. Some writers on these matters have suggested that this is a reason for rejecting the very idea of rights; the idea, they say, is incoherent.

Obligations conflict in the same way that rights conflict. In Plato's *Republic*, Socrates offers the example of someone who has promised to return in due time a weapon that he borrowed from a friend. The friend, in the meantime, has gone mad and is likely to use the weapon to harm himself or others. The borrower has an obligation to keep his promise; but he also has an obligation not to put a dangerous weapon in the hands of someone who is likely to use it to harm someone. Conflicting obligations.

The standard way in which philosophers deal with such conflicts is by distinguishing between prima facie duties and all-things-considered duties – the latter typically called *ultima facie* or *pro tanto* duties. Prima facie duties do, indeed, often conflict. But it is the view of most philosophers that all-things-considered duties do not conflict. If one considers just the promise the person made to return the weapon to his friend, he ought to do that; that is his prima facie duty. If one considers just putting a dangerous weapon in the hands of someone who has lost his sanity, he ought not to do that; that is his prima facie duty. Two conflicting prima facie duties or obligations. But if one asks what he ought to do *all things considered*, it seems clear that all things considered he ought to prevent his friend from harming himself or others by not keeping his promise to return the weapon. That is his ultima facie obligation. No conflict.

Along the same lines, we should distinguish prima facie rights from *ultima facie* (*pro tanto*) rights. If we consider just the promise made, the friend has a prima facie right to the borrower keeping his promise by returning the weapon. If we consider just putting a dangerous weapon in the hands of someone who has gone insane, the friend has a prima facie right to the borrower not putting a dangerous weapon in his hands. Two conflicting prima facie rights. But all things considered, surely the friend has a right to the borrower breaking his promise and not putting a dangerous weapon in his hands. That is his *ultima facie* right. No conflict.

From these observations about the nature of rights, let's move on to some points about the relation of rights to duties. In my brief, I affirmed a principle of correlation between rights and duties (obligations). Here is how I stated the principle: If you have a right to my treating you a certain way, then I have an obligation to treat you that way, and conversely.

This way of stating the principle fails to take account of third-party duties and rights. Rather than its being my duty to treat you a certain way, it may be my duty to you to treat Malchus a certain way. Correspondingly, rather than your having a right to my treating you a certain way, you may have a right to my treating Malchus a certain way. Taking account of third-party duties and rights, the way to state the principle of correlatives is this: If I have a duty to you to treat X a certain way, then you have a right to my treating X that way, and conversely.

An objection one sometimes hears to the existence of so-called *benefit rights* is that often it is impossible to specify a party responsible for honoring the right. Suppose, for example, that in a well-to-do modern society everybody has a right to adequate health care. If so, who is responsible for honoring that right? The question appears to have no answer. The principle of correlatives appears not to hold. Permission rights are different. If I have a right to assemble with others for religious worship, then *everybody* has a duty to permit me to assemble.

Here, too, thinking about duties helps us to get clear about rights. Immanuel Kant introduced the idea of what he called *imperfect* duties. An imperfect duty is a duty to treat *someone or other* a certain way without there being anyone such that it is one's duty to treat *him or her* that way. Many duties of charity are like that. I may have a duty to extend a certain kind of charity to *someone or other* without there being anyone such that it is my duty to extend that charity to *him or her.* I am free to choose.

I suggest that we think of rights along the same lines. Just as there are imperfect duties, so too there are imperfect rights: the right to be treated a certain way by *someone or other* without there being anyone such that one has the right to be treated that way by *that person.* Again, charity offers familiar examples. The beggar has a right to someone or other alleviating his need; if no one did, he would be wronged. But there may be no one such that he has the right to *that* person alleviating his need. The right to adequate health care is like that – a genuine right, albeit an imperfect right.

Return to the principle of correlatives between duties and rights. With that principle in mind, a natural question to ask concerning my analysis of justice – and a question some respondents did ask – is this: If duties and rights really are correlated in the way indicated, why not work out an account of justice in terms of duties rather than in terms of rights?

Let's make sure that we understand the proposal. In my Theology Brief, I devoted considerable space to considering why the recognition of rights is important – what would be lost if we never thought or talked in terms of rights. I argued that a number of things of great importance would be lost. The proposal we are now considering is not that we eliminate thinking and speaking about rights. The proposal is rather that we understand justice in terms of duties rather than in terms of rights.

It's a question I have never previously considered, and I don't feel entirely satisfied with my answer. I think it is the influence on me, and on most other writers in the West, of Ulpian's formula, transmitted to us by way of Justinian's *Digest.* Ulpian did not explain *iustitia* as the steady and enduring will to treat others as *one ought* to treat them. He explained *iustitia* as the steady and enduring will to treat others as *they* have *a right* to be treated. *Iustitia* is explained not in terms of *an agent's obligations* but in terms of *a recipient's rights.* The Latin pair, *iustitia* and *ius*, made this formula compelling.

We have all followed in Ulpian's footsteps, connecting justice to rights rather than to obligations, doing so in spite of the principle of correlatives. I don't know what a theory of justice developed in terms of duties rather than rights would look like. Perhaps not much different. Possibly quite different.

A Recent Publication on the History of the Idea of Natural Rights

An important, recently published book directly relevant to our discussion is *The Blessings of Liberty: Human Rights and Religious Freedom in the Western Legal Tradition*, by the legal historian John Witte.[7] In my brief I wrote that it is commonly said, by secular and Christian writers alike, that "the idea of natural rights was devised by the secular individualist philosophers of the Enlightenment," and that it continues to carry the DNA of its origins. Secular writers who tell this story about origins typically praise the idea on account of its origins; Christian writers who tell the story invariably condemn the idea for the same reason. I went on to note that "the medieval intellectual historian Brian Tierney showed decisively in his 1997 publication *The Idea of Natural Rights* that this historical claim is mistaken. He shows that the canon lawyers of the twelfth century were explicitly employing the idea" of natural rights.

I predict that *The Blessings of Liberty* will prove to be the decisive treatment of the matter. Based on a lifetime of scholarship, Witte goes far beyond Tierney's focus on the medieval period to tell the story of human rights and religious freedom from their earliest appearance in the Western legal tradition up to the present.[8] Summarizing his treatment of the early modern period, Witte writes, "Early modern Protestant theologians and jurists on both sides of the Atlantic expounded complex theories of natural law and natural rights" (76). And summarizing his opening discussion of Roman and medieval jurisprudence he writes,

> For Western jurists and judges, rights-talk was a common way to define and defend the law's protection, support, limitations, and entitlements of persons and groups in society as well as the proper relationships between political and other authorities and their respective subjects. For Western lawyers, subjective rights were not a modern invention. . . . Lawyers since classical Roman and medieval times used rights ideas and terms. (72)

The Blessings of Liberty should put to rest once and for all the claim that the idea of natural rights was an invention of the secular philosophers of the Enlightenment.

---

7. Cambridge: Cambridge University Press, 2022.

8. What Witte calls "human rights" are what I have been calling "natural rights."

In Conclusion

In my 2019 publication *Religion in the University*, I defend the thesis, against a number of objections, that religious voices have a place in the modern university. The argument remains purely abstract, of course, if it turns out that religious people have nothing significant to say on matters relevant to the academy, or if they remain silent because they feel insecure or intimidated. The project of the Global Faculty Initiative is to encourage and enhance the Christian voice on topics that are, or should be, of concern to the academy. Among those topics is justice, both within the academy and outside.

The Theology Brief on justice that I wrote for the GFI evoked responses that were, as I wrote in the opening sentence of this essay, "perceptive, inspiring, gratifying – and in some cases surprising." I have learned from them about the many ways in which Christian scholars are already thinking and speaking about justice, and seeking to act justly. Responding to their probing questions has been a gratifying experience.

References

Aquinas, T. 1274/1948. *Summa Theologica*. Complete English translation in five volumes. Notre Dame: Ave Maria Press.

Brueggemann, Walter. 2012. *Theology of the Old Testament: Testimony, Dispute, Advocacy*. Philadelphia: Fortress.

Deiss, Lucien. 1979. *The Springtime of the Liturgy*. Collegeville: Liturgical Press.

Jasper, R. C. and G. J. Cuming. 1980. *Prayers of the Eucharist: Early and Reformed*. Oxford: Oxford University Press.

Lynerd, Benjamin T. 2014. *Republican Theology: The Civil Religion of American Evangelicals*. Oxford: Oxford University Press.

Rawls, John. 1999. *A Theory of Justice*. Cambridge: Belknap Press.

Witte, John. 2022. *The Blessings of Liberty: Human Rights and Religious Freedom in the Western Legal Tradition*. Cambridge: Cambridge University Press.

Wolterstorff, Nicholas. 2009. *Justice: Rights and Wrongs*. Princeton: Princeton University Press.

———. 2011. "Reading Joshua." In *Divine Evil? The Moral Character of the God of Abraham*, edited by M. Bergmann, M. J. Murray, and M. C. Rea, 236–56. Oxford: Oxford University Press.

———. 2019. *Religion in the University*. New Haven: Yale University Press.

———. 2021. *United in Love: Essays on Justice, Art, and Liturgy*. Eugene: Cascade.

Subject Index

*Readers will find additional resources on Justice and Rights at the GFI website: Study Guides (globalfacultyinitiative.net/study-guide) and a Topical Guide (globalfacultyinitiative.net/topical-guides/justice).

A

abolitionism as a human rights movement 64

abortion, right to life 158–60

academic practices, justice in v, xvii, xix, xxiii, 28–29, 39–40, 51, 106, 134–35, 142, 179, 182, 205. *See also* hermeneutics

   academic publishing 174

   and social activism 174–75

   duty and calling of Christian academics 28–29, 43, 48, 50, 56, 63, 66, 89–92, 113, 149, 189, 198, 201–3, 207

   in academic institutions xviii, 9, 22, 25–26, 29–30, 54–101, 103, 107, 122, 129, 131–32, 137–46, 160, 169, 174–75, 182–83

   in interdisciplinary research 93, 102, 185–86. *See also* dialogue, encounter; interdisciplinary studies

   in preventing mass violations of human rights 134–36

   scholarly frontiers v, xix, 26–27

   scholarly pursuit of justice 28, 48, 61–62, 69, 153, 178, 185

   treatment of students 180, 184

academy/disciplines and justice 4–5, 26–28, 205. *See also* agriculture; architecture; biological science; business; economics; education; engineering; fine arts; history; international relations; language, linguistics; law; literature; management; medicine; philosophy; physical sciences; political science, political theory; public health; public policy; social sciences; sociology; theology

accountability for atrocities. *See* atrocities

agriculture 70, 149, 169

architecture 5, 27, 76, 138–39, 151

atrocities xix, 117, 131–33, 135–36, 176, 178–79

B

beauty, glory, and justice 24, 46, 48, 59, 102, 147, 197

biblical understanding of justice 3, 10–15, 42, 44–53, 56–60, 70, 75, 82–83, 90–92, 109, 115–16, 192–98. *See also* first-order justice; Scripture Index; second-order justice; theologies and classics of justice

   and government 107–8, 135, 197

   and injustice 3, 10–11, 40–41, 48, 82–83, 165, 194–95. *See also* injustice, forms of

   and love 3, 9–10, 12–13, 42, 48–49, 52–53, 59–60, 67, 90–92, 101, 161, 193–98, 200

   and neighborly love 13, 30, 48, 57, 101, 116, 161, 193, 196, 200

   and wellbeing/shalom 10, 13, 47, 75, 87, 91, 97, 101, 115, 194

   and worship 149, 157

   "correct justice" 56–60

   dignity and *imago Dei* 49, 63, 119

   eight-point biblical understanding of 189–98

quartet of the vulnerable. *See* vulnerable
justice, rights, and righteousness 131
universality of justice 79, 112, 182
biological science 145, 153
Black Lives Matter 65–66
business 19, 26, 31, 48, 66, 100, 106, 129, 138, 143, 178–79

C
church 47, 59, 78, 89–93, 96, 104–8, 112, 157, 161, 196–200. *See also* cognates of justice; Jesus Christ; restorative justice
and academy. *See* academy/disciplines and justice
and society 89–92, 106–7, 112, 120, 161, 196–200
faith/trust xii, xxi–xxiii, 51, 59, 87, 89–92, 102, 135, 142, 147, 153, 165, 215
in contexts, cultures, situations. *See* contexts and cultures; Global South, justice in; hermeneutics; peoples and places
mission of justice 46–47, 51, 54, 81, 93
people of God 15, 39, 45–47, 59, 70, 197, 205
climate change xix, 48, 125–30, 169, 178
cognates of justice. *See* dignity; faith and faithfulness; flourishing; judgment; love and justice; mercy; peace, peacemaking; public good; righteousness/uprightness; stewardship; virtues; wellbeing/shalom
communication 80, 84, 151–52
contexts and cultures 13–15, 38–40, 42–49, 60, 65, 71, 85, 87–88, 92, 106, 112–16, 124–26, 129, 132–35, 140, 153–54, 171, 174–75, 185, 194, 198. *See also* church; Global South, justice

in; hermeneutics; peoples and places
corruption 75–56, 78, 88–89
COVID-19 159, 165–72

D
dialogue, encounter v, xvii, xviii, xxii, 44, 53, 89, 95, 98, 124, 140, 274, 277, 182–83, 193, 196, 215. *See also* interdisciplinary studies
dignity 4, 9, 16, 18, 20, 24, 37, 49, 63–64, 80, 88, 96–97, 99–101, 106, 113, 117–20, 128, 135, 141–42, 146–47, 149, 165, 199, 201. *See also* sexual justice
disasters, justice in xx, 75–79
discrimination, inequality, inequity 4, 16, 18, 26, 61, 71, 74, 78–86, 101, 104–5, 109–20, 135–36, 146, 158, 165, 170, 174, 180–81
displacement, refugees 87–92, 177, 189
duties and obligations 9, 21–23, 36–37, 50, 63, 88, 92, 107, 131, 167–70, 172, 174, 201–3. *See also* displacement, refugees; family, parenting; health and justice; language, linguistics; linguistic justice; public health; rights and justice; vulnerable
to wealthy and poorer nations 130, 133, 167, 169, 172, 177
widening justice horizons 139, 169

E
economic justice 27, 69–70, 72. *See also* discrimination, inequality, inequity; lawmaking; rulemaking
and climate change 125–30
and human needs 37, 66, 71, 98, 100, 105, 120
distributive justice 15–16, 36–39, 117, 148, 176
efficiency and 74

of redistribution in modern Britain
69–73
social ethics and order 70–71
economics 4–5, 26–27, 36, 48, 69–74,
83, 91, 101, 105, 120–30, 138–39,
151, 155, 164, 168, 170, 177–82
education 26, 35–36, 71, 83, 87, 92,
111, 120, 159
engineering 27, 76, 145
environmental justice 79, 129. *See also*
climate change
epistemic justice 175, 182–83, 186

F
faith and faithfulness xxi–xxiii, 14–15,
45–47, 58–59, 78, 89–92, 107,
115, 142, 147–48, 153, 165–66,
215
family, justice in family law, family
courts, parenting 23, 35–39, 43,
70, 72, 106, 112–16, 155–59, 174
feminist perspectives on sexual dignity
and violence 117–19
fine arts xix, 5, 27
first-order justice 3, 9, 16–18, 24–25,
51, 69–73, 95, 97, 99, 101, 103,
112, 117, 121–22, 128–29, 134,
137, 140–42, 145, 147–48, 165,
173, 175, 182, 185–86. *See also*
Global South; second-order
justice
and economy 71, 122
and epistemological justice 175. *See
also* epistemic justice
and human needs, rights 18, 37, 66,
71, 98, 100, 105, 120
and interdisciplinary research 93,
102, 185–86
and ordinary affairs 9, 15–16, 25, 42,
69, 97, 117, 137
defined 3, 9, 16–18, 35–39, 69–73
in economic and social policy 71,
122. *See also* economic justice
in environmental economics 124–
30, 148–49, 167, 175, 177

in OT economy. *See* biblical understanding of justice; Scripture
Index
in psychiatric treatment 165–66
in transnational legal orders 137–43
flourishing 10, 17, 21, 24, 35, 47, 72,
74–75, 87, 91, 97, 101, 126, 129,
149–50, 157, 194, 200

G
gender injustice and sexual violence 5,
27, 72, 80, 178–79
global justice 125–43
and accountability for atrocities
131–36
and climate change 125–30
and transnational legal orders
137–41
Global South, justice in 171. *See also*
academy/disciplines and justice;
climate change; indigenous
peoples; language, linguistics;
lawmaking; linguistic justice
academic publishing in 29,
173–75, 186
epistemic injustice in. *See* epistemic
justice
first-order injustice in academy 173.
See also first-order justice; injustice, forms of.
government incapacity in 89, 189
human rights violations. *See* rights
and justice
God, Kingdom of, Trinity God, Trinity
31, 38, 47, 54, 107, 194. *See also*
Jesus Christ; theologies and classics of justice; Scripture Index
good, goodness 4–5, 9–15, 19–24,
35–51, 54, 59, 77, 82, 106–7, 110,
129, 140–41, 146–47, 151–62,
170, 176–77, 190, 193, 197–201.
See also public good
good news 11, 76, 183, 194. *See also*
Jesus Christ; Scripture Index

H

harms to civilians in civil war 87, 131–36

hate speech 131, 135–36, 152

health and justice
  challenges 166
  health as wholeness 101, 156–57, 160–63
  health rights 9, 118, 154–55, 158–59
  inequalities in 153–64, 167, 170
  love and justice 160–62
  mental health. *See* mental health care
  public health 26, 153–72
  World Health Organization 138, 154, 156, 158

health care 178. *See also* health and justice

hermeneutics 85. *See also* contexts and cultures; dialogue, encounter; first-order justice; interdisciplinary studies; second-order justice; theologies and classics of justice
  biblical interpretation. *See* biblical understanding of justice; Scripture Index
  communication, conversation 40–41, 47–48, 55, 67, 80, 84, 123, 142, 151–52, 176, 185, 202
  conception of justice 21–22, 38–43, 46–47, 51–53, 56, 62, 69–74, 95, 97, 100–109, 118–19, 128, 132, 142, 150, 154, 157–59, 167–68, 171, 186, 190, 192, 200
  differences, disagreement xviii, 3–4, 15–16, 18, 27, 30, 39, 42, 44, 46, 51, 81, 84, 98, 101, 104, 113–16, 159, 179, 185, 190, 193, 198, 203
  epistemology 175, 183. *See also* epistemic justice
  frames of justice 36, 43, 47–48, 95–96, 104, 116, 118, 122–26, 133–34, 138, 142, 165–71, 174, 185
  iconization 82, 86
  ideology 39, 81, 86, 105, 146

interpretation 12, 22, 30, 44, 46, 49, 84–85, 119, 156, 193, 195
language 22–24, 47–50, 62–67, 80–87, 104, 109–10, 129, 133, 135, 140, 150, 156–57, 168–69, 176, 189, 199, 201. *See* linguistic justice
method and process xxi, 9, 29, 44, 72, 96–99, 115, 121–24, 131–53, 185, 209
networking 84, 107, 134–35, 152, 174, 217
plurality, nuances 45–46, 49, 110, 178, 182, 185
translation 13–15, 18, 56, 69, 71, 140, 168, 190, 192, 194

history 10, 27, 39–40, 45, 52, 55, 61–69, 179, 190, 204
  and authentic Christian memory 66
  economic history in UK 69–73
  economic justice in OT 70
  economic policy in modern Britain 69–73
  genealogy of rights in Anglo-American history 62–65
  in biblical narrative 66
  informing policy 179–80
  intellectual history of human rights 62–65
  of racial injustice 65–66
  and tribal societies in India 68

human protection, trends in 132

human rights 3, 16–17, 69, 87, 89, 91, 97, 104, 117, 132–37, 154, 176, 178. *See also* rights and justice
  and Leveller Movement 62–63
  and Tolerationist Movement 63–64
  religious roots 65
  intellectual history of 62–65

humanities xix. *See also* history; language, linguistics; literature; philosophy

I

indigenous peoples 49, 96–97, 139, 177, 182

interdisciplinary studies 93, 102, 185–86. *See also* dialogue, encounter

injustice, forms of. *See* atrocities; climate change; communication; corruption; disasters; discrimination, inequality, inequity; displacement, refugees; gender and sexual injustice; hate speech; health and justice; language, linguistics; market failures; pandemics; perversion of just relations; poverty; protection of civilians; psychological trauma; race, racism; sin; slavery

international relations, organizations and governance 25–26, 36, 40, 63–64, 73–75, 78, 100, 112, 117, 120, 125–43, 157–58, 167–72, 176, 178, 180–81, 183. *See also* duties and obligations; human rights

 and vaccine nationalism 167–80

 global lawmaking 140. *See also* lawmaking

 global markets 73–74, 171

 nationalism and globalism 135, 167–72

 protection of civilians 131, 151

 public health 26, 153–72

 theological appraisal 25–26, 139–41

 United Nations 104, 131–32, 155

 wealthy nations 37, 73, 177, 198

 World Health Organization 138, 154, 156, 158

J

Jesus Christ 14, 59, 76, 82, 92, 107–8, 162. *See also* biblical understanding of justice; church; God, Kingdom of; Trinity; good news; restorative justice; salvation; Scripture Index

judgment (*mišpāṭ/krima*) 13, 42, 46, 57–58, 66, 84, 91, 97, 103–4, 109–10, 165

L

land use, justice in 124

language, linguistics 22–24, 47–50, 62–67, 80–87, 97–104, 109–10, 129, 133, 135, 140, 150, 156–57, 168–69, 176, 189, 192, 199, 201. *See also* linguistic justice

language of rights 22–23, 62, 67, 100, 104, 176, 201

languages, standard versus vernacular 83–84

law 3, 9–19, 22, 45–48, 52–53, 56–70, 76–77, 80, 95, 112–113, 115, 119, 204

lawmaking 121, 140–43. *See also* rule-making

linguistic justice 80–81, 85. *See* language of rights

 empire and ideology 107, 191

 sociolinguistics 80–83

 speech, language and justice 81

literature 5, 19, 27, 55, 66, 100, 133–36

love and justice 3, 9–10, 12–13, 17, 29–31, 35, 38–40, 48–49, 52–54, 58, 67, 90–92, 108, 131, 160–62, 166, 193–94, 196, 198, 200–201

M

management 4, 26, 77, 78–79, 178–79, 186

market failures 121–24

medicine xix, 150, 163–66, 182

memory, authentic Christian memory 66–67

mental health care 156–57, 161–63, 165

mercy xxi, 38–39, 41, 56, 58, 67, 75, 109, 136, 166

N

nationalists, vaccine nationalism 167–69

natural rights 9, 21, 49, 51, 62–63, 104, 146, 156, 158, 191, 204

P

pandemics 127, 138, 159, 165, 169–72, 178. *See also* health and justice
peace, peacemaking 10, 13, 36, 46–47, 75, 87, 91, 96–97, 99, 101, 115, 134, 136, 155, 194. *See also* well-being/shalom
peoples and places. *See also* Global South, justice in; indigenous peoples
    Africa 65, 118
    African Americans, black 64–65, 83
    Australia 115, 168, 171
    China, Han and Non Han 131, 139–40
    Colombia xx, 87–93, 182, 189
    Ethiopia 131
    Hong Kong 111
    India 78, 137
    Indonesia 81
    Japan 112
    Latin America 182
    Māori 96
    Moroccans 83
    Myanmar 131
    New Zealand 97–98
    Peru 83
    Singapore 112
    South Africa 118
    Ukraine 196
    United Kingdom 65
    United States of America 19, 112, 121, 123, 151
    Uyghurs 131
perversion of just relations 154, 180–81
philosophy 21, 25, 41, 43, 51, 106, 110–11, 119, 172, 180, 183, 185, 200
physical sciences xix, xxi, 145–72
political science, political theory 4, 16, 26, 36–39, 46, 48, 55, 61, 67, 70–78, 81, 91, 105–12, 117, 122,

131–32, 136–43, 155, 167–72, 175–79, 196, 199, 204
poverty 48, 71, 78, 177–78. *See also* vulnerable, quartet of the vulnerable
promoting justice 13, 183. *See also* climate change
    and retribution 133
    by epistemic humility 183
    by listening and giving voice 85
    in economic rulemaking 121
    in global lawmaking 140–41
    in transnational legal orders 137–43
    intercultural university 183
    promising sites for 135
    through climate change 48
    through crime prevention 134
    through healing, wholeness 160
    through redistribution policies 69–73
    through shared goals 157
    shared and divergent goals 157
    social-political transformation 46
protection of civilians 131, 136, 151
psychological trauma 165
public good 122, 151–52. *See also* good, goodness
public health xx, 26, 153–72
    and individual rights 159
    as a justice issue 153–54
    as wholeness 156, 161–62
    love and justice in 159–62
    rights and responsibilities 154–56
    tensions over rights in 158
public policy 69, 73–74, 76

Q

quartet of the vulnerable 196. *See also* vulnerable

R

race, racism 5, 9, 25, 27, 61, 65, 67, 104, 165
reconciliation 96, 100–101
    after atrocities 131–36

reductionism 171
refugees and displaced persons
177–78. *See also* displacement,
refugees
religious liberty 63–64
restorative justice 17, 70, 88, 95–102,
133–35, 165, 189. *See also* indigenous peoples; reconciliation
and compensation 70–71, 130
and retribution 15, 31, 98, 102, 133
as healing and repair 39, 96–100,
133
as second-order 100–101. *See also*
second-order justice
as shalom/peace 101. *See also* well-
being/shalom
Christian origins of justice 31
components of justice 80, 90, 98,
190, 194, 198, 200
righteousness/uprightness (*ṣĕdāqâ /
dikaiosynē*) 13–15, 45–49, 56,
58, 69, 97, 109, 197. *See also*
biblical understanding of justice;
church; Jesus Christ; judgment;
theologies and classics of justice
rights and justice 19, 21, 120, 159. *See
also* beauty, glory, and justice;
climate change; human rights;
language of rights; natural
rights; rights-talk
church fathers 63
conferred rights 9, 19, 97, 145, 156,
162, 191
Enlightenment 22, 31, 62–63, 65, 81,
104, 204
individual rights and common good
159
intellectual history of 62–65
intoxication with rights 112–13
medieval 22, 35, 38–42, 51, 62, 204
reproductive rights 158
rights-talk 9, 21–23, 69, 112–14, 176,
178, 190, 199–200, 204
rulemaking, justice in
administrative rulemaking 121–22

securities regulation 123–24
transnational legal orders 137–43

S
salvation, wholeness 14–15, 46–47,
101, 156–57, 160–63. *See also*
flourishing; Jesus Christ; sin;
wellbeing/shalom
science and technology, justice in 150
and injustice 64, 150, 152
and truthfulness 98, 148
global communications infrastructure 75
private and public goods 147, 159
scientific practices and research 115,
127, 151
second-order justice 3, 9, 17, 42, 69,
73, 76, 87–88, 91–92, 97, 103,
111–12, 115, 121–23, 130, 132,
136–37, 173, 186. *See also* first-
order justice
and accountability 96, 98, 131–34
atrocities against civilians 131, 151
compensation and redistribution 70
defined 3, 9, 17, 42, 87–88, 91–92,
111–12, 121–23, 130, 136–37
disaster relief 75–79
in environmental economics 79,
124–25, 128–30, 148–49, 177
in market failures 121–23
sexual justice. *See also* dignity; reproductive rights in rights and
justice
and *imago Dei* 49, 63, 119
sexual violence 117–19
sin 40, 45, 57–58, 60, 76, 78, 161, 182.
See also injustice, forms of; Jesus
Christ
sites of justice. *See also* climate change;
COVID-19; Global South, jus-
tice in; slavery
civil conflicts 62, 87, 89, 101, 131,
134–35, 137, 139, 170
disaster relief 75–79

economic deprivation 92, 106, 120, 128, 142. *See also* economic justice; international organizations

environment 5, 27, 55, 79, 98, 101, 111, 124–30, 148–49, 167, 175, 177

family 35–39, 70–72, 106, 112–16, 156–56, 159, 174

foreign aid 73, 168

global governance 101, 131–33, 136, 142

human protection 75–76, 99, 131–33, 136, 155. *See also* injustice, forms of; linguistic justice

persecution 63

public health 26, 153–72

sexual violence 25, 115–19, 137. *See also* sexual justice

universities, colleges iv, xvii, xxiii, 5, 9, 16, 25, 28, 36–40, 90, 107, 146, 174–75, 180–83, 205

urban design 76, 78

slavery xix, 61, 64–68

social sciences 44–46, 87, 120–21, 141–48, 182. *See also* economics; political science, political theory; sociology

sociology 26, 178–80

stewardship 74, 124, 129–30, 149

T

tax, income tax 70–74, 128, 170–71, 174

theology xix–xxii, 9–31, 35–60, 87, 90, 96, 147–48, 153, 167, 182, 185, 189–205

theologies and classics of justice. *See also* first-order justice; Jesus Christ; human rights; love and justice; mercy; righteousness/uprightness; rights and justice; second-order justice; varieties of justice. *See* Scripture Index

and holy eucharist, worship 63, 149, 197–98

and personhood 37, 41. *See also* dignity

Aquinas, Thomas 35, 38–39, 41–43, 103, 107, 110, 154, 160, 163, 191

Aristotle 4, 14–16, 18, 35, 107, 154, 190–93

Augustine 35, 38–39, 108

Catherine of Siena 39

Catholic Church 63, 71, 88, 106, 140

Greek 3, 14–15, 45, 107

Justinian 111, 191, 203

Medieval 22, 35, 38–42, 51, 62, 204

Plato 14, 30, 40, 54, 193, 196, 201

Reformation xx, 31, 46, 60, 63

Roman, Latin (*iustitia*) 4, 18, 62–63, 103–4, 106, 108–9, 140, 154, 190–92, 199, 204

Tertullian 63

U

university, religion in 205

V

vaccine nationalism 167–72

varieties of justice. *See also* duties and obligations; economic justice; first-order justice; judgment; second-order justice; restorative justice; rights and justice; virtues

commutative justice 36, 39

distributive justice 15–16, 36–41, 117, 148, 176

participatory justice 36, 39, 98–99, 101, 140–42

relational justice 91, 98, 100, 134, 142

virtues 17–21, 41–43, 54, 56, 103, 109–10, 148, 154, 166, 190, 198–200

vulnerable 37, 48, 63, 76, 78, 90–92, 131, 133, 165, 177, 196

W

wellbeing/shalom 10, 47, 75, 87, 91, 97, 101, 134, 157, 194. *See also* flourishing; peace, peacemaking

Scripture Index

OLD TESTAMENT

Genesis
1:25 24
1:31 .... 110, 147
3:14–19............110
9:6 50
9:8–17................128
11 84
12 45

Exodus
18:13–23............109
20:5 57
21:23–24............57
23:2 57

Leviticus
19:9–10...............70
19:15 ....13, 57
19:18 ....13, 201
25 70
25:8–22..............149

Deuteronomy
1:16–17...............57
1:16 109
5:12–14..............149
6:5 13
16:18–20.............15
16:18 109
24:16 57–58
32:4 46–47

Judges
12:5–6...............82

2 Samuel
8:15 109

1 Kings
10:9 109

2 Kings
23:25–26............57

2 Chronicles
9:8 109
12:6 47
18:14 109

Nehemiah
9:33 47

Job
29:16 47
31:21 47

Psalms
8 147
37:28 47
62 59
65:1 197
65:9–13..............147
67:4 46
72 197
95:4–5...............147
96:1–6...............147
96:7–8...............197
96:13 46
98:9 46
99:4 109
104 147
106:3 15

Proverbs
8:18 47
14:23 47

1 Kings
28:5 47
31:9 47

Isaiah
1:17 3
1:27 47
28:6 46
32:16–17............194
33:5 109
51:4–5 46–47
58:6 ....11, 195
61 .... 139, 195
61:1–2 11
61:1 183
61:8 193

Jeremiah
9:24 ....46, 109
23:5 109
31:28–30.............57
33:15 109

Ezekiel
18 57–58
18:2–3................57
18:3 58
18:4 58
18:10–13.............58
18:14–17.............58
18:20 58
18:21 58
18:24 58
34:16 46

Amos
5:7 109
5:24 109

Micah

4:4 70
6 75
6:8 ....67, 193
7:3 195

Habakkuk

1:1–4 45
2:3–4 45
2:4 45

NEW TESTAMENT

Matthew

5–7 4–6
5:6 ....14, 46
5:40–41 116
10:8 165
12:17–20 12
12:18–20 195
17:20 78
22:34–40 12
22:37–40 52
22:39 50
25 92
25:31–46 91
25:34–40 12
25:34 91
25:40 91
25:41 92
25:45 91
25:46 92
26:73 83

Mark

9:40 47
12:28–34 12

Luke

2:14 46
4 139
4:16–21 91
4:18–20 11
4:18–19 194
4:18 46
6:21 46
10:25–37 12
20:25 107

John

1:14 148
14:6 148

Acts

2 84
4:19 107
5:29 107

Romans

1:16–17 ....14, 110
1:17 45
2:13 60
2:6 59–60
2:10–13 59
2:13 59
2:14–15 59
2:26 59
2:26–29 59
2:29 59
3:10–18 60
3:19 60
3:19–20 60
3:20 ....58, 60
3:23 48
4 45
13:1 197
13:1–7 107
13:4 ....109, 197
13:9–10 161

1 Corinthians

5:8 148
13:4–7 53

2 Corinthians

3:3 60
3:6 60
5:20 107
6:7 148

Galatians

3 45
3:11 45

Ephesians

2:12 107
2:19 107
4:25 148
6:20 107

Philippians

3:20 107

1 Timothy

6:15 107

Hebrews

10:37–38 45

James

1:22 59
2:24 59

1 Peter

1:1 107
2:11 107
2:13–14 107
2:17 48

Revelation

17:14 107
19:16 107

Mission

The Global Faculty Initiative (GFI) promotes the integration of Christian faith and academic scholarship through cross-disciplinary dialogues between theologians and faculties in research universities worldwide.

Objectives

1. To bridge the gap between faith and scholarship in the world's universities by bringing theologians and Christian scholars into conversations inspired by great themes of the Christian faith that readily cross into the whole university
2. To equip disciplinary scholars effectively and efficiently with core theological concepts salient to their scholarship
3. To train advanced graduate students and early career scholars to think Christianly about research, teaching and writing
4. To stimulate university-wide conversations among Christians and other religious or non-religious scholars on mutually acceptable topics of great salience to the academy

Process

To equip busy scholars with Christian doctrines and themes salient to their work, GFI deploys a unique method in our Dialogues of Faith and Scholarship. GFI selects great themes of the faith relevant to research universities; invites distinguished theologians to write compact, accessible Theology Briefs on that theme; and calls for disciplinary scholars worldwide to reflect on ways the theology may be integrated into their work.

Vision

Through iterations of conversation between theologians and cross-disciplinary scholars, GFI envisions scholars and scholarly fields transformed by Christian thought, theologians energized by conversations with the university, universities spanning silos of scholarship and belief, and transformative influences on the church and world.

To learn more about GFI visit **globalfacultyinitiative.net**

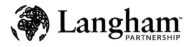

Langham Literature and its imprints are a ministry of Langham Partnership.

Langham Partnership is a global fellowship working in pursuit of the vision God entrusted to its founder John Stott –

to facilitate the growth of the church in maturity and Christ-likeness through raising the standards of biblical preaching and teaching.

Our vision is to see churches in the Majority World equipped for mission and growing to maturity in Christ through the ministry of pastors and leaders who believe, teach and live by the word of God.

Our mission is to strengthen the ministry of the word of God through:
- nurturing national movements for biblical preaching
- fostering the creation and distribution of evangelical literature
- enhancing evangelical theological education

especially in countries where churches are under-resourced.

Our ministry

Langham Preaching partners with national leaders to nurture indigenous biblical preaching movements for pastors and lay preachers all around the world. With the support of a team of trainers from many countries, a multi-level programme of seminars provides practical training, and is followed by a programme for training local facilitators. Local preachers' groups and national and regional networks ensure continuity and ongoing development, seeking to build vigorous movements committed to Bible exposition.

Langham Literature provides Majority World preachers, scholars and seminary libraries with evangelical books and electronic resources through publishing and distribution, grants and discounts. The programme also fosters the creation of indigenous evangelical books in many languages, through writer's grants, strengthening local evangelical publishing houses, and investment in major regional literature projects, such as one volume Bible commentaries like *The Africa Bible Commentary* and *The South Asia Bible Commentary*.

Langham Scholars provides financial support for evangelical doctoral students from the Majority World so that, when they return home, they may train pastors and other Christian leaders with sound, biblical and theological teaching. This programme equips those who equip others. Langham Scholars also works in partnership with Majority World seminaries in strengthening evangelical theological education. A growing number of Langham Scholars study in high quality doctoral programmes in the Majority World itself. As well as teaching the next generation of pastors, graduated Langham Scholars exercise significant influence through their writing and leadership.

To learn more about Langham Partnership and the work we do visit **langham.org**